D0872684

OTHER BOOKS BY DAVID JAUSS

AUTHOR

•

You Are Not Here

Black Maps

Improvising Rivers

Crimes of Passion

EDITOR

•

Strong Measures: Contemporary American
Poetry in Traditional Forms (co-edited with Philip Dacey)

The Best of Crazyhorse: 30 Years of
Poetry and Fiction

On Writing
FICTION

WRITER'S DIGEST
BOOKS

WritersDigest.com
Cincinnati, Ohio

On Writing
FICTION

Rethinking Conventional Wisdom
About the Craft

DAVID JAUSS
foreword by
BRETT LOTT

ON WRITING FICTION © 2011 by David Jauss. Manufactured in the United States. All rights reserved. No other part of this book may be reproduced in any form or by any electronic or mechanical means including information storage and retrieval systems without permission in writing from the publisher, except by a reviewer, who may quote brief passages in a review. Published by Writer's Digest Books, an imprint of F+W Media, Inc., 4700 East Galbraith Road, Cincinnati, Ohio 45236. (800) 289-0963. First edition.

Previously published as *Alone With All That Can Happen*.

For more resources for writers, visit www.writersdigest.com/books.

To receive a free weekly e-mail newsletter delivering tips and updates about writing and about Writer's Digest products, register directly at www.writers digest.com/enews.

15 14 13 12 11   5 4 3 2 1

Distributed in Canada by Fraser Direct
100 Armstrong Avenue
Georgetown, Ontario, Canada L7G 5S4
Tel: (905) 877-4411

Distributed in the U.K and Europe by F&W Media International, LTD
Brunel House, Forde Close, Newton Abbot, Devon, TQ12 4PU, UK
Tel: (+44) 1626-323200, Fax: (+44) 1626-323319
E-mail: enquiries@fwmedia.com

Distributed in Australia by Capricorn Link
P.O. Box 704, Windsor, NSW 2756 Australia
Tel: (02) 4577-3555

Edited by Kelly Nickell and Scott Francis
Designed by Terri Woesner
Production coordinated by Debbie Thomas

PN
355
38
011

This book is dedicated to the memory
of Delbert Wylder, George P. Elliott, and
Frederick Busch—master teachers, all.

BELMONT UNIVERSITY LIBRARY

ACKNOWLEDGMENTS

I am grateful to the editors of the following magazines, in which earlier versions of these essays first appeared:

North Dakota Quarterly: "Autobiographobia: Writing and the Secret Life"

The Writer's Chronicle: "From Long Shots to X-Rays: Distance and Point of View in Fiction"; "Lever of Transcendence: Contradiction and the Physics of Creativity"; "Remembrance of Things Present: Present Tense in Contemporary Fiction"; "Some Epiphanies About Epiphanies"; "Stacking Stones: Building a Unified Short Story Collection"; and "What We Talk About When We Talk About Flow"

I am also grateful for the support and encouragement of my students and colleagues at Vermont College of Fine Arts, where earlier versions of these essays were first delivered as lectures, and for the advice of Lisa Biggar, Andrea Hollander Budy, Philip Graham, Charlie Green, Jane Hirshfield, Lee Hope, Alison Jauss, Steve Jauss, Kaylie Jones, Maggie Kast, Kim Klement, Christopher Noël, Alicia Ostriker, Pamela Painter, Gabriele Rico, Chuck Rosenthal, Natasha Sajé, Linda Schneider, Betsy Sholl, Lisa Skoog de Lamas, Lawrence Sutin, Leslie Ullman, and Lisa Ventrella. I owe special debts of gratitude to Frederick Busch, Philip Dacey, Stephen Dunn, James Hannah, Bret Lott, Dennis Vannatta, David Wojahn, Delbert Wylder, and Edith Wylder, all of whom contributed to this book, and to my life, in ways above and beyond the call of friendship. Finally, I am thankful beyond measure to my wife, Judy, for nearly four decades of love and support.

ABOUT THE AUTHOR

David Jauss is the author of two collections of short stories, *Black Maps* and *Crimes of Passion*; two collections of poems, *You Are Not Here* and *Improvising Rivers*; a collection of essays on the craft of fiction, *Alone With All That Could Happen*; and a monograph on closure in literature and the arts, *A Crack in Everything: How We Know What's Done Is Done*. He has also edited three anthologies, *Strong Measures: Contemporary American Poetry in Traditional Forms* (co-edited by Philip Dacey), *The Best of* Crazyhorse: *Thirty Years of Poetry and Prose*, and *Words Overflown by Stars*, a collection of essays on the craft of poetry, fiction, and creative nonfiction by the MFA in Writing faculty of Vermont College of Fine Arts. His stories and poems have appeared in numerous magazines, including *The Georgia Review*, *The Iowa Review*, *The Missouri Review*, *The Nation*, *New England Review*, *The Paris Review*, *Ploughshares*, *Poetry*, *Prairie Schooner*, and *Shenandoah*, and his work has been reprinted in the *O. Henry Prize* and *Pushcart Prize* annual anthologies, *Best American Short Stories*, *The Pushcart Book of Stories: Best Stories from the First 25 Years of the Pushcart Prize*, *The Poetry Anthology, 1912-2002*, and elsewhere. He served as fiction editor of *Crazyhorse* for ten years and is currently on the Editorial Board of *Hunger Mountain*. The recipient of the AWP Award for Short Fiction, a National Endowment for the Arts Fellowship, the Fleur-de-Lis Poetry Prize, and a James A. Michener Fellowship, among other awards, he teaches at the University of Arkansas at Little Rock and in the low-residency MFA in Writing Program at Vermont College of Fine Arts.

www.davidjauss.com

TABLE OF CONTENTS

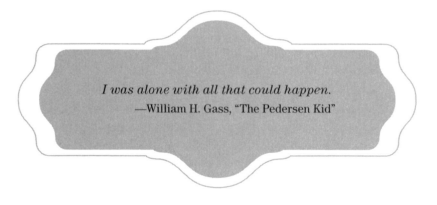

I was alone with all that could happen.
—William H. Gass, "The Pedersen Kid"

FOREWORD

I have never written a foreword for someone else's book before, and now that I am sitting down to do this, I am filled with a certain kind of apprehension, or perhaps it is a sort of inadequacy. Maybe both.

Not because this is my first foreword, but because I am writing one for a writer whose work I respect and admire utterly, and from whom I myself have learned a great deal about writing.

I met David Jauss at a very peculiar moment in my life. This was in January of 1999 at Vermont College in Montpelier, Vermont, where I was teaching in the low-residency M.F.A. program. David was the new guy on the faculty—I had been with the program for five years by that time—and though I had read and admired his fiction and poetry, knew of his superb work as editor of the literary journal *Crazyhorse* as well, I hadn't met him before, and when I was introduced to this mild-mannered, bespectacled and distinguished gentleman, I remember thinking, *Here's a nice guy.*

During that eleven-day residency in the cold New England winter, I got to know him a little better and found that my first assessment of his being a nice guy was truer than true. He was and remains a gentleman, a kind soul whose gentle voice and thoughtful demeanor reveal a man of great character.

But here is the peculiar circumstance under which we met: On the next-to-last day of the residency, I got a call from Oprah Winfrey, who had found me up in Vermont; it was on this day that she gave me the news a book of mine had been selected for her book club.

Though this might seem to have been an occasion for *Huzzahs!* from the Vermont College writing community, the circumstances in which I found myself that day made this an absolute impossibility. For reasons too complex and convoluted to go into here, this news from Oprah became the most humbling moment in my literary career and precipitated my writing, a couple of months later, a lengthy essay attempting to describe the entire sequence of events that had forced upon me this clarifying sense of humility.

Once I'd finished the essay, uncertain of what it was or whether or not it worked—it was and still is unlike anything else I have ever written—I sent it to David. I did so because of his demeanor during that strange and tumultuous residency; I did so because of his calm, and his smile, and what I had come to see as his honest sense of what it means to be a teacher and a writer. So I decided to send it to him, and to listen to what he had to say.

My life as a writer hasn't been the same since.

He brought to what I had written a quality of vision that saw not only where I had bungled words, but also where I had bungled thoughts. He saw at once and in detail what my essay was trying to do and to be, saw where it was failing and where it was working, and saw just what the heck I needed to do with *this* word *here* and *that* word *there* so my essay might ring as true as it could.

And perhaps the most important part of this exchange was that all of his acumen was delivered with generosity, with love, and with respect.

That essay ended up being published first in the journal *Fourth Genre*, and was then reprinted in *Utne Reader*; later that year it received a Pushcart Prize, and later still appeared in the Pushcart collection of the best essays published in its twenty-five-year history, and has since appeared in a dozen or so anthologies and textbooks.

I give you this story not to toot my own horn. Believe me, I know better than any person alive that the last person anyone needs to hear from about *me* is *me*.

Rather, I tell you all this as a means to express my apprehension and inadequacy at writing this foreword. Most everything I have written since handing David that essay I have passed before him for both his practical and spiritual editorial input. Rest assured I will continue to send him what I write so as to help me understand, finally, what it is I truly mean to say, and the best way in which I can say it. I will even send him this foreword so it might benefit from his gift at making my writing all the better.

What you hold in your hands this moment is now a gift to *you*. It is the gift of a man who is beloved by his students, beloved by his colleagues, and beloved by his readers. You will find in these pages, whether he is writing about such practical matters as point of view or such seemingly esoteric issues as Janusian thinking, a teacher who cares deeply about his students and a writer who cares just as deeply about the power of words and all they can mean. His is a fierce kind of caring—he takes this vocation seriously—and yet it is also a nurturing kind, as you will soon see.

The best way I know to discover how words do their work, and to understand how they can become *art*, is for the apprentice to study with a fierce and compassionate master of that art. David Jauss is just such a master, and this book grants its readers— you who desire to know what it means *to write*—an invaluable course of study, all at the hands of this extraordinary teacher, writer, and human.

—Bret Lott, author of *Jewel*; *A Song I Knew by Heart*; *Before We Get Started: A Practical Memoir of the Writer's Life*; *Ancient Highway*; and other books

INTRODUCTION

"I was alone with all that could happen": This comment, by the narrator of William H. Gass's "The Pedersen Kid," seems to me the quintessential description of the fiction writer's situation. The way I see it, Emily Dickinson missed the mark when she said that poets "dwell in Possibility— / A fairer House than Prose": Possibility is the place where *all* writers of imaginative literature hang their hats, regardless of their genre. Each time we sit down to write a work of fiction, we face a vast panorama of possibilities—and not just "all that could happen" but also all the narrative strategies and techniques we could possibly use to convey the people and events we imagine.

The process of writing a work of fiction is ultimately the process of making choices among this panorama of techniques and strategies. But before we can make these choices, we need to know what the possibilities are, and in my opinion, too much of what's been written about the craft of fiction restricts the possibilities we can, and should, be exploring. In this book, I have tried to take a descriptive, rather than prescriptive, approach to the craft of fiction. The seven essays that follow attempt to describe the technical possibilities available to us and, further, to analyze the advantages and disadvantages of each possibility, the effects each choice we make has on the work as a whole. Instead of *Do this* and *Avoid that*, this book aims to delineate the possibilities, then say, **If** *you do this* ... and *Avoid that* ***unless*** ...

Although the essays are grounded in literary history and tradition, they frequently depart from the reigning dogma of our time, as expressed both in standard creative writing textbooks and in the practice of many contemporary fiction writers. For example, much fiction today is written to the tune of the restrictive and ubiquitous mantra "Write what you know," but in my essay

"Autobiographobia," I argue for writing what you *don't* know—for what is fiction if not something we haven't literally experienced? In "From Long Shots to X-Rays," I counter the inaccurate and generally unhelpful advice about point of view we commonly find stated in textbooks, and as a result illustrated in much of the fiction of our time, by providing definitions and examples of a wide spectrum of points of view that have been successfully employed in fiction (including that ostensibly "impossible" point of view, first-person omniscience). And in "Remembrance of Things Present" and "What We Talk About When We Talk About Flow," I question the current hegemony of the present tense and minimalist syntax and diction, respectively, and explore the advantages and disadvantages of other tenses, syntax, and diction. "Some Epiphanies About Epiphanies" challenges the current extremist attitudes, both pro and con, toward those life-altering moments of revelation (cue the trumpets and celestial choir!) and surveys a plethora of possible ways to write satisfying and successful epiphanies. In "Stacking Stones," I likewise survey the many possible ways to create unity and order in collections containing stories that are disparate in form, style, and content, and in the book's final essay, "Lever of Transcendence," I argue for an understanding of the creative process that I believe vastly increases the technical—and therefore intellectual and emotional—possibilities of fiction.

In all of these essays, then, my goal has been to describe as accurately and thoroughly as I can what has actually been done in fiction and to assess the relative value of these various possibilities, many of which contemporary writers have ignored, to the detriment of our fiction, because of prevailing attitudes that have been all too readily accepted. I hope these essays will help you the next time you sit down to write and find yourself alone with all that could happen.

AUTOBIOGRAPHOBIA:
WRITING AND THE SECRET LIFE

1. YOU'RE NOT ALONE

Recently, I received two phone calls that made me think about the kind of fiction I tend to write. One was from a man who told me he had just read a story of mine called "Rainier," which is about a divorced alcoholic whose son dies in a car accident. "The same thing happened to me," the caller said, then proceeded to tell me about the anguish he suffered after the death of his son and how AA had helped him overcome not only his alcoholism but his grief. He did not cry, but I could tell he was fighting tears. When he finished telling me his story, he paused, then said, "I just wanted you to know that you're not alone."

I couldn't tell him that *he*, at least at that moment, was alone. My story is not autobiographical. I have never lived in Montana or Wyoming, where the story takes place; I am not now, nor have I ever been, divorced; I am not an alcoholic, recovering or otherwise; and my son, I'm happy to say, is very much alive. Nothing in that story happened to me, or to anyone I know. I made it up. I didn't have the heart to tell the caller this, however; for the duration of the phone call, I pretended that the story was true, and that I shared his grief not only imaginatively but literally.

The other phone call was from a Vietnam vet who had read my short story "Freeze," which is about a soldier in Vietnam who steps on a mine that doesn't explode yet nonetheless has devastating effects on his life. The caller wanted to know if we'd ever met. "I remember that guy you wrote about," he said. "The lieutenant. And I think we must have been at Lai Khe at about the same time. Did you know Larry Kelvin? Or Rick Hammond?" When I told him I'd never been in Vietnam, or even in the military, he was more than disappointed, he was outraged. "What gives you the right to write about a war when you weren't even fucking *there*?" he demanded. Clearly, he felt as if he'd been taken in by a con man. And in a way, he had, for what is a fiction writer if not a confidence artist, someone who trades words for your trust, and—if he's lucky—your money? And how can writers blame their readers for failing to recognize that fiction is *fiction*, not truth, when we do everything we can to make them believe something we imagined is true? Still, I wish he had realized that writers, like magicians, work in the realm of illusion, not reality. He would never assume that the magician actually sawed the lady in half, yet he was quick to assume that the soldiers I killed had bled real blood.

I didn't get a chance to defend myself to this caller—he hung up almost immediately after accusing me of the crime of lying in a work of fiction—but if I had, I would have told him that "Freeze," like "Rainier" and the rest of my stories, *is* a true story, but not true in the way he wanted. Its truth is not the kind that can be captured by a surveillance camera but the kind that appears in our dreams, a truth heightened by distortion and the odd juxtaposition of a lifetime's accumulation of images. Like a dream, a story, if it's any good, tells the truth about the author's secret, inner life, and as often as not it does so by telling lies about her public, outer life, for, as Oscar Wilde said, "One's real life is so often the life that one does not lead." And about the nature of that truth the reader sometimes knows more than the author.

Perhaps the most repeated advice in the history of creative writing workshops is "Write what you know." For writers who have a talent for negotiating between the demands of facts and the demands of the imagination, this may be valid advice. But for most of us, I believe, writing what we know can only result in nonfiction, whether thickly or thinly disguised. This is why Graham Greene suggested that a good memory was incompatible with good fiction writing. "All good novelists have bad memories," he said. As Robert Olen Butler explains, "What you remember comes out as journalism. What you forget goes into the compost of the imagination."

Knowing also creates aesthetic problems that imagining doesn't. As Garrett Hongo has said, "Sometimes, in writing about 'what you know,' … autobiography gets in the way. If you write 'Grandfather's backyard,' *you* may see his amazing collection of hybrid lilies, but the reader won't unless you put them into the poem. It's easier to describe something that you've invented than something that's so deeply familiar you take it for granted." Furthermore, writing about what you already know can be a prescription for boring yourself—and if you bore yourself, you'll bore your reader. For my money, Grace Paley got it exactly right when she said, "You write *from* what you know but you write *into* what you *don't* know." You can't avoid what you know—it's who you are, after all—but if you're trying to write into what you don't know, you'll discover things about yourself that you didn't know. In short, you'll discover your secret life, and so will your readers.

All literature, I believe, is predicated on the desire to reveal the author's essential, secret self, to be known by others. This is most obviously true of the work of writers like Walt Whitman, Allen Ginsberg, and Robert Lowell, whose strategy, and sometimes subject, is candor. Yet there are many writers—including some of our greatest—who reveal their essential selves by eschewing candor and adopting the strategy of disguise. Both candor and disguise are valid—even indispensable—ways of approaching the secret life in literature, and both can result in great art, though I believe disguise improves your chances, because the less you rely on autobiographical fact, the more your imagination is of necessity invoked. For the last several decades, however, the dominant approach in American literature has been candor. Our literature has become more overtly factual in its pursuit of the inner life than at any previous point in literary history. Since so many writers believe that the subject of fiction and poetry is and should be their factual experience—"what they know"—it's no wonder so many readers assume the same thing.

In my stories, and in my poems, I have tried to write my way into many characters whose lives I know nothing, or next to nothing, about. On paper, I have been—or at least tried to be—a nun, a serial killer, a bag lady, a nine-year-old boy, a ninety-nine-year-old man, a woman afflicted with hysterical blindness, a teenager who witnesses his father's nervous breakdown, a man with an artificial hand, a divorcée, a girl from Bangladesh, a minor league baseball player from the Dominican Republic, a Hmong refugee, a sixteenth-century Spanish priest, a nineteenth-century Russian dwarf, the biblical Lazarus, and various other characters, including several actual jazz musicians and authors. One of those authors—Gustave Flaubert—wrote a letter to Louise Colet about the pleasure of writing about lives other than his own. Of his day's work on *Madame Bovary*, he wrote:

> It is a delicious thing to write, whether well or badly—to be no longer yourself but to move in an entire universe of your own creating. Today, for instance, man and woman, lover and beloved, I rode in a forest on an autumn afternoon under the yellow leaves, and I was also the horses, the leaves, the wind, the words my people spoke, even the red sun that made them half-shut their love-drowned eyes. Is this pride or piety? Is it a silly overflow of exaggerated self-satisfaction, or is it really a vague and noble religious instinct?

It may be evidence of my own pride, but I'll opt for piety as the correct answer. I believe that escaping the self, imagining the life of another, is a noble, even religious, act. But I also believe that we learn as much or more about Flaubert's true self through the people he invents than we would through any overt autobiographical account, for imagining the other is ultimately a way of discovering the self. Flaubert clearly knew this, for when he was asked how he was able to create such a convincing female character, he answered, "Madame Bovary, c'est moi." And Jorge Luis Borges understood this, too, as his summary of the life of an artist indicates:

> A man sets himself the task of portraying the world. Through the years he peoples a space with images of provinces, kingdoms, mountains, bays, ships, islands, fishes, rooms, instruments, stars, horses, and people. Shortly before his death, he discovers that that patient labyrinth of lines traces the image of his face.

I cannot see my own face yet, but I trust that I am drawing it, if badly, each time I sit down and attempt to enter another person's central nervous system. And that's the face I want my readers to see, my true face, not the false ones I wear in order to reveal it.

But what will they see if they see my true face? Their own faces, I believe. As Charles Simic has said, "Poems are other people's snapshots in which we recognize ourselves." The same goes, of course, for stories.

Here's the paradox: Just as you reveal your secret life when you imagine others', you reveal others' secret lives when you reveal your own. As Donald Hall once remarked, literature "starts by being personal but the deeper we go inside the more we become everybody."

Everybody, c'est moi. And c'est *vous*.

2. THE SECRET WANTS TO CROSS OVER

In his great story "The Lady With the Pet Dog," Anton Chekhov says this of his protagonist, Gurov:

> He had two lives: an open one, seen and known by all who needed to know it, full of conventional truth and conventional falsehood, exactly like the lives of his friends and acquaintances; and another life that went on in secret. And through some strange, perhaps accidental, combination of circumstances, everything that was of interest and importance to him, everything that was essential to him, everything about which he felt sincerely and did not deceive himself, everything that constituted the core of his life was going on concealed from others; while all that was false, the shell in which he hid to cover the truth ... went on in the open. Judging others by himself, he did not believe what he saw, and always fancied that every man led his real, most interesting life under cover of secrecy as under cover of night.

Chekhov believed that the public life, not only of a character but also of its author, is the false, "accidental" one, the inner, secret life the real, "essential" one. As this suggests, he also believed that autobiographical fiction, if it is devoted to the "conventional truths" of the public life (as it often is), must therefore also be false. No wonder, then, that this man who abhorred falsehood above all things also abhorred autobiographical writing. In an 1899 letter, he diagnosed his abhorrence in medical terms: "I have a disease," he said, "called autobiographphobia." Writing about himself was like sticking a knife in his side, he claimed, and he just couldn't do it. Nor did he want to. Nor, I should add, did he have to, for I believe we learn as much or more about Chekhov from his work than we learn about such conventionally autobiographical authors as Jack Kerouac or Henry Miller from theirs. What we learn—*feel* or *sense* might be more accurate words—is his essential, secret self, not the arbitrary, accidental facts of his life, which would only mask his real nature. Few writers in history have put less of their public lives, and more of their secret lives, into their work. And he did it, paradoxically, by creating an extraordinary range of characters whose lives, on the surface, differed dramatically from his. In this he resembles Shakespeare, the greatest of our writers, who wrote that "the truest poetry is the most feigning." Reading Chekhov and Shakespeare, and others like them, we inhabit their essential selves and dream their dreams along with them. When we read overtly autobiographical writers, however, all too often we stand apart and watch, from a greater or lesser distance depending on the gifts of the author, the arbitrary and accidental circumstances of their public lives.

Oscar Wilde once said, "Man is least himself when he talks in his own person. Give him a mask, and he will tell the truth." Lionel Trilling seconds that opinion, saying "disguise is not concealment" but revelation, for "the more a writer takes pains with his work to remove it from the personal and subjective, the more—and not the less—he will express his true unconscious." Some writers are gifted enough to tell the truth about their inner lives without the aid of a mask, but most of us, I believe, are not. Even if we know our secret selves (and that's a big *if*), it's almost impossible to draw our true faces for our readers merely by reporting what seems to be the "truth." Instead, like Shakespeare, like Chekhov, we have to imagine we are someone else, we have to wear a mask; in short, we have to *lie*. For a lie is nothing more, nor less, than the means to make a secret public while still keeping it secret. As Jorie Graham has put it,

> The secret cannot be
> kept.
> It wants to cross over, it wants
> to be a lie.

Writing about the secret life is not, then, a matter of revealing actual secrets but of distorting and altering them, consciously or unconsciously, so they tell a larger kind of truth. If you simply reveal a secret—tell the god's honest truth about it—you may in fact tell a lie about your real, inner life. At the very least, you will be false to the primary characteristic of the secret, which is that it is *secret*. There have been times in my life when I've told someone a secret I'd suppressed for years, and once it was spoken, it suddenly felt false and insignificant. On the other hand, a secret that remains buried under the oppressive weight of silence increases in significance and value, the way carbon buried under the weight of the earth turns into a diamond. To reveal this "diamond" factually is to return it to carbon, but to reveal it in a way that conceals it—in other words, to tell a lie about it—allows the secret to retain the luster that silence has given it.

As this suggests, a lie is a form of silence, for it is a refusal to reveal the secret. But, as Wilde suggests, a lie tells the truth all the more fully and honestly by refusing to tell it. Or, as Emily Dickinson would put it, it tells the truth but tells it slant. Dickinson's poetry is a good example of literature that reveals through its reticence. Her poems convey a stunning inner life while concealing the specifics that would claim the spotlight in a confessional poem. In an article in *The New York Times Book Review*, Elizabeth Schmidt asks, "Why do readers feel so close to [Dickinson] in spite of her attempts to push her audience away?" The answer, I believe, is that her poems reveal her essential life more compellingly *because* of the aura of secrecy rather than *in spite of* it. Clearly, Dickinson knew that reticence can be a form of revelation. C.P. Cavafy recognized this, too. In his poem "Hidden Things," he says, "From my most unnoticed actions, / my most veiled writing— / from these alone I will be understood." If Dickinson and Cavafy and writers like them had revealed their secret selves nakedly, we would not *feel* their inner lives so much as *know* them, and feeling is a deeper, more vital form of knowing. What brings a poem to life more than anything else, I believe, are its secrets and the feelings they engender in the reader. Stanley Kunitz agrees: "A poem without secrets," he once said, "lies dead on the page."

The principal paradox of literature, then, is that by lying it simultaneously reveals and represses the truth about the author's secret life. Ted Hughes goes so far as to suggest that this combination of revelation and repression is the very *definition* of literature. "Maybe all poetry," he has said, "… is a revealing of something that the writer doesn't actually want to say, but desperately needs to communicate, to be delivered of." And, he concludes, "Perhaps it's the need to keep it hidden that … makes it poetry."

The secret cannot be kept and it must be kept. The only way to satisfy both demands, the only way the secret can cross over without being recognized, is to don the disguise of a lie.

3. THE GENERATIVE SECRET

As the quotation from Hughes suggests, literature has its origin in secrets that the author feels compelled both to reveal and conceal. In other words, secrets, and the secret life, *generate* literature. As I said earlier, literature ends, if it's successful, by expressing everybody's secrets, but it begins in the personal life of the author. Let me give two examples of personal secrets that "cross over" as lies in works of literature that, in my opinion, rise well beyond their personal origins.

Some time ago, a former student of mine whose poetry I admire revealed a secret that she has kept from everybody, including her husband, for more than twenty years: When she was a teenager, she ran away from home and, after working as a waitress in various cities and towns, married a middle-aged bartender in one of the western states. They lived as man and wife for several years, then one day she left him—she's still not sure why—and returned to her home state, where she eventually met and married her current husband without ever divorcing her first. When she revealed this secret to me, she mentioned a poem of hers that is perhaps her most harrowing, one in which a teenage girl witnesses her father's fatal heart attack. I knew the poem wasn't factual—her father is alive and healthy—but I didn't know, until she told me, that the man described in the poem is her first husband (who is also, as far as she knows, still alive). The poem ends with a reference to a button that's missing on the father's shirt. "That's my husband's shirt," she said. "That's what he was wearing the day I left him." The fiction she made to surround one small fact—the missing button—reveals far more about her inner life, I believe, than a straightforward history of her first marriage possibly could. By transforming her husband into a father, and his heartache after she left him into a heart attack, she reveals the extremity of her sorrow and guilt over abandoning him—and simultaneously expresses a desire, perhaps secret even to herself, that he in fact die, so she won't have to worry about having her past revealed to her current husband. However we interpret the transformation of facts in her poem, the description of her first husband's shirt is the only overt reference to him in all of her work, and it's as oblique as can be: No one reading the poem could possibly guess the secret of its significance to the author. And now that I know this secret, I cannot read that poem, or others by her, without seeing how it informs and generates her poetry.

Similarly, Charles Dickens had a secret that informs much of his work—most especially *David Copperfield*, *Oliver Twist*, and *Little Dorrit*, though its traces are virtually everywhere—and this secret appears to have generated not only those works but, to a large extent, their very author. As his biographer Edgar Johnson reveals, when Dickens was twelve, his parents' financial straits became so dire that they sent him to work at a grimy, rat-infested blacking warehouse (*blacking* being the English term for shoe polish). There, the young Dickens labored from eight in the morning until eight at night pasting labels on pots of blacking. The six shillings he earned each day did not prevent his father from being imprisoned for debt, however; eleven days after Charles began his degrading work, his father entered Marshalsea Prison, bringing further shame to Dickens and dashing whatever hopes he had of one day distinguishing himself in the world. Though both he and his father were released from their respective prisons within four or five months, those months felt like an eternity to the young Dickens, who could not have known when, or even *if*, his or his father's bondage would end. Dickens would have taken the secret of his family's shame to his grave had it not been for a chance encounter between his friend John Forster and a man named Charles Wentworth Dilke. Dilke told Forster, who was writing a biography of Dickens at the time, that he recalled seeing Charles working in the blacking warehouse when he was a child. When Forster mentioned Dilke's comment to Dickens, Dickens abruptly changed the subject. "I felt," Forster later wrote, "that I had unintentionally touched a painful place in his memory." After several weeks of silence about the matter, Dickens gave Forster a fragmentary written account of his childhood. Of his work at the blacking warehouse and his father's imprisonment, he said, "From that hour until this at which I write, no word of that part of my childhood which I have now gladly brought to a close, has passed my lips to any human being. ... I have never, until I now impart it to this paper, in any burst of confidence with any one, my own wife not excepted, raised the curtain I then dropped ..."

Of course Dickens *did* raise that curtain throughout his life— though only in his fiction, where he raised it again and again. But, importantly, each time it appears, it appears in disguise: The secret crosses over in the form of a lie. In *David Copperfield*, for example, Dickens alters the autobiographical facts, making his protagonist—whose initials are his own reversed—younger (ten instead of twelve) and putting him to work for a wine merchant, pasting labels on wine bottles instead of blacking pots. These are minor alterations, of course, and as such they're typical of your garden-variety autobiographical fiction. Another alteration takes us a little farther from the "conventional truths" of his public life, however: Instead of Copperfield's father going to prison for debt, it's his surrogate father, Mr. Micawber, who is imprisoned. More importantly, Dickens also made a major alteration, one that departs from the facts of his public life so completely that it reveals his secret life nakedly: He made Copperfield an orphan. This alteration reveals more than any recitation of the facts possibly could just how alone and abandoned Dickens felt then, and would feel as long as he lived. Furthermore, the fact that he "murders" his parents in his imagination may even suggest how much he secretly blamed and hated them for causing him such shame and misery. In any case, one thing is clear: For all his efforts to keep his secret, Dickens couldn't keep from telling it, in fictional form, throughout his life.

These two examples involve secrets that eventually became public, but I think it is fair to assume that much of literature—if not all of it—is similarly informed and generated by secrets that have remained secret. Reading literature, we feel these secrets the way we feel, rather than see, subliminal advertisements for popcorn and drinks at a movie theater. They're there but not there at the same time, yet their effect is nonetheless palpable: We suddenly feel hunger and thirst, and don't know why.

4. SECRECY AND IMMORTALITY

One of Chekhov's greatest stories, "The Bishop," is about a dying man who judges the external facts of his life a success yet nevertheless feels dissatisfied. As Chekhov says, Bishop Pyotr "had attained everything in life that it was possible for a man in his position to attain; his faith was unsullied, and yet all was not clear to him; something was lacking, and he did not want to die. It still seemed to him that he was leaving unfound the most important thing of all." That "most important thing of all," the story goes on to reveal, is "someone to whom he could unburden his heart." Like Chekhov's early story "Misery," which recounts a cabdriver's vain attempts to find someone to whom he can tell his sad story, "The Bishop" traces the bishop's failure to find that all-important someone to whom he could unburden his heart. He wishes to confide in his mother, who has come to visit him, but though she is "so natural and simple with strangers," she is "silent and awkward" with him, because he is a bishop. Pyotr wishes desperately to be known by someone—he even tries to reveal his feelings to the cantankerous Father Sisoi—and his tragedy is that he dies paradoxically both famous and anonymous: His public life is famous, but his secret life, the one that really matters, is utterly unknown. (No doubt the famous Chekhov feared the same fate, but rather than attribute his anxieties to an overtly autobiographical character—say, an atheistic writer—he attributes them to a devout bishop.) After the bishop's death, it is as if he had never truly lived at all, for even his public life soon fades from memory. "A month later a new bishop was appointed," Chekhov writes, "and everyone forgot his Reverence Pyotr." Only his mother remembers him, and though she tells people about him, she can't keep his memory alive. In fact, as Chekhov movingly suggests, the very effort to keep his memory alive helps *erase* it: When she tells people about her famous son, they believe she's lying in an attempt to increase her prestige. As a result, the bishop's life becomes, for most people, nothing more than a fiction, and his reality fades further into oblivion.

The desire to be known, not only now but also after our deaths, is one of the most basic of human desires. Ultimately, it's not celebrity the bishop, or Chekhov, wants, but immortality, our real life surviving beyond our public life. Everyone seeks immortality in some form or another. The very fact that we tend to judge the value of the present in terms of the future—"And would it have been worth it, after all?" Prufrock asks—reveals the premise that life lacks meaning unless it continues in some way after its biological close. Death, then, is the enemy of meaning, unless something more valuable than the physical body survives. All systems of thought, in order to assert meaning, deny death and posit some kind of afterlife. Religion touts the immortality of the soul, and science the perpetuation of the species or the replenishment of the earth (which our bodies renew as they decompose). To my way of thinking, neither of these forms of "immortality" provides consolation. Heaven, hell, and their relatives strike me as feeble fictions, and the afterlife science offers is meager indeed. I take little comfort from the thought that someday I'll be fertilizer for weeds, and not much more from the fact that, as a father, I will live on in future generations through my children and their children and so on, for as time passes my individual contribution to the species will diminish at an astronomical rate. In his book *The Dance of Life: Courtship in the Animal Kingdom*, Mark Jerome Walters points out that we are able to pass on only half of our genetic material when we reproduce and that our genetic contribution erodes drastically with each new generation. "After nine generations," he writes, "fewer than one in every 415 million genes is a direct offshoot of the original parents," and "Successive generations dilute the contribution at a geometric rate, rapidly driving the genes of the ancestral parents from the picture." If our lives derive meaning from the presence of our genes in those who follow us, that meaning diminishes just as geometrically as our surviving genes.

The only kind of immortality that truly exists, to my way of thinking, is the immortality of fame, if we define fame as Donald Hall does in *Their Ancient Glittering Eyes*—as "the love that everyone wants, impersonal love, love from strangers for what we are, what we do or make" that will last "forever and ever, as long as the language exists and maybe longer." But fame is tenuous at best: The artist whose stock is high today may be off the board tomorrow. (In the nineteenth century, for example, Philip James Bailey was ranked with Wordsworth, Shelley, and Tennyson, but today he's forgotten.) And fame is not only tenuous but, in relation to eternity, short-lived: Ozymandias may erect a glorious monument to himself, but it will eventually crumble; Shelley can resurrect that monument, and Ozymandias, in verse, but his poem too will crumble—and so, one day, as Hall acknowledges, will the English language itself. Still, there is no other "afterlife," however tenuous or short-lived, available to us than that earned through fame. And the fame accruing to a historical figure is a relatively paltry one, for it is based only on the public life, not the secret life that is the real life. Genghis Khan's *name* may be immortal, but his inner life isn't. The truest kind of fame is that based on "what we are"—on our real, secret selves—as revealed through "what we do or make." And the best—perhaps the only— way the secret life can continue after our deaths is through art, and especially, I believe, literature, which Hall has aptly defined as "human inside talking to human inside."

Reading Shakespeare, Dickinson, Chekhov, all the masters, we find, wherever we look, the literary equivalent of their DNA, all their genes surviving intact.

5. CYRANO

There is another reason I praise autobiographobia: Ever since I was a child, I have believed that secrecy and virtue are largely synonymous. If you did a good deed in public—helped an old lady across the street, say, as the Boy Scouts advocated—how could you be sure you were doing it for virtuous motives rather than vain ones? If an act was public, there was always the danger that you were doing it so that someone—the old lady, a bystander, God, Santa Claus—would think you were a good person. And if that was your motive, your act was not, in fact, a virtuous one.

In 1990 I saw the film *Cyrano de Bergerac*, starring Gerard Départedieu, and wrote a poem about it that addresses this issue of the relationship of virtue and secrecy. The poem is a fictive attempt to deal with my actual reaction to the film. Here it is:

CYRANO

How we admire Cyrano's suffering,
>   his noble silence, the purity
of a love kept secret, as he whispers

into the ear of his dying rival
>   *It's you she loves.* Unwitnessed,
his lie wins him neither praise

nor Roxanne, for goodness is nothing
>   if not a form
of privacy. But what if he believed

God was watching, as all-knowing and voyeuristic
>   as a moviegoer?
An audience taints every good act, a judge

corrupts it utterly. So is faith the greatest obstacle
>   to virtue? I'm falling
through this thought when I hear her,

a woman two rows down,
>   weeping so loudly I suspect
a grief too personal to be expressed

except in public. Hands over her face,
>   she whips her head back
and forth, as if saying *no* over and over

to someone not there. Or is she
>   talking to her life? Sympathy
is one disguise curiosity wears:

if I comfort her, I wonder, would she tell me
        the sorrow that sits down with her
each day for dinner, the pain

that makes her bed each morning?
        I believe she would, and I'm tempted
to be the audience that would give her grief

its twist of pleasure. But I turn back
        to the movie and try not to listen
as her sobs gradually subside. In an hour

we sit through twenty-seven minutes of darkness—
        the black spaces between frames—
and though we can't see it, we feel it

behind the images light casts
        on the blank screen: the blue sky,
the green lawn, and Roxanne's face,

beautifully ignorant, as Cyrano, old now
        and dying, visits one last time,
his secret the only thing

holding him, and us, up.

Perhaps it is my association of secrecy and virtue that makes me suspicious of those writers who, to echo Norman Mailer, "advertise" themselves. Even when they're advertising their vices, as is often the case, they seem to be congratulating themselves, as if they believe their candor is sufficiently virtuous to absolve them of those vices. As much as I love the work of many writers who choose nakedness over disguise, I sometimes find that love compromised by the suspicion that their work, however beautiful and moving, is motivated to some extent by self-admiration. The writers who most move me—the writers I, vainly, aspire to emulate—are those who most disguise themselves. (And we must remember that fact can sometimes serve as a brilliant disguise—witness Tim O'Brien's richly imagined stories about a character named Tim O'Brien.) By cloaking their selves in secrecy, these writers create works that renounce the self in order to discover, and reveal, the other. In Sherwood Anderson's opinion, "the whole glory of writing lies in the fact that it forces us out of ourselves and into the lives of others." Antonio Machado made much the same point: "What the poet is looking for," he said, "is not the fundamental I, but the deep you." But, paradoxically, the more a writer focuses on "the deep you"—the other—the more his secret life enters the work, and enters it with the mystery and power—and virtue—of a secret.

6. ZORRO'S SERVANT

What better way to end an essay on autobiographobia than with some autobiography?

In my youth, I saw a movie that, like *Cyrano de Bergerac*, taught me the virtue and value of the secret life. If, as Chekhov wryly suggested, autobiographobia is a disease, I was first exposed to it in the fall of 1958, when I was seven, and I caught it from an unlikely, and quite corny, source—the movie *The Sign of Zorro*. The movie was a distillation of the first thirteen episodes of the *Zorro* television series that had shown the previous fall and spring on ABC, and as far as I could tell, its characters and plot were familiar to virtually all the children who went to the theatre in my small hometown to see it that Saturday afternoon. My family did not yet own a television, however, and none of my friends had one either, so I knew almost nothing about Zorro. A few weeks before, one of my first-grade classmates had worn his Zorro costume to school for show-and-tell and all during recess he'd carved *Z*s in the playground dirt with his plastic sword. Ever since then, I'd been begging my mother to buy me a Zorro costume—I'd seen them for sale at our local Ben Franklin store—but she did not then, or ever, relent. Evidently, many of the kids at the movie that day had waged similar campaigns more successfully, for they were wearing Zorro capes and masks. The theatre had promised free admission to anyone wearing a Zorro costume (hats and swords had to be checked behind the candy counter, however) and they even let in a few girls who were carrying Fresh-Up Freddie dolls, stuffed roosters wearing Zorro outfits. (I'd seen these dolls at Ben Franklin also—along with Zorro games, puzzles, watches, and paint-by-number sets—but I had no idea what a rooster had to do with Zorro until the following year, when my parents finally bought a television and I saw an animated version of Fresh-up Freddie advertising 7-Up during *Zorro*'s commercial breaks.) When the movie began, the theater full of Zorros sang along with the theme song—"Out of the night, / when the full moon is bright, / comes the horseman known as Zorro"—and I felt I was the only one who didn't know the words. Despite my youth, I was already accustomed to feeling like an outsider, even when I was with my friends and family, but I had never felt more like an outsider than I did that day. As much as I'd looked forward to the movie—I had seen only a few others in my short life—now that I was there watching it, I felt as if I were the only person who wasn't in on the secret.

Like most kids, I wanted to fit in, and at this time and place, that meant knowing about Zorro. But the more I watched the movie, the more I found myself fascinated not so much with Zorro but with his faithful servant, Bernardo, played by the virtually unknown, then or now, Gene Sheldon. Sheldon did not have the looks or style of Guy Williams, the teen idol who played Zorro; he was a short, dumpy, baby-faced man whose double chin was accentuated by the cord that held his Spanish hat on his head. Like Cary Grant and Kirk Douglas, he had a cleft in his chin, but that fact only emphasized his difference from them and other stars. Nonetheless, I was fascinated by the character of Bernardo in a way that I wouldn't be by the other sidekicks of dashing heroes I'd encounter in the coming years—Friar Tuck, Tonto, Jimmy Olsen, Robin, and their like—and for a long time after I saw the movie I pretended to be Bernardo the way other kids my age pretended to be Zorro. No one ever knew I was doing this, but that was the whole point. For in watching Bernardo, I fell in love with the idea of the secret life.

Bernardo is a mute who pretends to be deaf in order to overhear secrets that he can pass on, via sign language, to his master, Don Diego de la Vega, whom he and he alone knows is Zorro. Because of this pretense, Bernardo's real self is hidden from the rest of the world—and not just metaphorically either. Don Diego's hacienda is full of false walls and secret passageways, and beneath it is the secret cave where Zorro's horse, Tornado, is hidden—these are the special provinces of Bernardo, the places where he lives his most essential life, hiding in order to spy on his master's enemies, caring for Tornado, and helping Zorro plot his heroic deeds. Like Don Diego/Zorro, Bernardo leads two lives—a public and a private one—and the secret life is the one that matters. But unlike Don Diego, who hides his identity with a mask, Bernardo requires no costume change. Or, to put it another way, he is always in disguise. And whereas Don Diego affects a glib, foppish eloquence to deflect suspicion, chattering away about trivial matters whenever he's in public, Bernardo dons the mask of silence and "speaks" only in secret and only about matters of grave importance. Stephen Dunn once said that writers are those people who are "hungry for essential speech" and that phrase goes a long way, I believe, toward explaining my interest in Bernardo as a metaphor for the kind of writer I have tried to be. Nothing Bernardo said—or signed, rather—was less than a matter of life and death. He wasted no time on the amenities of small talk, the dance of conventions that define most of our daily conversations. Even as a seven-year-old, I preferred his deceptive silence to Don Diego's deceptive talk, and for months after I saw the movie, I practiced being silent, even timing myself to see how long I could go without speaking, and whenever I was around strangers, I pretended to be a deaf mute, looking blankly at them and pointing at my ear or signing imaginary sign language when someone asked me a question.

I could not have explained my fascination with Bernardo at the time, of course, but now I suspect I admired him mostly because, unlike me, he only *appeared* to be an outsider while in fact he was the ultimate insider, the only one who knew Los Angeles's biggest secret. Pretending to be Bernardo, I could be the one who knew the secret, not the one who felt left out. But perhaps there was another reason, too. Perhaps I was hungry, even then, for essential speech, even if it required something akin to a vow of silence. And perhaps I knew, somewhere deep down in the cave below my surface life, that our real lives are the ones we hide from everybody. Whatever the motives for my fascination with this character, it strikes me now, nearly fifty years later, that Bernardo taught me the lesson that still guides my writing life: To be most truly yourself requires hiding yourself, and serving someone else.

II

FROM LONG SHOTS TO X-RAYS:
DISTANCE AND POINT OF VIEW IN FICTION

1. A DESCRIPTIVE APPROACH

Point of view is arguably the most important element of fiction writing, for it is inextricably linked to characterization, style, and theme, yet it is perhaps the least understood of all aspects of fiction. This lack of understanding is due in part to the fact that the term *point of view* has several different meanings. In common usage, of course, it refers to an opinion (as in "That's just your point of view"), but in literary discussions, it refers to three not necessarily related things: the narrator's person (first, second, or third), the narrative techniques he employs (omniscience, stream of consciousness, and so forth), and the locus of perception (the character whose perspective is presented, whether or not that character is narrating). Since there is no necessary connection between person, technique, and locus of perception, discussions of point of view in fiction almost inevitably read like relay races in which one definition passes off the baton to the next, and the result is confusion about what, exactly, constitutes the point of view of a particular work. The lack of understanding about point of view is also due to the tendency of authors of creative writing and literature textbooks to write prescriptively rather than descriptively about point of view, asserting that certain techniques are available only to certain types of narrators and that a work's point of view should be consistent. In this essay I will attempt to present a more accurate conception of point of view by closely examining the actual practice of authors and explaining how they use point of view to manipulate the degree of emotional, intellectual, and moral distance between a character and a reader.

Let's begin with Ernest Hemingway's "Hills Like White Elephants." In this story, Hemingway seats us at a table outside a train station in Spain. Sitting at a table near us are a man and a woman who are waiting for the train to arrive, and for the bulk of the story we eavesdrop on their conversation, just as we might in real life. And also just as in real life, we cannot enter into their minds; we can only hear what they say and see what they do. This objective point of view is commonly called "dramatic," for it imitates the conventions of drama, which does not reveal thoughts, only words and deeds.

Like a play, Hemingway's story consists largely of dialogue. At first, the dialogue is the smallest of small talk—the man and the woman discuss what they should drink, etc.—but it's clear there's some tension between them, something unmentioned that's lurking beneath their trivial conversation, and our interest is piqued. Two pages into this five-page story, the man finally broaches, however indirectly, the subject that is causing their tension: The woman is pregnant, and she wants to have the baby but he doesn't. Though the man repeatedly says that he's "perfectly willing" to go through with the pregnancy, it's clear he's doing his best to pressure her into having an abortion. Eventually, his protestations of selfless concern for her wear out her patience, and she asks him to "please please please please please please stop talking." The conversation over, he picks up their suitcases and carries them to the other side of the station, and we follow him there.

At this point, Hemingway momentarily abandons the dramatic point of view for only the second time in the story (the first time occurs when he says that the woman "saw the river through the trees") and tells us that the man "looked up the tracks but could not see the train." In this sentence, Hemingway reveals something that cannot be externally observed—what the man was *unable* to see—and so moves us a little way into his mind, reducing the distance between us and him ever so slightly. And two sentences later, Hemingway completes the segue that sentence begins, taking us even farther inside the character and reducing the distance significantly. He writes that the man "drank an Anis at the bar and looked at the people. They were all waiting reasonably for the train." Notice that word *reasonably*. This word violates the objective, dramatic point of view even more than the statement that the man did not see the train, for it tells us not just what the man sees—or, in this case, fails to see—but the man's *opinion* about what he sees. Just as Hemingway could have written "He looked up the tracks" without going on to tell us whether the man saw the train, so he could have written "They were all waiting for the train" without conveying the man's opinion that they were all waiting "reasonably."

If Hemingway had done these things, he would have maintained consistency of point of view, and according to virtually every discussion of the subject I've ever read or heard, consistency of point of view is an essential element of good fiction writing. But for my money, the word *reasonably* is the most important word in the story, and Hemingway's point-of-view shift is the single smartest move in a story full of smart moves. In the context of their argument over the abortion, this word implies that the man considers the woman *un*reasonable, unlike these people in the bar—and, of course, unlike him. This implication complicates the story considerably, for if the man didn't believe he was being reasonable, we would see him as a relatively simple villain, someone who consciously manipulates the woman into doing what he wants—all the while absolving himself of any responsibility for the decision—and we would see the woman, who agrees to have the abortion, as a victim (albeit a knowing one) of his manipulation. The story would therefore veer in the direction of melodrama, which thrives on the simple, knee-jerk emotions that result from villains' mistreatment of victims. But if the man truly believes what he's saying, then he is a relatively complex character, someone whose behavior stems from self-delusion, not one-dimensional villainy, and the story immediately becomes too complex to evoke the simple responses of melodrama. It is essential, then, that the reader know what the man thinks about himself and the woman. If Hemingway had maintained the same point of view throughout the story, as most commentators on point of view would recommend, we'd never know whether the man was a conscious, Machiavellian villain or merely a self-deluded person. But Hemingway wisely shifts his point of view, twice moving in from outside to reveal, with increasing depth, the man's thoughts. In my opinion, this is a brilliant example of how a writer can use the technical resources of point of view to manipulate distance between narrator and character, and therefore between character and reader, in order to achieve the effect he desires.

Similarly, Anton Chekhov violates the so-called "rule" against shifting point of view in his story "A Trifle From Real Life" in order to manipulate distance and achieve the effect he desires. For all but two sentences of this story, the unidentified first-person narrator reports the thoughts and feelings of only one character, Nikolai Belayeff, who discovers during a conversation with his lover's eight-year-old son Aliosha that the boy has been secretly seeing his father against his mother's wishes. Although Nikolai promises not to reveal this secret to the boy's mother, as soon as she returns home, he does. Distraught, Aliosha's mother turns to her son and asks him if what Nikolai has said is true. At this point, Chekhov steps slightly closer to the boy's mind for a moment, telling us that Aliosha "did not hear her," then he immediately returns to Nikolai's point of view. It isn't until the story's final sentence that Chekhov closes the distance between his narrator and Aliosha enough to tell us the boy's thoughts: "This was the first time in his life that he had come roughly face to face with deceit; he had never imagined till now that there were things in this world besides pastries and watches and sweet pears, things for which no name could be found in the vocabulary of childhood."

As this sentence suggests, the true protagonist of this story is Aliosha, not Nikolai, for he is the character who undergoes a completed process of change. Yet, except for the two sentences I've mentioned, the story restricts itself to Nikolai's point of view. Why does Chekhov shine the spotlight of point of view on a minor character rather than on his protagonist? The answer, I believe, is that by focusing on Nikolai, Chekhov forces us to make the same mistake Nikolai does: the mistake of assuming that it's the adult's experience that is important, not the child's. By abruptly shifting to Aliosha's point of view, Chekhov reveals that the story is not really about Nikolai and his trifling grievance but about Aliosha and his devastating discovery of an adult's capacity for duplicity and betrayal. This revelation allows Chekhov to complicate our response to Nikolai's despicable act by making us "accomplices" of sorts—for we, too, have been guilty of underestimating the importance of this "trifle from real life" to Aliosha. In a way, then, by abruptly reducing the *narrative* distance between Aliosha and us at the end of the story, Chekhov reduces the *moral* distance between Nikolai and us, and a potentially "trifling" story becomes a serious and complex one.

As these two examples suggest, perhaps the most important purpose of point of view is to manipulate the degree of distance between the characters and the reader in order to achieve the emotional, intellectual, and moral responses the author desires. Outside of Wayne C. Booth, who makes this argument persuasively in his book *The Rhetoric of Fiction*, few writers have stressed this aspect of point of view. Of the creative writing textbooks I know, only two discuss the issue of narrative distance at any length—Janet Burroway's *Writing Fiction* and Richard Cohen's *Writer's Mind: Crafting Fiction*—and neither one goes into much depth about the subject. Generally, textbook authors define point of view in terms of "person," focusing on the *angle* of perception—who's telling the story—instead of the various degrees of depth available within that angle. Even Richard Cohen, who does go on to discuss narrative distance briefly, defines point of view this simplistically. "There is no mystery about point of view," he says. "There are basically two of them: first person ('I') or third person ('he, she')." (He says "basically two" because there are relatively few works of fiction written in second person—examples include Carlos Fuentes's *Aura*, Jay McInerney's *Bright Lights, Big City*, and some of the stories in Lorrie Moore's *Self-Help*.) The more complex discussions of point of view, like Burroway's, go on to divide each of Cohen's two basic points of view into various types: First person is usually divided into "first-person central" and "first-person peripheral," depending on whether the narrator is the main character or a secondary one; and third person is divided into "omniscient," "limited omniscient," and "dramatic," depending on whether the narrator tells us the thoughts and feelings of several characters, just one character, or none.

In my opinion, classifying works of fiction according to their person tells us virtually nothing about either the specific works or point of view in general. If we think all we need to do to define the point of view of a work is identify its person, we're missing not only the boat but also the ocean. As Booth has said, "We can hardly expect to find useful criteria in a distinction that would throw all fiction into two, or at most three, heaps." Furthermore, as Christian Paul Casparis has noted, "The 'I' is a 'she' to the reader" and hence "Whole novels are read without leaving any particular impact as to whether they are written in the first or third person." Booth again: "To say that a story is told in the first or the third person … will tell us nothing of importance unless we … describe how the particular qualities of the narrators relate to specific desired effects." In other words, we need to focus on the *techniques* a narrator uses, not the *person* he uses. And as Booth has pointed out, *all* narrative techniques are found in "both first- and third-person narration alike." For example, both first- and third-person narrators can, and do, tell us the thoughts and feelings of other characters. We may call this technique "omniscience" when a third-person narrator uses it, or "inference" or "speculation" when a first-person narrator uses it, but the terminology cannot hide the fact that the technique is the same: In each case, the narrator assumes what Booth calls "privilege," the right to inform the reader of the contents of a character's heart and mind. While I'd like to see us abandon the term *omniscient* and replace it with *privileged*, I know that word would cause at least as many problems as it'd solve, so I'll continue to use the conventional word *omniscient* throughout this essay. But please be aware that when I talk about omniscience, I'm not referring to its ostensible meaning—"all-knowing" and "truthful"—but to the narrative technique of reporting—*whether accurately or not*—characters' thoughts and feelings. It seems to me that we cannot begin to understand how point of view actually works in fiction until we put more emphasis on technique than we do on Truth.

In short, despite what the textbooks tell us, the technique of omniscience is not the sole property of third-person narrators. As Booth tells us, "There is a curious ambiguity in the term 'omniscience.' Many modern works that we usually classify as narrated dramatically, with everything relayed to us through the limited views of the characters, postulate fully as much omniscience" as we find in third-person works. The only difference between first- and third-person omniscience (and it can of course be a *crucial* difference) is not in the narrator's technique but in the reader's response: We never question the truth of a third-person narrator's statement, but sometimes we do question a first-person narrator's statement.

Sometimes, but not always. Often, we respond to a first-person narrator's omniscience exactly as we do to a third-person narrator's omniscience—with complete trust. Chekhov's "A Trifle From Real Life" is one example. Joseph Conrad's *Heart of Darkness* is another. In it, Conrad's principal narrator, Charlie Marlow, tells us not only the thoughts and feelings of Kurtz and other characters but also the thoughts and feelings of the *jungle*. If that's not omniscience, I don't know what is. And though we certainly may question some of Marlow's editorial comments on the nature of women and so forth, we do not question the accuracy of his omniscient statements about other characters' thoughts.

Madame Bovary is another work whose first-person omniscience we accept without question. Flaubert's narrator, who identifies himself as one of Charles Bovary's former classmates, enters as fully into the minds of both Charles and Emma as any third-person narrator could, telling us about thoughts and events he could not have known anything about, and yet at no point do we question his omniscience. Because we have been taught—erroneously—that omniscience is the sole province of third-person narrators, readers tend to consider first-person omniscience a "mistake" on the part of the author. A scholar I know once had the audacity to claim that Flaubert—possibly the most fanatically meticulous artist who ever lived—simply *forgot* that he was writing in first person and began writing from a third-person omniscient perspective. (If he was afflicted with authorial amnesia, it apparently vanished from time to time, for the first-person point of view recurs in all three parts of the novel.) Mario Vargas Llosa's explanation isn't much different, I'm afraid. In *The Perpetual Orgy: Flaubert and Madame Bovary*, he explains the co-existence of a first-person narrator and omniscient narration by asserting that the novel actually has two separate narrators: the "character-narrator" who narrates in first-person plural, and the "omniscient narrator" who uses third-person singular and "witnesses and recounts with equal ease what takes place in the outside world and in the heart of hearts of the characters." In Vargas Llosa's view, these narrators take turns narrating the first chapter, and then from that point on, the character-narrator "disappears, never to return" and the omniscient narrator takes over for the remainder of the novel. (In fact, as I mentioned above, the first-person plural point of view recurs throughout the novel. While it's most evident in chapter one, it also appears two more times in part one, twice in part two, and four times in part three.) Unlike the character-narrator, Vargas Llosa continues, the omniscient narrator exists apart from the fictional world he describes and so is "invisible." But at times, he admits, this "invisible" narrator "manifests himself … in the form of intrusions which betray … the existence of a being who is a stranger to the fictitious reality." These intrusive comments range from such trivial opinions as "It is here that the worst Neufchâtel cheeses of the entire district are made" to such philosophical observations as "every notary carries within himself the remains of a poet." Vargas Llosa considers these intrusions mistakes—"involuntary … lapses"—in Flaubert's handling of the point of view. Well, if they're mistakes, Flaubert certainly made a lot of them: Although Vargas Llosa says there are "no more than fifty" of these "involuntary lapses" in the novel, in fact the number is at least double that amount. The effect of these "mistakes," Vargas Llosa argues, is to create yet another narrator: the "philosopher-narrator." I submit that there's a much less convoluted and far more logical way to explain these intrusions than by positing the use of a third narrator: They are the comments of the first-person narrator, who "disappears" only insofar as he stops referring to himself as overtly and regularly as he does in the first chapter. Furthermore, I submit that the first-person narrator and the omniscient narrator are also one and the same. In short, the novel has only one narrator, not two or three. The narrator's *techniques* may change, but the narrator himself does not.

Vargas Llosa's assumption is, sadly, a common one: that first-person narration and omniscience are mutually exclusive. At the heart of this assumption is the notion that since individuals are not omniscient in life, they cannot be omniscient in fiction. It's particularly ironic that Vargas Llosa would subscribe to this view, since he says in his *Letters to a Young Novelist* that "Life as described in fiction … is never just life as it was lived … but rather … what [authors] were obliged to fabricate because they weren't able to live it in reality." One of the things we can't do in reality is know what other people are thinking; in fiction, however, we can.

To those who, like Vargas Llosa, would maintain that first-person omniscience violates the most basic of all "rules" about point of view, I would point out that there isn't, and never was, such a rule. An abundance of first-person omniscience can be found in every period of literature. We see it in the oldest-known collection of stories, the Egyptian *Tales of the Magicians*, which was written between 5000 and 2000 B.C.E.; we see it in such medieval works as the *Gesta Romanorum* and Boccaccio's *The Decameron*; we see it in such early novels as Cervantes's *Don Quixote*, Fielding's *Tom Jones*, Defoe's *Moll Flanders*, Sterne's *Tristram Shandy*, Thackeray's *Vanity Fair*, Eliot's *Middlemarch*, and we see it in Melville's *Moby-Dick*, Hawthorne's *The House of the Seven Gables*, Hugo's *Les Miserables*, Dostoevsky's *The Devils*, Gogol's "The Overcoat," and James's *The Turn of the Screw*. And first-person omniscience isn't just some "old-fashioned narrative liberty" we've outgrown; it's still very much with us today. Among the many contemporary writers who have used it to superb effect are John Barth, Samuel Beckett, Jorge Luis Borges, Frederick Busch, Junot Díaz, Jeffrey Eugenides, Gabriel García Márquez, Günter Grass, Milan Kundera, Alice Munro, Tim O'Brien, Alain Robbe-Grillet, Marilynne Robinson, Salman Rushdie, Alexander Solzhenitsyn, and Eudora Welty. First-person omniscience has a long and noble pedigree; the prejudice against it is of more recent birth. If this attitude persists, I'm afraid we fiction writers will be deprived not only of a narrative technique that has served the masters well for centuries but also of the complex effects it can achieve.

Our misunderstanding of first-person omniscience is not the only problem that results from defining point of view primarily in terms of person rather than technique. Because it is generally a bad idea to shift person in a work of fiction—to have a first-person narrator suddenly morph into a third-person narrator, for example—we leap to the conclusion that point of view should be singular and consistent. In fact, however singular and consistent the *person* of a story may be, the techniques that truly constitute point of view are inevitably multiple and shifting. For example, the point of view we call third-person omniscience may be consistently third person but it is not consistently omniscient, for the narrator must of necessity shift from omniscience to the dramatic point of view whenever she deals with a character whose mind she does not enter.

Defining point of view largely in terms of person ignores the fact that whenever a third-person narrator presents a character who is telling a story, that character in effect takes over as narrator, if only briefly. (Consider, for example, the many first-person narrators who combine to tell the story of Thomas Sutpen and his descendents in Faulkner's third-person novel *Absalom, Absalom!*.) Defining point of view in terms of person also ignores the fact that first-person narrators, when they talk about other characters, use *third* person. And it ignores the fact that sometimes a first-person narrator uses third person to talk about *himself*. (Examples include Thackeray's *Henry Esmond*, Günter Grass's *The Tin Drum*, Charles Baxter's "Media Event," and Kevin Brockmeier's "These Hands," the last of which opens, "The protagonist of this story is named Lewis Winters. He is also its narrator, and he is also me.") How, then, are we to classify these narratives? First person? Third person? Both? Clearly, defining a work's person doesn't tell us much about its point of view.

I agree with Booth that the term *point of view* should be understood to refer not only to person but also to the various techniques that allow fiction writers to manipulate the degree of distance between characters and readers. Some of these techniques have the effect of long shots in a film—they keep us very distant from the characters—and others resemble close-ups. Still others are like X-rays: They take us all the way inside characters, so we're thinking and feeling with their central nervous systems. For most of "Hills Like White Elephants," for example, we watch Hemingway's protagonist with the distance and detachment of a surveillance camera, then Hemingway zooms in for a close-up of the man and, finally, a quick one-word X-ray of his soul. Chekhov follows this same pattern with Aliosha in "A Trifle From Real Life." (In terms of technique, these two stories are virtually identical, though one is written in third person and the other in first.)

Good fiction writers, like good filmmakers, know how to use these techniques to manipulate the reader's distance from the characters, sometimes moving in for a close-up and other times moving back for a panoramic view. And, often, going where the camera can't, into the mind and heart and soul of a character.

2. A SPECTRUM OF DISTANCES

What I want to do now is define, and provide examples of, the principal techniques we can use in our fiction to manipulate narrative distance. Though we don't have enough space to discuss how each point of view, and each shift from one point of view to another, can affect the reader's response to a story, please remember that directing the reader's response is the ultimate purpose of these techniques, as I hope my comments on "Hills Like White Elephants" and "A Trifle From Real Life" have demonstrated.

Most, if not all, of the techniques that constitute point of view will be familiar. What may not be familiar is the fact that all of these techniques are available to any narrator, whether that narrator uses first, second, or third person. Since second-person narrators are rare, we'll focus here on first- and third-person narrators. And we'll look at the techniques these narrators use in order of decreasing distance—from long shots to X-rays. As we'll see, some of the resulting points of view keep us entirely outside the characters; some allow us to be simultaneously outside and inside; and others take us all the way in. We'll also see that point of view is more a matter of where the language is coming from than it is of person. The points of view that keep us outside a character require the narrator to use *his* language, not his character's, whereas the points of view that allow us to be inside a character require the narrator to use the *character's* language, at least some of the time.

Outside

Dramatic

There is only one point of view that remains outside all of the characters, and that's the dramatic point of view, the point of view Hemingway uses almost exclusively in "Hills Like White Elephants." In this point of view, the narrator assumes maximum distance from the characters he describes and writes about them in language appropriate to him but not necessarily to them. We are so distant from Hemingway's characters, for example, that we don't even know their names—they're simply "the man" and "the girl." As James Joyce says in *A Portrait of the Artist as a Young Man*, a writer who uses the dramatic point of view is "like the God of the creation": He is "within or behind or beyond or above His handiwork, invisible, refined out of existence, indifferent, paring His fingernails." The narrator who uses this point of view imitates the conventions of drama, restricting himself to presenting dialogue, action, and description but not thoughts. The excerpt from "Hills Like White Elephants" that follows is a good example. Like a play, it consists solely of dialogue and "stage directions."

> "It's really an awfully simple operation, Jig," the man said. "It's not really an operation at all."
>
> The girl looked at the ground the table legs rested on.
>
> "I know you wouldn't mind it, Jig. It's really not anything. It's just to let the air in."
>
> The girl did not say anything.
>
> "I'll go with you and I'll stay with you all the time. They just let the air in and then it's all perfectly natural."
>
> "Then what will we do afterward?"
>
> "We'll be fine afterward. Just like we were before."
>
> "What makes you think so?"

"That's the only thing that bothers us. It's the only thing that's made us unhappy."

The girl looked at the bead curtains, put her hand out and took hold of two of the strings of beads.

"And you think then we'll be all right and be happy?"

"I know we will. You don't have to be afraid. I've known lots of people that have done it."

"So have I," said the girl. "And afterward they were all so happy."

"Hills Like White Elephants" is written in third person, but Hemingway also uses the dramatic point of view extensively in some of his first-person stories. In the following excerpt from "The Light of the World," Nick Adams, the narrator, reports action and dialogue but no thoughts, either his own or those of any other character.

When he saw us come in the door the bartender looked up and then reached over and put the glass covers on the two free-lunch bowls.

"Give me a beer," I said. He drew it, cut the top off with the spatula and then held the glass in his hand. I put the nickel on the wood and he slid the beer toward me.

"What's yours?" he said to Tom.

"Beer."

He drew that beer and cut it off and when he saw the money he pushed the beer across to Tom.

"What's the matter?" Tom asked.

The bartender didn't answer him. He just looked over our heads and said, "What's yours?" to a man who'd come in.

Because the dramatic point of view allows the narrator to report only the externals of a story, it requires a mastery of what

T.S. Eliot called the "objective correlative," an objective, sensory detail or action that correlates to a character's subjective thought or feeling. (In "Hills Like White Elephants," for example, we know that the woman doesn't want to discuss having an abortion because she looks at the ground instead of responding to the man. And in "The Light of the World," we know that the bartender thinks Nick and Tom don't have much money because he covers the free-lunch bowls and waits to see the nickels before he gives them their beers.) When an author is a master of this technique, as Hemingway is, the story that results is inevitably subtle. Careless or inexperienced readers will often be confused by stories employing this point of view.

Outside and Inside

There are two points of view that allow the narrator to be simultaneously outside and inside a character to various degrees: omniscience and indirect interior monologue.

Omniscience

Most textbooks distinguish between two kinds of omniscience: "limited" and "regular." In limited omniscience, the narrator relates the thoughts and feelings of only one character whereas in regular omniscience, he relates the thoughts and feelings of at least two and usually more. I don't believe dividing omniscience into "limited" and "regular" tells us anything remotely useful. The technique in both cases is identical; it's merely applied to a different number of characters. And as I see it, all omniscience is "limited": I don't know of any work of fiction that goes into the minds of *all* of its characters. Although we call the point of view of *War and Peace* "omniscient" rather than "limited omniscient," Tolstoy stays outside of far more minds—hundreds, in fact—than he enters. So I propose that we use the term *omniscience* to describe the point of view used when the narrator reports, in *his* language, the thoughts of any number of characters. The fact that the narrator retains his own language keeps him "outside" while the fact that he reports a character's thoughts allows him to go "inside"; hence this point of view allows the narrator, and the reader, to be simultaneously outside and inside a character.

Let's start by looking at two relatively simple examples of omniscience, one in third person and the other in first. The following passage is from Dostoevsky's third-person novel, *Crime and Punishment*:

> The triumphant sense of security, of deliverance from overwhelming danger, that was what filled his whole soul that moment without thought for the future, without analysis, without suppositions or surmises, without doubts and without questioning. It was an instant of full, direct, purely instinctive joy.

As I suggested earlier, "where the language is coming from" is one of the most important issues in point of view. The language here clearly belongs to the novel's third-person narrator. At this particular moment, Raskolnikov would not have used these rational, abstract, insightful words to describe his "purely instinctive joy"—in fact, he *could not* have used them because the moment was "without thought" and "without analysis." For Raskolnikov, the moment was "purely instinctive," not reflective, as the passage is. And if these are supposed to be his thoughts, they amount to the absurdly contradictory thought "I'm not thinking." If Raskolnikov is not thinking and analyzing at this moment, then, these thoughts and analyses—and the language that conveys them— must be the narrator's. As a result, we are conscious of someone outside the character peering into his soul and telling us what he sees. We are therefore both inside and outside Raskolnikov at the same time—inside in the sense that we witness his feelings, and outside in the sense that we are conscious that those feelings are being defined and articulated by an omniscient observer. In omniscience, then, the narrative perspective is still external to the character, as in the dramatic point of view, but we have moved, if only tentatively, into his mind and heart.

The next example is from Fitzgerald's *The Great Gatsby*, in which the first-person narrator, Nick Carraway, occasionally assumes an omniscient understanding of Gatsby.

> One autumn night, five years before, they [Gatsby and Daisy] had been walking down the street when the leaves were falling, and they came to a place where there were no trees and the sidewalk was white with moonlight. They stopped here and turned to each other. Now it was a cool night with that mysterious excitement in it which comes at the two changes of the year. The quiet lights in the houses were humming out into the darkness and there was a stir and bustle among the stars. Out of the corner of his eye Gatsby saw that the blocks of the sidewalks really formed a ladder and mounted to a secret place above the trees—he could climb to it, if he climbed alone, and once there he could suck on the pap of life, gulp down the incomparable milk of wonder.
>
> His heart beat faster and faster as Daisy's white face came up to his own. He knew that when he kissed this girl, and forever wed his unutterable visions to her perishable breath, his mind would never romp again like the mind of God. So he waited, listening for a moment longer to the tuning-fork that had been struck upon a star. Then he kissed her. At his lips' touch she blossomed for him like a flower and the incarnation was complete.

Like the example from *Crime and Punishment*, this passage employs the language of the narrator, not of the character the narrator is discussing. Whereas Carraway's style is often lyrical and poetic, Gatsby's is nothing if not laconic, though he dresses it up with his affected use of British expressions like "old sport." Can you imagine him saying, "So I waited, listening for a moment longer to the tuning fork that had been struck upon a star, old sport"? Me, neither. Clearly, Carraway is translating Gatsby's overwhelming, inchoate feelings into language that conveys what his own could not. Technically, then, both Dostoevsky's and Fitzgerald's passages employ the same point of view, though one is in third person and the other is in first person. Indeed, if we didn't know the excerpt from *The Great Gatsby* was narrated by one of the novel's characters, we would almost certainly assume it was another example of conventional third-person omniscience. That fact alone should indicate that we need to pay more attention to technique than to person.

Now let's look at two examples of omniscience that are a little more complex, one from Tolstoy's third-person novel *War and Peace* and another from Delmore Schwartz's first-person story "In Dreams Begin Responsibilities."

> When Boris came into the Rostovs' drawing room, Natasha was up in her room. Hearing of his arrival she almost ran down to the drawing-room, red in the face and radiant with a more than friendly smile.
>
> Boris was still thinking of the little Natasha he had known four years ago dressed in a short frock, with brilliant black eyes darting out from under her curls, all wild whoops and girlish giggles, so when he saw a totally different Natasha coming into the room he was quite taken aback, and the surprise and delight showed on his face. Natasha was thrilled to see him looking like that.
>
> "Well, do you recognize your little playmate and sweetheart?" said the countess.

...

Finally my mother comes downstairs, all dressed up, and my father being engaged in conversation with my grandfather becomes uneasy, not knowing whether to greet my mother or continue the conversation. He gets up from the chair clumsily and says "hello" gruffly. My grandfather watches, examining their congruence, such as it is, with a critical eye, and meanwhile rubbing his bearded cheek roughly, as he always does when he reflects. He is worried; he is afraid that my father will not make a good husband for his oldest daughter.

If we define the points of view of these passages in the conventional, person-oriented way, the passage from Tolstoy is an example of "regular omniscience" (despite the fact that its omniscience is limited to two of its three characters) and the passage from Schwartz is an example of "first-person central." But classifying these passages according to person can only mislead the reader into thinking that they are diametric opposites when in fact their techniques are essentially identical. Both Tolstoy's third-person narrator and Schwartz's first-person narrator omnisciently enter the minds of two characters (Boris and Natasha, the father and grandfather) while presenting a third character (Countess Rostov, the mother) dramatically, reporting only her actions or dialogue, not her thoughts or feelings. In terms of technique, then, there is virtually no difference between these two passages, yet most scholars would put them into two separate categories, based on person.

These two passages not only illustrate that all omniscience is limited to some extent but also that point of view is inevitably multiple and shifting, not singular and consistent. Unless the omniscient narrator enters the mind of *every* character, she will of necessity use the dramatic point of view for one or more characters. Imagine, for example, a hypothetical short story containing five characters. If the narrator—whether first- or third-person—uses the omniscient point of view for one character, she would have to use the dramatic point of view for the remaining four. And if she uses omniscience for two characters, she'd have to treat the remaining three from the dramatic point of view. And so forth.

It is of course theoretically possible for a story to employ only one point of view, but I can't think of a single example that does. More than any other story I know, "Hills Like White Elephants" consistently employs one point of view, but even it departs from that point of view three times, as we've noted. Since the major function of point of view is to manipulate the degree of distance between reader and character, it shouldn't surprise us that writers use more than one point of view in a story: How else can they create different degrees of distance between the reader and the various characters? And how else can they keep the story from feeling static? Imagine a film in which the camera stays the same distance from the characters, never moving back or in. Boring, right? The same is true for fiction.

Indirect Interior Monologue
The second technique that allows the narrator and reader to be simultaneously outside and inside a character is indirect interior monologue. This technique was invented by Flaubert, who uses it extensively in *Madame Bovary*, and it has become ubiquitous in twentieth- and twenty-first-century fiction. Indirect interior monologue—or, as the French call it, *style indirect libre*—differs from omniscience in one very important way: Whereas the omniscient point of view requires the narrator to translate the character's thoughts and feelings into his own language, indirect interior monologue allows him to use his character's

language. As a result, the character becomes a kind of "co-narrator," even though he is not, properly speaking, narrating at all. Henry James called this kind of character a "reflector," for indirect interior monologue functions like a mirror that reflects a character's thoughts. But just as mirrors distort what they reflect, inverting left and right, so indirect interior monologue distorts what it reflects. A narrator using this technique doesn't report a character's thoughts verbatim. Take, for example, that sentence from "Hills Like White Elephants" we discussed earlier: What the man is actually thinking is "They **are** all waiting reasonably for the train" but Hemingway's third-person narrator says "They **were** all waiting reasonably for the train." As this example reveals, indirect interior monologue involves altering the *tense* of a character's thought. Further, it often involves transforming the *person* of the thought from first to third. These alterations make us aware that the narrator is outside the character, reflecting the character's thoughts. In this point of view, then, we witness the character's interior monologue, but we do so *indirectly*, through the narrator's alterations. The result is, as Vargas Llosa has said, "an ambiguous form of narration," one in which "the narrator tells what he is recounting from a viewpoint so close to the character's that the reader at times has the impression that it is the character himself who is speaking." Like omniscience, indirect interior monologue allows the narrator to be simultaneously outside and inside a character, but because he is giving us the character's thoughts in the character's language, not his own, he is farther inside than in the other points of view we've examined so far.

The following passage from *Madame Bovary* demonstrates this technique. In it, Emma is recalling the romantic afternoons she spent in a garden with her former lover Léon. I have italicized the passages that employ indirect interior monologue.

With his head bare he would read aloud as he sat on a footstool of dried sticks. The fresh breeze from the meadow would blow on the pages and on the nasturtiums in the arbor. *And now he was gone, the one pleasure of her life, the one possible hope for happiness. Why hadn't she seized this happiness when it first appeared? Why hadn't she held him back with her hands or by begging on her knees when he wanted to leave?* She cursed herself for not having loved him.

Clearly, the italicized sentences are not the narrator's thoughts and questions; they're Emma's, reflected via indirect interior monologue. If they were presented directly, they would read as follows: "And now he **is** gone, the one pleasure of **my** life, the one possible hope for happiness. Why **didn't I seize** this happiness when it first appeared? Why **didn't I hold** him back with **my** hands or by begging on **my** knees when he wanted to leave?" Because Emma's thoughts are presented indirectly, through alterations in their tense and person, when we read them we feel as if the narrator and character are somehow talking to us at the same time. As the distinction between narrator and character blurs, the distance between them shrinks, and so does the distance between the reader and character. In no other point of view is the boundary line between narrator and character as thin as it is in indirect interior monologue.

While indirect interior monologue is most often employed by third-person narrators reflecting a character's thoughts, it can also be used by first-person narrators reflecting the thoughts of another character. In *Midnight's Children*, for example, Saleem, Salman Rushdie's narrator, uses this technique to reflect the thoughts his grandfather Aziz had when he visited the holy city of Amritsar before Saleem was even born: "Aziz stood at the window, inhaling the city. The spire of the Golden Temple gleamed in the sun. But his nose itched: something was not right here." What Aziz actually thought, of course, was "something **is** not right here." First-person narrators also use indirect interior monologue to reflect their own *prior* thoughts. In such cases, the first-person narrator treats his previous self as if it were a separate character. In *Heart of Darkness*, for example, Charlie Marlow uses indirect interior monologue to present thoughts he had during his voyage up the Congo River. "I turned my shoulder to him [the manager of the Central Station] in sign of my appreciation and looked into the fog," he says, then adds, "How long would it last?" Marlow is not asking *now*, at the moment he's narrating the story, how long the fog would last; rather, he's reflecting the thought he had at that time, the thought "How long **will** it last?" Clearly, he is reflecting his previous self's interior monologue just as a third-person narrator would reflect a character's.

Jeffrey Eugenides' *Middlesex* also offers excellent examples of first-person indirect interior monologue. In the following example, his hermaphroditic narrator, Cal/Calliope, reflects the thoughts she had twenty-seven years earlier, when she discovered she was genetically male, not female, and had her long hair cut in a male's style:

> Ed the barber put a comb in my long hair. He lifted it experimentally, making snipping sounds with his scissors. The blades weren't touching my hair. The snipping was only a kind of mental barbering, a limbering up. This gave me time for second thoughts. What was I doing? What if Dr. Luce was right? What if that girl in the mirror really *was* me? How did I think I could defect to the other side so easily? What did I know about boys, about men? I didn't even like them that much.

Cal/Calliope is not asking herself these questions, now, as she narrates; she's reflecting, through the change in tense, the "second thoughts" she had all those years ago, the thoughts, "What **am** I doing? What if Dr. Luce **is** right? What if that girl in the mirror really *is* me?" and so forth.

As the preceding examples of indirect interior monologue suggest, a narrator using this point of view reflects not only the diction of the character's thoughts but also the grammar, syntax, and associational movement of those thoughts. In passages employing indirect interior monologue, we frequently find rhetorical questions, exclamations, sentence fragments, and associational leaps as well as diction appropriate to the character rather than the narrator. The following example is from Joyce's *A Portrait of the Artist as a Young Man*. It portrays Stephen Dedalus, Joyce's protagonist, well before he became the young man of the title—at this point in the novel, he's a young boy, a student in a boarding school.

> It pained him that he did not know well what politics meant and that he did not know where the universe ended. He felt small and weak. When would he be like the fellows in poetry and rhetoric? They had big voices and big boots and they studied trigonometry. That was very far away. First came the vacation and then the next term and then vacation again and then again another term and then again the vacation. It was like a train going in and out of tunnels and that was like the noise of the boys eating in the refectory when you opened and closed the flaps of your ears. Term, vacation; tunnel, out; noise, stop. How far away it was! It was better to go to bed to sleep. Only prayers in the chapel and then bed. He shivered and yawned.

Clearly, the adult narrator of Joyce's novel is not asking the question "When **would he** be like the fellows in poetry and rhetoric?" Rather, he is reflecting the child's question "When **will I** be like the fellows in poetry and rhetoric?" Similarly, the adult narrator would not characterize the young boys Stephen looks up to as having "big voices and big boots": Those words come from the character, not the narrator. And the narrator, whose sense of time is certainly more sophisticated than young Stephen's, wouldn't measure it in vacations and school terms, nor would he think the year or two that separates Stephen from the older boys he admires is an extraordinary amount of time. The exclamation "How far away it **was**!" is not the narrator's thought, therefore; it's a reflection of Stephen's thought, "How far away it **is**!" And of course it's Stephen, not the narrator, who associates the alternation between term and vacation with a train going in and out of tunnels and the noise of the boys eating in the refectory. As this example shows, the change in person and tense allows the narrator to remain outside the character while simultaneously reporting, *almost* verbatim, the language, grammar, syntax, and associational movement of a character's interior monologue.

This example also illustrates the extremely important but rarely acknowledged fact that narrators often shift points of view not only within a story or novel but also within a single paragraph. The first two sentences, which summarize Stephen's thoughts in the narrator's diction, employ omniscience. The next nine reflect Stephen's thoughts indirectly, by changing their tense and person, and are therefore examples of indirect interior monologue. And the final sentence, which reports action only, uses the dramatic point of view. If we were to graph the point of view of this paragraph, we'd see that it begins on the outside edge of Stephen's consciousness, then goes deeper and deeper inside, and finally retreats to being completely outside.

As I hope this example suggests, handling point of view is much more than a matter of picking a person or a narrative technique and sticking with it; rather, it involves carefully manipulating the distance between narrator and character, moving closer one minute, then farther away the next, so as to achieve the desired response from the reader. In this case, Joyce manipulates the distance to allow the reader to enter into the psychological drama of what, on the surface, might appear to be a moment of extreme boredom. If he had employed only the omniscient point of view, our sense of this drama would be significantly diminished. As evidence, here's a purely omniscient rendering of the paragraph's opening sentences: "It pained him that he did not know well what politics meant and that he did not know where the universe ended. He felt small and weak. He wanted to be like the older boys at the school, who studied poetry, rhetoric, and trigonometry, but several terms and vacation would have to pass before he was their age. That seemed like a long time to him."

Or, worse yet, imagine how the moment's drama would utterly disappear if Joyce had used only the dramatic point of view. This entire paragraph would shrink to the simple and unevocative sentence, "Stephen shivered and yawned."

Inside
There are two points of view that to differing degrees eliminate the distance between character and reader and take us all the way inside, abandoning either temporarily or permanently the mind and diction of the narrator. They are direct interior monologue and stream of consciousness.

Direct Interior Monologue
In direct interior monologue, the character's thoughts are not just "reflected," they are presented *directly*, without altering person or tense. As a result, the external narrator disappears, if only for a moment, and the character takes over as "narrator." Unlike a conventional first-person narrator, however, the character is

not consciously narrating. Elizabeth Bowen's story "The Demon Lover" provides an example of this point of view.

> As a woman whose utter dependability was the keystone of her family life she was not willing to return to the country, to her husband, her little boys, and her sister, without the objects she had come up to fetch. Resuming work at the chest she set about making up a number of parcels in a rapid, fumbling-decisive way. These, with her shopping parcels, would be too much to carry; these meant a taxi—at the thought of the taxi her heart went up and her normal breathing resumed. I will ring up the taxi now; the taxi cannot come too soon: I shall hear the taxi out there running its engine, till I walk calmly down to it through the hall. I'll ring up—But no: the telephone is cut off … She tugged at a knot she had tied wrong.

Like the excerpt from Joyce we looked at a moment ago, this passage demonstrates how a great writer can manipulate distance within a brief paragraph. The first two sentences here are examples of omniscience. The third sentence slides into indirect interior monologue, altering the thoughts "These **will** be too much to carry" and "these **mean** a taxi" to "These **would** be too much to carry" and "these **meant** a taxi," then the sentence shifts back to omniscience. The next three sentences are direct interior monologue—her actual thoughts presented without alteration, comment, or even attribution by the narrator—and the final sentence is dramatic.

Sometimes the transition from external third-person narration to direct interior monologue is even more abrupt than in this passage. In the following sentence from *Ulysses*, Joyce leaps from a description of Leopold Bloom's external behavior to the thought that accompanies it with the aid of nothing more than a colon: "He sighed down his nose: they never understand." Jean-Paul Sartre uses the same technique in his short story "Intimacy," though he uses a comma more often than a colon to separate the external from the internal. And sometimes he makes the transition into direct interior monologue without any punctuation at all, as in this sentence: "She didn't even take the time to comb her hair, she was in such a hurry and the people who'll see me won't know that I'm naked under my grey coat."

As with indirect interior monologue, direct interior monologue is most common in third-person narration, but it is sometimes used by first-person narrators also. Again, Conrad's Charlie Marlow provides an example when he says, "I caught sight of a V-shaped ripple on the water ahead. What? Another snag!" The last two sentences report directly, without altering person or tense, the thoughts that occurred to him *then*, not thoughts he's having *now*, as he tells his story to his shipmates. Another example of this technique occurs in Hemingway's *A Farewell to Arms*:

> At a quarter to five I kissed Catherine good-by and went into the bathroom to dress. Knotting my tie and looking in the glass I looked strange to myself in the civilian clothes. I must remember to buy some more shirts and socks.

Frederic Henry is clearly not reminding himself now, as he narrates the novel, to buy some shirts and socks; instead, he's reporting the thought he had at a quarter to five on that now-distant day.

Stream of Consciousness

The other point of view that takes us completely inside a character is stream of consciousness. The term comes from William James, who coined it in his book *The Principles of Psychology* to describe the incessant, associational movement of our thoughts. Writers and critics have adopted this term as the name for a point of view that, as Burroway puts it, "tries to suggest the process as well as the content of the mind." Like direct interior monologue, stream of consciousness presents a character's thoughts and feelings directly, without transforming either their person or tense, but unlike direct interior monologue, it presents those thoughts as they exist before the character's mind has "edited" them or arranged them into complete sentences. Because our thoughts are continually moving, each one rippling into another, writers who want to convey the process as well as the content of a character's mind often eschew punctuation. But sometimes writers use a kind of "shorthand" approach to the character's constantly flowing thoughts, giving us brief fragments from the stream of associations. Joyce does this regularly throughout *Ulysses*. In the following example, he sandwiches nineteen fragments from Leopold Bloom's stream of consciousness between two sentences of external action:

> He walked on. Where is my hat, by the way? Must have put it back on the peg. Or hanging up on the floor. Funny, I don't remember that. Hallstand too full. Four umbrellas, her raincloak. Picking up the letters. Drago's shopbell ringing. Queer I was just thinking that moment. Brown brilliantined hair over his collar. Just had a wash and brushup. Wonder have I time for a bath this morning. Tara street. Chap in the paybox there got away James Stephens they say. O'Brien.
>
> Deep voice that fellow Dlugaacz has. Agenda what is it? Now, my miss. Enthusiast.
>
> He kicked open the crazy door of the jakes.

In the final chapter of *Ulysses*, Joyce uses the "longhand" version of the stream of consciousness technique. By telling us everything Molly Bloom thinks, without interrupting for so much as a comma, he takes us as far inside her mind as an X-ray takes us inside a body. The chapter, which consists of forty-some pages of Molly's unpunctuated thoughts as she falls asleep, opens with the following words:

> Yes because he never did a thing like that before as ask to get his breakfast in bed with a couple of eggs since the City Arms hotel when he used to be pretending to be laid up with a sick voice doing his highness to make himself interesting to that old faggot Mrs Riordan that he thought he had a great leg of and she never left us a farthing all for masses for herself and her soul greatest miser ever was actually afraid to lay out 4d for her methylated spirit telling me all her ailments she had too much old chat in her about politics and earthquakes and the end of the world let us have a bit of fun first God help the world if all the women were her sort down on bathingsuits and lownecks of course nobody wanted her to wear I suppose she was pious because no man would look at her twice I hope I'll never be like her a wonder she didn't want us to cover our faces ...

If we define point of view solely in terms of person, stream of consciousness is "first-person point of view." But there's an enormous difference between stream of consciousness and your garden-variety first-person narration, and that difference stems from the all-important fact that in stream of consciousness the character is not conscious of narrating. As Chuck Rosenthal has said, "Consciousness does not narrate itself. It's exposed to us by a narrator" whose presence is implied but not overtly revealed, either through self-reference or the use of third person. What's more, this implied narrator stakes claim to the ultimate form of omniscience, the ability to know, and present verbatim, absolutely every thought that passes through his character's mind. Other points of view *report*, in the *narrator's* language, a character's conscious thoughts, or they *reflect*, in the *character's* language, that character's conscious thoughts. But this point of view *presents*, directly and without any apparent mediation, a character's conscious—even, sometimes, *un*conscious—thoughts. In a way, then, this point of view resembles its diametric opposite, the dramatic point of view, which remains completely outside a character's mind. As with that point of view, the author is—to quote Joyce once more—"like the God of creation": "within or behind or beyond or above His handiwork, invisible, refined out of existence, indifferent, paring His fingernails."

The last chapter of *Ulysses* uses only stream of consciousness, but sometimes a narrator will mix stream of consciousness into passages that employ other points of view. In the second chapter of *The Sound and the Fury*, for example, Faulkner inserts brief italicized passages of stream of consciousness into Quentin Compson's first-person narration of his conscious thoughts and actions as he walks through the streets of Boston. Here is a representative passage:

> *The street lamps would go down the hill then rise toward town* I walked upon the belly of my shadow. I could extend my hand beyond it. *feeling Father behind me beyond the rasping darkness of summer and August the street lamps* Father and I protect women from one another from themselves our women *Women are like that they dont acquire knowledge of people we are for that they are just born with a practical fertility of suspicion that makes a crop every so often and usually right they have an affinity for evil for supplying whatever the evil lacks in itself for drawing it about them instinctively as you do bed-clothing in slumber fertilising the mind for it until the evil has served its purpose whether it ever existed or no* He [the deacon] was coming along between a couple of freshmen. He hadn't quite recovered from the parade, for he gave me a salute, a very superior-officerish kind.

Within the stream of consciousness point of view, as within every other point of view, there are various degrees of depth possible. Most passages of stream of consciousness go only as deep as conscious thought, but in this passage Faulkner gives us two levels of Quentin's mind, both his conscious thoughts and those that lie just beneath them. In *Light in August*, he goes even deeper, giving us *three* levels of a character's mind:

"I dont even know what they are saying to her,' he thought, thinking *I dont even know that what they are saying to her is something that men do not say to a passing child* believing *I do not know yet that in the instant of sleep the eyelid closing prisons within the eye's self her face demure, pensive ...*

As Dorrit Cohn has noted in *Transparent Minds: Narrative Modes for Presenting Consciousness in Fiction*, "A sort of stratification of Joe Christmas's consciousness is suggested here, with each successive mental verb ("he thought, thinking ... believing") descending into lower depth, less clear articulation, and more associative imagery." In short, Faulkner quotes Joe Christmas's *conscious* thought and then, in italics, presents first a *semiconscious* thought that exists simultaneously with it and then the *unconscious* thought that underlies them both.

3. OTHER CONSIDERATIONS

These, then, are the basic techniques fiction writers may use to manipulate distance between the reader and the characters. It's important to note, however, that there are other ways that writers manipulate distance, and a more complex description of point of view would have to take them into account. Consider, for example, the question of a narrator's reliability. Both Melville's *Moby-Dick* and Grass's *The Tin Drum* are first-person novels that employ omniscience, but we feel substantially "closer" morally, intellectually, and emotionally to Ishmael than we do to Oskar Matzerath because Ishmael is clearly a reliable narrator—even when he reports thoughts Ahab has when he's alone, we never question the truth of what he says—and Oskar is an unreliable one—he is an inmate in a mental institution, after all, and he credits his omniscience to his toy drum, which he claims "tells him" about people and events he never witnessed. (There are degrees in our response to a narrator's unreliability, of course: We feel much closer to Oskar than we do to, say, the narrator of Ring Lardner's "Haircut," who thinks destroying someone's life with a practical joke is great fun.)

And just as we feel closer to a character in a play who breaks through the "fourth wall"—that imaginary wall that separates us from the actors—and speaks directly to us, so we feel closer to narrators who are conscious of addressing an audience. Both Twain's *The Adventures of Huckleberry Finn* and Hemingway's *A Farewell to Arms* are first-person novels that focus on the thoughts, feelings, and experiences of their narrators, but we feel closer to Huck, whose very first word is "You" and who addresses us throughout his narration, than we do to Frederic Henry, who tells his story as if the fourth wall were reality, not metaphor. I do not mean to suggest that Twain succeeded where Hemingway failed—far from it. Each author created the kind of distance that best directs our response to his protagonist. We are supposed to feel an affinity to Huck, who behaves nobly while thinking he's behaving badly, and we are supposed to feel some distance from Frederic Henry, who sometimes behaves badly while thinking he's behaving nobly.

When we think about point of view in our fiction, then, we should pay attention not only to the person we're using but to all the techniques that manipulate our narrator's distance from the characters. And if we remember that manipulating distance is the primary purpose of point of view, we'll write stories and novels that take fuller advantage of this all-important narrative resource.

III

WHAT WE TALK ABOUT
WHEN WE TALK ABOUT FLOW

1. THE "F" WORD

We all have our pet peeves. One of mine is the word *flow*. In my three decades as a creative writing teacher, I've heard it literally thousands of times. It's a rare class in which I don't hear "It flows" or "It doesn't flow" offered as an explanation of what's good or bad about a story we're discussing. What bothers me about the word—beyond the fact that I hear it so often—is that my students generally don't seem to understand what they mean by it. They intuitively recognize flowing prose when they read it, but they're not sure what constitutes it. If I ask them what makes a particular sentence or story "flow," they'll answer with semi-synonyms that are equally vague: "It's the rhythm," they'll say, or "the pace," "the style." They can't really define it.

I'm afraid I can't either, at least not adequately. My response to flow is undoubtedly as intuitive as theirs, for when we talk about flow we're talking about an element of writing that is more music than meaning and thus beyond rational explanation—perhaps even beyond language itself. Hence it's extremely difficult to discuss, much less define or teach.

Difficult, but not impossible. While there is much about the flow of prose that will inevitably remain instinctual, there are some aspects of it that can be discussed, understood, and even practiced. The principal purpose of this essay is to try to make our unconscious understanding of flow conscious, so that those of us who don't instinctively write flowing prose can practice the skills and strategies involved until they become so habitual they are, for all practical purposes, instinctive.

Let's begin by looking at a paragraph that—my students and I agree—flows extremely well. It's the opening paragraph of a story submitted to Ford Madox Ford in 1909, when he was editor of the *English Review*. According to Ford, the story was sent to him by a schoolteacher from Nottingham who informed him that it had been written by a young, unpublished author who was "too shy to send his work to editors." Ford didn't expect the story to amount to much, of course, but the moment he finished reading the first paragraph, he laid the story in the basket reserved for accepted manuscripts and announced to his secretary that he had discovered a literary genius—indeed, "a big one." And that night, he told his dinner companion H.G. Wells the same thing, and Wells passed the word on to people seated at a nearby table. Before the night was out, two publishers had asked Ford for first refusal rights to the young author's first book. All of this happened before the author even knew his work had been submitted to an editor, and it all resulted from a single paragraph. What was it about this paragraph that impressed Ford so much that, without reading a single word further, he accepted the story and judged its unknown author a genius? In his explanation of his decision he points out many of the paragraph's virtues, but he stresses two in particular that convinced him he could trust the author "for the rest" of the story: The author employs "the right cadence," Ford says, and "He knows how to construct a paragraph." In my opinion, cadence and paragraph construction are two of the principal things we talk about when we talk about flow. If I'm right, the paragraph's flow is a major reason—perhaps even the *principal* reason—Ford recognized genius in it.

Lest this turn into an essay on how to create suspense, let me say now that the then-unknown author of this paragraph is D.H. Lawrence and that it is the opening of "Odour of Chrysanthemums," his first published story. Here's the paragraph:

> The small locomotive engine, Number 4, came clanking, stumbling down from Selston with seven full wagons. It appeared round the corner with loud threats of speed, but the colt that it startled from among the gorse, which still flickered indistinctly in the raw afternoon, out-distanced it at a canter. A woman, walking up the railway line to Underwood, drew back into the hedge, held her basket aside, and watched the footplate of the engine advancing. The trucks thumped heavily past, one by one, with slow inevitable movement, as she stood insignificantly trapped between the jolting black wagons and the hedge; then they curved away towards the coppice where the withered oak leaves dropped noiselessly, while the birds, pulling at the scarlet hips beside the track, made off into the dusk that had already crept into the spinney. In the open, the smoke from the engine sank and cleaved to the rough grass. The fields were dreary and forsaken, and in the marshy strip that led to the whimsey, a reedy pit-pond, the fowls had already abandoned their run among the alders, to roost in the tarred fowl-house. The pit-bank loomed up beyond the pond, flames like red sores licking its ashy sides, in the afternoon's stagnant light. Just beyond rose the tapering chimneys and the clumsy black headstocks of

> Brinsley Colliery. The two wheels were spinning fast up against the sky, and the winding engine rapped out its little spasms. The miners were being turned up.

When I show this paragraph to my students, they invariably praise its flow. Even those who complain that the prose is too "descriptive" or "old-fashioned" (words that many students consider synonymous these days, alas) find the flow of this overly descriptive, old-fashioned prose to their liking. When I press them for an explanation of what makes the passage flow, however, I rarely get more than the verbal equivalent of shrugged shoulders. To help clarify for them, and me, what makes Lawrence's paragraph flow, I offer them a revision that, we all agree, does *not* flow. I won't subject you to the entire revision; my point should be painfully obvious after you see how I've butchered Lawrence's first two sentences.

> The small locomotive engine came down from Selston. It was Number 4. It clanked and stumbled. It had seven full wagons. It appeared round the corner. It made loud threats of speed. It startled a colt from among the gorse. The gorse still flickered indistinctly in the raw afternoon. The colt out-distanced the train at a canter.

Awful, isn't it? But why? My sentences contain the same content as Lawrence's, and that content is presented in essentially the same order, yet the passage is as stagnant as the afternoon light Lawrence describes. So clearly neither content nor order determines flow. (For further evidence, take a look at Raymond Queneau's *Exercises in Style*, in which he tells the same brief incident ninety-nine times, keeping its content and order intact and changing only the style and, therefore, the flow.) Nor does ease of reading determine flow, since the revision is significantly easier to read than the original—even a grade-schooler could follow it. So what is the essential difference between the two versions? Nothing more, or less, than variety of sentence structure. That sentence structure is related to flow is an obvious point, no doubt, but if there's one thing I've learned as a writer and a teacher, it's that when something is obvious, we tend not to pay it sufficient attention. So let's pay closer attention to the relationship of sentence structure and flow in Lawrence's paragraph.

There are, of course, four basic types of sentence structure—simple, compound, complex, and compound-complex. But within these four general categories, there are many different types of structure, as the grammarian Virginia Tufte has demonstrated so superbly. In her book *Grammar as Style*, Tufte defines—and illustrates—innumerable ways to structure sentences, using left-, mid-, and right-branching modifiers, balance, repetition, coordination, inversion, apposition, and a vast array of other techniques. Significantly, Lawrence uses all four sentence types in his paragraph, not to mention many of the structural techniques Tufte describes. More importantly, seven of his ten sentences are either complex or compound-complex, the two types that permit most variation in structure. For example, both the fourth and seventh sentences are complex, but one contains five dependent clauses and the other only one.

Because of the variety of sentence structure in the paragraph, Lawrence's sentences range from 6 to 62 words. I use only the simple sentence pattern in my revision, however, and so my sentences range—if they can be said to "range" at all—from 4 to 9 words. According to Tufte, "The better the writer, … the more he tends to vary his sentence length. And he does it as dramatically as possible." Since variation of sentence length results from varying sentence structure, ultimately it's our syntax that determines whether our prose flows or not. As Stephen

Dobyns tells us, syntax is like a landscape: If it's too uniform, as in my revision, our prose will look more like Nebraska than Switzerland. A variety of sentence structure—and therefore of sentence length—will give our prose a more flowing, and appealing, landscape.

But because we don't think enough about syntax when we read, we don't think enough about it when we write, either. As a result, our work—my own, as well as my students'—tends to rely far too heavily on the two most basic sentence structures, the simple and compound. There's nothing inherently wrong with either, of course. In fact, the simple sentence is the base structure, the ground note of all prose. We can't, and shouldn't, do without it. But it is also the structure with the least possibility for variation in syntax and length since there are no other clauses, dependent or independent, attached to its single independent clause. The compound sentence structure is only slightly more complicated since it merely connects simple sentences with a conjunction. Because these two sentence types so dominate our writing, they prevent our prose from achieving that flowing cadence that marks the best fiction. As Robie Macauley and George Lanning have said, the simple, minimalist style "has its Spartan virtues but it also has its Spartan vices." And chief among those vices is a lack of flow.

Why are the simple and compound sentence types so dominant in our prose today? I asked my students and colleagues this question, and virtually everyone gave me the same answer: It all goes back, they confidently asserted, to the influence of Hemingway. But I disagree: Hemingway's simplicity is far more a matter of diction than of syntax. Like Lawrence, Hemingway knew how to vary sentence structure so his paragraphs flow. If you look at random paragraphs from his work, you'll notice how the simplicity of his diction exists within the context of complex syntax. The opening paragraph of "A Clean, Well-Lighted Place" is a good example.

> It was late and every one had left the café except an old man who sat in the shadow the leaves of the tree made against the electric light. In the daytime the street was dusty, but at night the dew settled the dust and the old man liked to sit late because he was deaf and now at night it was quiet and he felt the difference. The two waiters inside the café knew that the old man was a little drunk, and while he was a good client they knew that if he became too drunk he would leave without paying, so they kept watch on him.

The prose here is admirably straightforward and clear, but its syntax is by no means simple. All three of these sentences are compound-complex, and no two share the same structure. The number and placement of dependent and independent clauses in each varies significantly; the sentences have two, five, and three independent clauses, respectively, and one, four, and three dependent clauses. And the placement of the dependent clauses varies widely, too: The one in the first sentence *follows* an independent clause whereas three of the four in the second sentence *precede* independent clauses. And in the third sentence, two dependent clauses are embedded in the *middle* of independent clauses. Flaubert once said that "The sentences in a book must quiver like the leaves in a forest, all dissimilar in their similarity," and these sentences do exactly that.

I don't believe for a millisecond that Hemingway was thinking consciously about varying the placement of dependent clauses in these sentences—at least not when he first drafted them. No doubt he was responding to an instinctive sense of what would make the paragraph flow. We, too, should do our best to follow the ebb and flow of our rhythmic instincts, but to ensure that we have the skills needed to follow our instincts, we should also practice varying the structures and lengths of our sentences as rigorously as concert pianists practice scales.

While I don't think Hemingway can be held accountable for the current dominance of simple sentence patterns, I do think it's true that many of his followers have tended to use syntax as simple as their master's diction. This is certainly true of Raymond Carver—or, at least, of Raymond Carver as edited by Gordon Lish (as D.T. Max has revealed, Carver's hyper-minimalist style was due largely to Lish's drastic editing)—and it is also true of many of the writers who were influenced by the stories in *Will You Please Be Quiet, Please?* and *What We Talk About When We Talk About Love.* But the best of Hemingway's followers use syntax nearly as complexly. Even Carver, once he no longer allowed Lish to edit his work, varied his sentence structure and length considerably more than many of Hemingway's other disciples (not to mention Carver's own devotees). Witness the opening paragraph of "Menudo," whose four sentences use three different structures and vary in length from 4 words to 35.

> I can't sleep, but when I'm sure my wife Vicky is asleep, I get up and look through our bedroom window, across the street, at Oliver and Amanda's house. Oliver has been gone for three days, but his wife Amanda is awake. She can't sleep either. It's four in the morning, and there's not a sound outside—no wind, no cars, no moon even—just Oliver and Amanda's place with the lights on, leaves heaped up under the front windows.

There's nothing wrong with simplicity, in short, if it's only apparent, not actual. The best simple writing is, at its deepest level, the level of structure, complex.

So if we can't blame the current tendency toward simplicity of syntax on Hemingway's example, or even on Carver's, why is it so dominant? It's not, I'm sure, because we lack the linguistic skills to write more complexly (provided, of course, that we practice those skills). And it's not, I hope and pray, because we agree with Robert Bly's ludicrous assertion that "The use of subordinate clauses in sentences reveals the writer's tendency to fascism." One reason simple syntax dominates our writing, I believe, is that such sentences are just plain easier to write. They take less effort, less thought. Plus, there's less risk of grammatical mistakes or—a worse crime in these dumbed-down times—of appearing pretentious. To some of us, it seems, writing a compound-complex sentence is about as embarrassing as wearing an ascot to a hoedown.

But I suspect the most important reason we overuse simple structures is that we're excessively afraid of not writing clearly. Often, in the struggle to express a complicated, only half-understood idea or emotion, we sacrifice the truth we're trying to convey in order to write simply and clearly. As Wright Morris has said, "When we give up what is vague in order to be clear, we may have given up the motive for writing." Donald Barthelme also questions the value, even the possibility, of creating art that is simple and clear. "However much the writer might long to be, in his work, simple, honest, and straightforward," he says, "these virtues are no longer available to him. He discovers that in being simple, honest, and straightforward ... he speaks the speakable, whereas what we are looking for is the as-yet unspeakable, the as-yet unspoken."

So am I—or Morris or Barthelme—advocating the overthrow of English grammar and the production of vague, convoluted prose? Hardly. What we *are* advocating, however, is a conscious struggle against our natural inclination to simplify, for the sake of clarity and ease of reading, the complex, uncertain ideas and emotions that constitute our experience. And the best way to struggle against this inclination is to struggle against our tendency toward simplicity in syntax. The more we experiment with syntax, then, the more opportunities we give ourselves to discover our thoughts and express what would otherwise either remain vague or be sacrificed in the name of clarity.

Thus, altering our syntax does more than help us write flowing prose; it allows us to get our thoughts off the normal track on which they run. Syntax is nothing if not the very structure of our thought, so if we change the way we think, we can sometimes change *what* we think. But don't take my word for it; take Yeats's. In the introduction to his collected plays, he wrote, "As I altered my syntax I altered my intellect." Morris also believes that changing our syntax changes the way we think. According to him, "syntax shapes the mind … and does our thinking for us. If the words are rearranged, the workings of the mind are modified." And if the words are rearranged, the rhythm of those words is modified, too, of course. According to Robert Hass, it's this alteration in rhythm, more than the alteration in meaning, that changes our intellect. "New rhythms," he has said, "are new perceptions." In any case, the more we concentrate on altering our syntax, the more we free ourselves to discover other modes of thought. I'm not sure I'd go as far as Yeats, Morris, and Hass do, though, and assert that changing our syntax actually changes our intellect. Rather, I believe that as we alter our syntax, we *discover* our intellect—i.e., we find ways to say what we always knew but never knew we knew, our deepest beliefs and feelings. And it just may be that we discover not only the self but also the world. Bertrand Russell certainly believed syntax revealed the nature of outer as well as inner reality, for he concludes his *An Inquiry Into Meaning and Truth* with these words: "For my part, I believe that, partly by means of study of syntax, we can arrive at considerable knowledge concerning the structure of the world."

Given this relationship between syntax, thought, and discovery of both self and world, it shouldn't be so surprising that some of our greatest writers blossomed when they abandoned their native languages to write their work. As Morris says, "In this release from the overfamiliar, the apparently exhausted, and immersion into new resources, we may understand better than we did in the past the flowering of a talent like Conrad's. The new and strange language is part of a new consciousness." Nabokov is another example. He was so dissatisfied with his original Russian version of *Lolita* that he destroyed it. Only when he began to rewrite the novel in English, he says, did he find the syntax appropriate for the book, the syntax that made the book conform to what he calls "its prefigured contour and color."

We may not alter our own intellects when we alter our syntax, but by discovering and expressing them, we just may alter our *readers'* intellects. Indeed, it's possible that one of the things we talk about when we talk about flow is the feeling that the writer's syntax is altering our consciousness, making us think—and therefore feel—in new ways.

2. SYNTAX AS SOUNDTRACK

But just how does syntax do this? How can merely changing the structure of our sentences change how we think and feel? The answer is that syntax is more than mere sentence structure. As Tufte says, "Syntax has direction, not just structure," and the particular "sequence" of a sentence, its movement in time and space, "generate[s] its own dynamics of feeling." Pascal made this same point in his *Pensées*: "Words differently arranged have a different meaning, and meanings differently arranged have different effects." What alters our consciousness, then, is not so much syntax but the effects—the feelings—evoked by its sequence. As "a stylistic analysis of syntax considered as sequence," *Grammar as Style* is not your run-of-the-mill grammar textbook; rather, it is an indispensable guide to the ways writers can create different effects through different sentence structures. In the words of Lisa Biggar, it demonstrates that syntax is "a means of delay, suspense, emphasis, focus, direction—in essence, a tool to control the reader's sensory and emotional experience." One of the things we talk about when we talk about flow, then, is "the sequence of syntax" and the way it generates and controls the dynamics of the reader's emotional response.

Given that syntax is not just structure but a sequence—a *flow*—that generates "dynamics of feeling," it stands to reason that one purpose of syntactical variation is to convey rhythmically the emotion we wish to create in the reader. If we fail to create the appropriate rhythm, we will most likely also fail to convey fully the appropriate emotion—and that can have disastrous effects on the story as a whole. (Hence Truman Capote's comment, "A story can be wrecked by a faulty rhythm in a sentence.") Whether through instinct or conscious labor (or, more likely, a combination of both), the greatest writers skillfully modulate the sequence of their syntax to modulate their readers' emotions. Lawrence is certainly one writer who had this skill; as Morris has said, in his prose "emotion and syntax seem to be of one substance." In Stuart Dybek's opinion, this skill is essentially a musical one. "There's a story," he says, "and the writer then finds the words that serve as beats and notes to capture the invisible music. And like all music, that soundless thrum, now represented in language ... conveys deep emotion." As a result, he concludes, every well-written story has "its own interior soundtrack, one that a reader who listens might almost detect."

But sometimes the syntax does more than convey the appropriate emotion; sometimes it also rhythmically *imitates* the very experience it is describing, as when Beethoven mimics a thunderstorm in his "Pastoral Symphony" or when Duke Ellington mimics a train in his "Daybreak Express." The fourth sentence of the opening of "Odour of Chrysanthemums" is a good example of this sort of "rhythmic mimesis" in fiction. Let's take a close look at it. (To convey the sentence's rhythm, at least as I hear it, I've put the stressed syllables in capitals, and the most heavily stressed ones in bold.)

> The **TRUCKS THUMPED HEAV**ily **PAST, ONE** by **ONE**, with **SLOW** inEVitable MOVEment, as she **STOOD** INsigNIFicantly **TRAPPED** beTWEEN the **JOLT**ing **BLACK WAG**ons and the **HEDGE**; then they **CURVED** aWAY towards the **COP**pice where the WITHered OAK LEAVES dropped NOISElessly, while the **BIRDS**, PULLing at the SCARlet **HIPS** beSIDE the **TRACK**, made OFF into the **DUSK** that had alREADy **CREPT** into the SPINney.

Both structurally and rhythmically, this sentence divides itself into two almost equal halves, breaking at the semicolon. In the first half, the words rhythmically imitate the jolting rhythm of the passing railway cars. Seven of the first twelve syllables "thump" as heavily as the trucks—and five of those seven abut another stressed syllable, making us read the sentence's opening very slowly and thus reinforcing the sense of the train's slowness. (Imagine how different the effect would be if Lawrence had written "**ONE** after aNOTHer" instead of "**ONE** by **ONE**.") What's more, the heavy stresses evoke an oppressive mood, helping convey how the woman feels, trapped between the train and the hedge, unable to move. As the trucks fade away, however, so does the thumping rhythm: In the second half of the sentence, the stressed syllables are no longer either as heavy or as clustered, and thus the rhythm imitates the diminishing noise of the train as it gradually disappears, as well as the woman's sense of relief that she's no longer trapped. When Ford praised Lawrence's prose for having "the right cadence," I suspect he was referring at least in part to its rhythmic mimesis.

While I believe that rhythmic mimesis is one of the things we talk about when we talk about flow, it's important to recognize that it is not *synonymous* with flow. It results from the same impulse that creates flow—the impulse to make the sequence of syntax serve as an appropriate "soundtrack" for the story—and therefore it's a common feature of writing that flows. However, there are situations in which we can achieve rhythmic mimesis only if we *avoid* a flowing variety of syntax. In the following passage from *Light in August*, for example, Faulkner uses a sequence of short, choppy sentences to convey the simple, halting thought patterns of Joe Christmas, the novel's mentally challenged protagonist. There's just barely enough variety of sentence structure and length here to keep this passage from being as stagnant as my revision of Lawrence's paragraph.

> "Yes," Joe said. His mouth said it, told the lie. He had not intended to answer at all. He heard his mouth say the word with a kind of shocked astonishment. Then it was too late.

This passage is rhythmically mimetic but it doesn't flow. Nevertheless, I consider it successful. However important flow is, it is by no means the only criterion for judging the quality of our prose. As this example illustrates, there are times when flow would actually be detrimental to our fiction, if it were achieved at the expense of appropriateness. If Faulkner had tried to convey Joe Christmas's simple thoughts with the same flowing prose he uses for the maniacally intellectual thoughts of Quentin Compson in *The Sound and the Fury*, this passage would fail to convey Joe's experience and therefore to generate the appropriate response in the reader. Like flow, rhythmic mimesis is an element of good writing, not a condition of it.

Ezra Pound would disagree. In his essay "Vorticism," he argues that "every emotion and every phase of emotion has some ... rhythm-phrase to express it," and that it is the writer's responsibility to find it. But this is an impossible ideal, for identical rhythms can, and do, convey opposite meanings. As D.W. Harding says in his study *Words Into Rhythm*,

> The idea that rhythms have expressive value will easily be discredited if we take it to mean that a particular rhythm is peculiarly appropriate to one emotion rather than another. ... 'I adore her', 'I abhor her', 'It's appalling', 'It's enthralling', all these phrases with their diverse emotional value share the same rhythmical form ...

Harding goes on to suggest that although there are no simple one-to-one correspondences between rhythms and ideas or emotions, rhythm can "contribute appreciably" to the meaning of a sentence. In other words, while it may not be possible to make *every* sentence rhythmically mirror its meaning, it is possible to make *some* of them do so. Tufte makes this same point. Generally speaking, she says, a good sentence is one in which the rhythm and meaning are merely not "at odds with" each other. Sometimes, though, she adds, "the rhythm and sequence of syntax begin to act out the meaning itself" and "the drama of meaning and the drama of syntax coincide perfectly." This perfect coincidence of syntax and meaning, which I've been calling "rhythmic mimesis," and which Pound calls "absolute rhythm," she calls "syntactic symbolism." Whatever we call it, it is the result of the same impulse that engenders flow, the impulse to turn the sequence of syntax into a soundtrack for the story, and as such it is frequently part of what we talk about when we talk about flow. And when the rhythm of the syntax both flows and corresponds perfectly to meaning, the prose approaches poetry.

3. THE MUSICAL UNCONSCIOUS

And it approaches music. Ultimately, I believe, what we talk about when we talk about flow is music. As E.M. Forster says, "In music fiction is likely to find its nearest parallel." Helen Benedict seconds this opinion. "A composer would understand the analogy," she says. "Each syllable is a note, each word a bar of music, each transition from one word to the next an interval, each sentence a phrase or motif, and so on." As we've already seen, Stuart Dybek also understands this analogy, comparing as he does the rhythm of our prose to a soundtrack. Importantly, Dybek stresses that this soundtrack is not an afterthought or some kind of ornamentation but rather an essential part of the writing process itself. "One aspect of prose rhythm that is usually wholly ignored," he says, "is that a writer attentive to it, even if simply operating instinctively, often hears the rhythm before he writes the words. There is a rhythmic ebb and flow in mind that slightly precedes and certainly participates in the selection of language." Dybek is not alone in hearing the music before he discovers the words that correspond to it. Gerard Manley Hopkins wrote that his ear had long been haunted by "the echo of a new rhythm" before he finally realized that rhythm in the writing of "The Wreck of the Deutschland." And, as David Malouf notes, "Flaubert said that the last pages of *Madame Bovary* already existed as music before he had words for them." Malouf, too, often knows the rhythm of the words before he knows the words themselves and so frequently writes "a notation of long and short stresses" for the as-yet-unknown words. Alice Mattison notes further that sound, like rhythm, can also precede the selection of language: "Sometimes all I know about what I'm going to write is the sound. I know that something important happens in the story and it sounds like 'aaah.' I'll run around for days, going 'aaah'—is it a cat, is it a camera?" The philosopher Jacques Maritain has commented on these aspects of the creative process too, noting that it begins with a kind of "musical stir" in the unconscious that precedes "the production of words" and is "audible only to the heart," not the ear.

I've felt this sort of "musical stir" myself (though not nearly as often as I'd like), and so have most writers I've talked to. But where does this preverbal sense of rhythm come from? I suspect it comes at least in part from the language and music we grow up listening to, from the literature we've read, and even from nature—the rhythmical motion of waves, the drumming of rain on a roof, and so forth. But in recent decades, philosophers, linguists, psychoanalysts, and cognitive scientists have developed an intriguing theory that suggests an additional possible origin: They posit that we are all born with a private, innate "language of thought"—a sort of linguistic equivalent of Jung's "collective unconscious"—which we must *translate* into whatever public, learned language we speak. (What these thinkers call a "language of thought" Maritain calls the "*musical* unconscious," a spiritual, innate unconscious whose "primal expression" is the "musical stir" that precedes language.) In their view, behind our conscious language is an unconscious one, a proto-language if you will, which has its own semantics and syntax—and rhythm. And for the psychoanalyst Jacques Lacan, the unconscious does more than just contain a language, it is itself "structured like a language." All languages have their origin, he suggests, in the innate syntax of our collective unconscious.

The theorists who posit the existence of a "language of thought" believe we are wrong to believe that we think in English or any other known language. As the philosopher Jerry A. Fodor has said, "The obvious … refutation of the claim that [public, learned] languages are the medium of thought is that there are nonverbal organisms that think"—among them human children. If we need to know English in order to think, how is it that children are capable of thought before they learn the language? And how could they ever learn the language if learning requires the ability to think and thinking requires knowledge of the very language they're attempting to learn? As Fodor asserts, "you cannot learn a language whose terms express ... properties not expressed by the terms of some language you are already able to use." Therefore, like Noam Chomsky and his fellow transformational-generative linguists, Fodor argues that human beings must be preprogrammed with an innate knowledge of linguistic properties and rules that enables them to transform the syntax of thought into a public language. "[W]hat happens when a person understands a sentence," he says, "must be a translation process basically analogous to what happens when a [computer] 'understands' ... a sentence in its programming language."

If writing is indeed the act of translating an innate, unconscious language of thought into a learned, conscious one, it makes sense that we might "hear," at least on some level, the rhythm of the former language before we translate it into the latter. And it also makes sense that this rhythm might, as Dybek suggests, "participate" in our "selection of language." Virginia Woolf certainly believed this to be the case. In a letter to Vita Sackville-West, she says, "Style is a very simple matter, it is all rhythm. Once you get that, you can't use the wrong words. ... This is very profound, what rhythm is, and goes far deeper than words. A sight, an emotion, creates this wave in the mind, long before it makes words to fit it; and in writing ... one has to recapture this, and set this working (which has nothing apparently to do with words) and then, as it breaks and tumbles in the mind, it makes words to fit in." The source of this rhythm that apparently has nothing to do with words is, according to Fodor, our unconscious language of thought. Robert Hass seems to agree, for he has said that "rhythm is an idiom of the unconscious." And Rilke, too, expressed a belief in the unconscious, irrational source of rhythm. In a letter to Rodin, he says, "[T]o make prose rhythmic, one must go deep into oneself and find the anonymous and multiple rhythm of the blood."

Whatever the source of the preverbal rhythm Woolf, Dybek, and others talk about, it is important for us to listen to it. And we should listen to the *post*verbal rhythm of our prose as well, of course. As Benedict says, if we read our prose out loud, listening attentively to its music, we will hear "that too many sentences of the same length create a monotonous beat; that forced transitions are like the wrong bridge between riffs; that overlong, breathless sentences can be the same as music without rests, those essential silences that are as important for emphasis as the notes themselves." We will hear, in short, where the prose flows, and where it doesn't.

4. FORM AS RHYTHM

It's important to note that when we talk about flow in prose we're not just talking about the music of a particular sentence or even passage, we're also talking about the music of the work as a whole—its entire soundtrack. The word *flow* refers not only to style, then, but also to form, to the rhythmic relationship of sentences to paragraphs, paragraphs to scenes, scenes to chapters, and chapters to an entire novel. As the jazz musician and composer Tom Harrell has said, "Form is rhythm on a larger scale."

In *Aspects of the Novel*, E.M. Forster discusses at length the formal relationship of a novel's parts to the whole, and he discusses this relationship in the same terms Harrell does. He says "there appears to be no literary word" for this aspect of fiction, so "we will borrow from music and call it rhythm." In Forster's view, there are two kinds of rhythm. The first kind is stylistic, the kind we recognize in the syntax of an individual sentence, and we respond to it physically. The second kind is structural, the "syntax" of the work as a whole, and we respond to it less with our bodies than with our minds. "Beethoven's Fifth Symphony," Forster says, "… starts with the rhythm 'diddidy dum,' which we can all hear and tap to. But the symphony as a whole has also a rhythm—due mainly to the relation between its movements—which some people can hear but no one can tap to." This second kind of rhythm involves the entire structure of the fiction, the way its parts flow together to form the work's soundtrack. And just as a paragraph will flow if its sentences vary in structure and length, a complete work of fiction will flow if its scenes and chapters vary in structure and length. This kind of rhythm is simultaneously cerebral and emotional, something that makes our mind and soul "tap their feet." It is this holistic, formal kind of rhythm Dybek is referring to when he says, "Hemingway talks about the need for a writer to hear his way through a story, a fact missed terribly by his many tone-deaf imitators who manage to recreate his mannerisms but miss the underlying rhythmic coherence of his best stories." *Underlying rhythmic coherence*: That's another thing we talk about when we talk about flow.

Like Forster and Dybek, Milan Kundera uses musical analogies to talk about the underlying rhythmic coherence of fiction. He says his novels *The Book of Laughter and Forgetting* and *The Unbearable Lightness of Being* employ "polyphonic" structure and "counterpoint." And when he talks about the rhythmic relationships of a novel's parts to its whole, he uses the term *tempo*. Like Benedict, who says tempo is as important to fiction as its content, Kundera stresses the significance of this musical element of prose. "Contrasts in tempi are enormously important to me," he says. "They often figure in my earliest idea of a novel, well before I write it." He goes on to describe the seven sections of his novel *Life Is Elsewhere* as if they were movements in a symphony. Part one, he notes, is *moderato*, since it has eleven chapters in seventy-one pages. Part seven, on the other hand, is *presto* because it has twenty-three chapters in just twenty-eight pages.

But the tempo of a section is not determined solely by the relation between its length and the number of chapters it contains. As Kundera says, the "tempo is further determined by … the relation between the length of a part and the 'real' time of the event it describes." For this reason, he labels part six, which deals with only a few hours of actual time, as *adagio*, not *presto* or *prestissimo*, even though it has seventeen chapters in only twenty-six pages.

As Benedict, Dybek, Forster, and Kundera all suggest, rhythm, tempo, or flow—whatever we choose to call it—is essentially a holistic issue, one that addresses virtually every aspect of a work of fiction. (E.K. Brown has demonstrated that flow also manifests itself in a writer's handling of dialogue, character, plot, symbols, and themes. I recommend you read his critical study *Rhythm in the Novel* to see how he applies Forster's term *rhythm* to these elements of fiction, which are beyond the scope of this essay.) When we talk about flow, then, we're not only talking about syntax and rhythmic mimesis but also about the tempo and structural proportion of every part of a work in relation both to each other and to the work as a whole. When we first start writing fiction, we tend to focus on the syntax of the sentence but not on the "syntax" of the paragraph. As we progress in our craft, however, we begin to think about structure in larger and larger terms. We begin to vary not only the structure and length of sentences within paragraphs but the structure and length of paragraphs within scenes and the structure and length of scenes within chapters, and so forth. And we try to make the flow of each of these parts rhythmically mimetic, or at least appropriate, to the story's events and the characters' states of mind.

When we begin to think about flow on a macro as well as a micro level, we realize that consecutive scenes with the same structure and length have the same monotonous rhythm, only on a larger scale, as consecutive sentences of identical structure and length. It's possible, therefore, to write a story that does not flow as a whole although its individual parts do.

An example: Recently, one of my most talented undergraduates turned in a story that was, sentence by sentence and paragraph by paragraph, very well written. Several of his classmates praised the flow of his prose, but a couple of them went on to say that the story as a whole didn't flow. And they were right. So we spent the rest of the class doing an analysis of its structure to try to figure out why the parts didn't work together.

What we found was this: The story was divided into six scenes, each of which was almost exactly two pages long—the shortest was one and three-quarters pages and the longest was two and a third pages. All six scenes covered approximately the same amount of "real" time as well—about five to ten minutes. The sameness of length made the story's rhythm seem choppy, almost staccato, and, worse, it implied that each scene was somehow of "equal" importance, when some were clearly more dramatic and life-altering than others.

But the equal length wasn't the only problem; indeed, it was only a symptom of a deeper problem: The reason the scenes were of relatively the same length was that they had relatively the same structure. Each scene began with a paragraph or two describing either a character or a setting or both, then followed that with several paragraphs of dialogue, then one to two paragraphs of the protagonist's thoughts, and finally one brief paragraph—

sometimes, just a single sentence long—of action. While each individual scene was well written, the effect of six consecutive sections of similar structure and length was oppressive. According to Forster, rhythm requires "repetition plus variation." This student's story failed to flow because it was, structurally, repetition *without* variation.

While this story is obviously an extreme example, the problem it illustrates is hardly a rare one. Just as we tend to repeat certain pet sentence structures, so we tend to repeat certain pet scenic structures. We need to remember that scenes have their own kind of syntax—in a way they, too, can be simple, compound, complex, or compound-complex.

Let's look now at a story that varies the syntax of its scenes in such a way as to make the story as a whole flow: Tobias Wolff's "The Chain." This story consists of a chain of causally connected events, but Wolff doesn't make the mistake of making each link in the chain uniform. The story is composed of eight sections of differing lengths, structures, and tempos. The sections range in length from less than a page to nearly four pages, and the number of paragraphs per section ranges from two to forty-nine. One might suspect that the section with the fewest paragraphs is the shortest one, but in fact, that section is almost twice as long as the shortest one, and the shortest one contains more paragraphs than three that are significantly longer. And two sections of relatively equal length have eleven and forty-nine paragraphs, respectively. What Tufte said about the best writers varying sentence length dramatically also applies to the larger units of a fictional work: The best writers—and Wolff is certainly one of our best—vary the syntax of their scenes, sections, chapters, and so forth much as a composer varies the structure and tempo of a symphony's movements. And they do it for the same reason: to modulate the emotional response of the audience. For just as the sequence of syntax in a sentence "generates its own dynamics of feeling," so does the sequence of syntax in a scene, section, or chapter.

The first section of Wolff's story is a masterful example of how the sequence of syntax in a section generates feeling. It consists of two long paragraphs describing a man's frantic dash down a hill through deep snow to rescue his daughter from a dog that is attacking her. As the man says later in the story, "The whole thing took maybe sixty seconds. ... Maybe less. But it went on forever." Wolff manages to convey both the headlong speed of the events—its actual time—and the sense that it "went on forever"— its psychological time—chiefly through the way he handles the syntax of both his sentences and his paragraphs. Here's the story's opening section:

> Brian Gold was at the top of the hill when the dog attacked. A big black wolf-like animal attached to a chain, it came flying off a back porch and tore through its yard into the park, moving easily in spite of the deep snow, making for Gold's daughter. He waited for the chain to pull the dog up short; the dog kept coming. Gold plunged down the hill, shouting as he went. Snow and wind deadened his voice. Anna's sled was almost at the bottom of the slope. Gold had raised the hood of her parka against the needling gusts, and he knew that she could not hear him or see the dog racing toward her. He was conscious of the dog's speed and of his own dreamy progress, the weight of his gumboots, the clinging trap of crust beneath the new snow. His overcoat flapped at his knees. He screamed one last time as the dog made its lunge, and at that moment Anna flinched away and the dog caught her shoulder instead of her face. Gold was barely halfway down the hill, arms pumping, feet sliding in the boots. He seemed to be running

in place, held at a fixed, unbridgeable distance as the dog dragged Anna backwards off the sled, shaking her like a doll. Gold threw himself down the hill helplessly, then the distance vanished and he was there.

The sled was overturned, the snow churned up; the dog had marked this ground as its own. It still had Anna by the shoulder. Gold heard the rage boiling in its gut. He saw the tensed hindquarters and the flattened ears and the red gleam of gum under the wrinkled snout. Anna was on her back, her face bleached and blank, staring at the sky. She had never looked so small. Gold seized the chain and yanked at it, but could get no purchase in the snow. The dog only snarled more fiercely and started shaking Anna again. She didn't make a sound. He flung himself onto the dog and hooked his arm under its neck and pulled back hard. Still the dog wouldn't let go. Gold felt its heat and the profound rumble of its will. With his other hand he tried to pry the jaw loose. His gloves turned slippery with drool; he couldn't get a grip. Gold's mouth was next to the dog's ear. He said, "Let go, damn you," and then he took the ear between his teeth and bit down with everything he had. He heard a yelp and something cracked against his nose, knocking him backwards. When he pushed himself up the dog was running for home, jerking its head from side to side, scattering flecks of blood on the snow.

The fact that there are only two paragraphs in this section helps convey the headlong quality of the events; we pause only once in our mad dash through the deep, heavy paragraphs. The same sentences, divided into, say, six paragraphs, wouldn't have nearly the same effect. Furthermore, many of Wolff's sentences convey the same headlong hurry that the two long paragraphs do, each clause tumbling downhill after another. (He creates this "downhill" sensation chiefly by ending sentences with a cluster of dependent clauses.) But mixed into these frantic, fast-moving sentences are occasional short sentences, sentences that seem to stop the pell-mell movement of time for one brief instant much like a snapshot, thus conveying the character's sense that he's "running in place," moving as slowly as we do in dreams. Such sentences as "Snow and wind deadened his voice," "His overcoat flapped at his knees," and "She didn't make a sound" force us to pause briefly in the midst of the frenzy. Thanks to these time-stopping sentences, the opening section accomplishes an amazing feat: It conveys both speed and slowness at once.

As brilliant as this section is, if Wolff had followed it with seven sections of similar structure, the story would have failed despite its superb prose and moving content. By varying the syntax of his eight sections expertly, Wolff creates the kind of rhythm that Forster talked about, the kind you can sense but can't tap your foot to: a rhythm that's simultaneously cerebral and emotional: in a word, flow.

5. THE "F" WORD (REPRISE)

Flow. As I said at the outset, I'm weary of that vague, all-purpose term. But I think we're stuck with it. Though I've tried for years, I haven't been able to think of an alternative that contains all of its implications. (*Rhythm* comes close, but I think rhythm is ultimately more of a characteristic of flow than a synonym for it.) So I've concluded that the next best thing to finding a new term is trying to understand the old one better. As I hope I've made clear, I believe that when we talk about flow we're talking about the variation of sentence structure and length; about "the sequence of syntax" and its effects on the reader's emotional response; about rhythmic mimesis and the way it contributes to those effects; and about the rhythmic relation of the work's parts to the whole. Thus, if we want to write fiction that flows, we need to explore the syntax of our prose on all levels, from the micro level of the sentence to the macro level of the complete work. We need to develop our sense of a work's "underlying rhythmic coherence" by developing, first, our sense of our sentences' rhythmic coherence, then that of our paragraphs, our scenes, our sections, and so forth. The more we explore all these levels of syntax, the more we'll increase our chances of discovering both our story's content and our own intellects. And we'll also increase our chances of creating an "interior soundtrack" for our story, a silent symphony that transcends the events of the story, the denotations and connotations of the words, and moves the reader in ways as mysterious and powerful as music.

IV

REMEMBRANCE OF THINGS PRESENT:
PRESENT TENSE IN CONTEMPORARY FICTION

I'd like to begin this discussion of the past and present of present-tense narration with a prediction about the future: When the literary historians of 3000 write about the fiction of our time, I believe they will consider our use of the present tense to be its most distinctive—and, perhaps, problematic—feature. Whereas present-tense narration was once rare, it is now so common as to be commonplace. In 1987, Robie Macauley and George Lanning dubbed it "the most frequent cliché of technique in the new fiction," and since then, it's appeared with even greater frequency. And although there are signs that its use is diminishing among established writers, it's becoming the default choice for many younger writers. Recently, I asked one of my talented undergraduate students why she wrote all of her stories in the present tense. "Isn't that the way fiction's supposed to be written now?" she said, then added, "The past tense makes a story seem kind of 'nineteenth-century,' don't you think?" Why, I wondered, did a tense that has served authors since the very inception of fiction suddenly lose favor? What made the past tense passé? And why was the present tense now omnipresent?

In this essay, I will first speculate about some possible answers to these questions, then I will examine the advantages and disadvantages of the present tense in fiction.

1. A BRIEF HISTORY OF THE PRESENT TENSE

Some of the influences on our current use of present tense are direct—they are aesthetic examples that writers have more or less consciously imitated. But others are indirect—influences that have filtered into the culture and become part of the very air we breathe. Chief among the direct influences are, of course, the novels and stories written in the present tense, virtually all of which are products of the contemporary period. In his essay "A Failing Grade for the Present Tense," William H. Gass comments on the paucity of present-tense narratives in pre-twentieth-century literature, saying, "The present tense is a parched and barren country. In the past, writers rarely went there." But while it's true that past writers rarely visited that country, not all of its terrain is parched and barren; some of it is lush and verdant, as I hope to illustrate when I discuss the tense's advantages. Nonetheless, we must deal with the fact that, with some important exceptions, fiction managed to get along without the present tense for thousands of years but now employs it regularly, even obsessively.

Although the occasional use of present tense dates back at least to 59 B.C.E.—Virgil uses it at times in *The Aeneid*—it appears as the principal, or a principal, tense in no more than a few dozen works published before 1960. Five of these works are by Charles Dickens, who was the first major figure to experiment extensively with present tense. None of his novels is written solely in the present tense, but *Dombey and Son*, *David Copperfield*, *Our Mutual Friend*, *The Mystery of Edwin Drood*, and, especially, *Bleak House* contain significant, extended sections in present tense.

(For example, ten of the twenty-three chapters in *The Mystery of Edwin Drood* and thirty-seven of the sixty-seven chapters in *Bleak House* are in present tense. And, ironically, all the chapters in *David Copperfield* titled "Retrospect" are in present tense.) But fiction writers were slow to follow Dickens's lead. In the ninety years between the publication of *The Mystery of Edwin Drood* and 1960, few works composed wholly or partially in present tense appeared. Among them were Édouard Dujardin's *We'll to the Woods No More*, James Joyce's *Ulysses*, Gertrude Stein's *Tender Buttons* and *A Long Gay Book*, Virginia Woolf's "The Evening Party" and "The String Quartet," Katherine Mansfield's "The Wind Blows" and "Spring Pictures," Samuel Beckett's *The Unnamable*, Katherine Anne Porter's "Flowering Judas," William Faulkner's *As I Lay Dying*, Jolán Földes's *The Street of the Fishing Cat*, Joyce Cary's *Mister Johnson*, and Norman Mailer's *The Naked and the Dead*. Dujardin's 1887 novel *We'll to the Woods No More* was especially important since it pioneered present-tense stream-of-consciousness narration and greatly influenced James Joyce, who of course has greatly influenced us all. Faulkner's *As I Lay Dying* was also an important influence, since it, unlike most stream-of-consciousness fiction by Joyce, Woolf, and Faulkner himself, used present tense not only for thoughts but also for action, dialogue, and description. The same is true of Földes's *The Street of the Fishing Cat*, which was published seven years after *As I Lay Dying*, in 1937, and became an international bestseller, thus calling worldwide attention to present-tense narration. But it was the publication in 1960 of John Updike's *Rabbit, Run* that was most immediately responsible for the contemporary vogue of the present tense. Since its publication, present tense has become pervasive. While there were relatively few examples of it published in the thousands of years before 1960, there have been thousands of examples of it published in the few decades since.

Significantly, the principal influence on *Rabbit, Run* was not the work of Dujardin, Joyce, Faulkner, Földes, or any other previous writer. Rather, it was the work of Hollywood. Originally subtitled *A Movie*, the novel was Updike's attempt to "make a movie" on the page by capturing what he called "cinematic instantaneity." "The present tense was in part meant to be an equivalent of the cinematic mode of narration," he told an interviewer in 1967. "The opening bit of the boys playing basketball was visualized to be taking place under the titles and credits. This doesn't mean, though, that I really wanted to write for the movies. It meant I wanted to make a movie. I could come closer by writing it in my own book than by attempting to get through to Hollywood." No doubt many of the writers who've used present tense, both before and after *Rabbit, Run*, were under the influence to some extent of film, whether consciously or not. Gass suggests that these writers were, and are, under the influence of television as well, noting that "there was no particular fondness for the present tense until television (and now the VCR) upped our exposure to pictures from two hours a week to six or ten a day."

Another possible influence, one that bridges the gap between literature and film, is drama. Ever since Henry James introduced, and Ernest Hemingway popularized, the so-called dramatic method, a great deal of fiction has imitated the conventions of drama, focusing on dialogue and action as a way to imply thought and feeling. Even though most of these stories were written in the past tense, their avowed purpose was to place the reader in the position of a playgoer, someone who witnesses the events as they happen, right then, before his very eyes. As a result, it is perhaps only a short step from such past-tense stories as "Hills Like White Elephants" to the dramatic present-tense stories we find everywhere today.

And present-tense fiction may also owe something to the influence of lyric poetry. As many have noted, poetry and prose have been cross-fertilizing each other for the past two centuries, the most obvious results being the prose poem and its kissin' cousin, the short short story. Like lyric poems, short shorts are often written in the present tense. Nearly a third of the short shorts in the popular anthology *Flash Fiction* are present-tense narratives, for example.

Another influence, one that is perhaps more indirect than direct, is music—and I don't just mean the present-tense lyrics of some popular songs, those descendants of lyric poems. We see the apotheosis of the present most clearly in jazz. In most forms of music (as in drama), the performer and the audience share the same present, but the composer does not. In jazz, however, the performer is also the composer, or at least co-composer, since he improvises the music on the spot. The Beat writers were obsessed with jazz and the idea of spontaneous composition, so it's not surprising to find present tense in the work of Jack Kerouac, William S. Burroughs, and their cohorts. It is surprising, though, to find it in Eudora Welty's work. The fact that Welty turns to present tense only when she turns to the subject of jazz, as she does in her story "Powerhouse," seems to me evidence that present-tense fiction stems in part from our attempt to capture the spontaneity and immediacy of our most American art form.

Philosophy's influence on the rise of present tense has largely been indirect, affecting us through its general influence on our culture, but it is nonetheless very pervasive and important. Henri Bergson was perhaps the first philosopher to call writers' attention to the present in a significant way. In his 1889 treatise *Time and Free Will*, he argues that what we generally, and wrongly, think of as time is "nothing but the ghost of space haunting the reflective consciousness." He says that if we stop thinking about time in terms of space—if we stop thinking that the past is "behind" us, the future "before" us—we will realize that time truly exists only *now*, in—as the subtitle of his book says—"the imme-diate data of consciousness."

Bergson's contemporary William James had a similar view. Ac-cording to the scholar Robert Bartlett Haas, he believed that "all knowledge (whether of the present or the past) is held within the experience of the present" and hence reality exists only in "the now." The influence of James—and, through James, Bergson—is perhaps most apparent in the work of Gertrude Stein, who studied with James at Radcliffe. Haas argues that James's influence led her to believe that, to be "real," fiction "must be a description of the 'now'," or, as she put it herself in "As Fine as Melanctha," "a history of a moment." Haas's summary of James's influence on Stein could be read as applying to many contemporary writers as well: "The past as past could thus no longer be the content of her writing," he says. "Goodbye history. Goodbye traditional narrative which employed a beginning, a middle and an ending. … Goodbye past tense."

As influential as Bergson and James were, a more immediate and important influence is the existentialist philosophy of Jean-Paul Sartre, Albert Camus, and others, or at least the pop culture version of it that permeated our society in the 1960s, when the obsession with the present tense first took root. For Sartre, the present is paramount. It is the locus of human self-definition and responsibility, the moment in which we make "radical choices" about who we are. These choices are not caused by past events, heredity, environment, society, or any other so-called motivation or reason. In *Being and Nothingness*, Sartre says that choice is "absurd" and "beyond all reasons"; indeed, he asserts that choice actually brings "reasons … into being," not the other way around. In short, instead of being shaped by our past selves, we invent ourselves wholesale in every moment. Camus echoes this idea, stressing that the absence of a meaningful connection between past and present is precisely what allows us the freedom to invent ourselves, to make those radical choices. And though this freedom causes torment, because it makes us responsible for who we are every instant of our lives, it is also what ennobles us. In Camus's words, "This hell of the present is [humankind's] Kingdom ..."

According to Sartre, to affirm causality is to deny both our freedom and our responsibility for our current actions and thus to be in "bad faith," his term for self-deception. It stands to reason, then, that to write fiction that suggests that past events, beliefs, and desires motivate—or even elucidate—a character's present actions is to be ourselves in a state of bad faith. Sartre's ideas not only suggest why many writers have turned to the present but also why they have rejected causality and plot in favor of simple sequence and episodic structures. The stream-of-consciousness novel—which the scholar A.A. Mendilow has called "a kind of picaresque novel of the day-dreaming mind"—is a prime example of this tendency, and so are the many present-tense stories that depict little more than a "slice of life."

It's not a very long trip from the existentialist attitude toward the past to the "Live for the present" mantra of the 1960s. William Rueckert's "Boxed in the Void: An Essay on the Late Sixties in America" is a thought-provoking analysis of this obsession with the present, and it suggests that existentialism wended its way into that generation's—*my* generation's—view of history. His analyses tend to be overstated, but I suspect there are several large grains of truth in them. According to Rueckert, the generation that came to adulthood in the 1960s repudiated, in a way no previous generation had, conventional attitudes toward history because, for them, history was a record of "futility, helplessness, despair—or at its most extreme, the VOID." Because they found no meaning in history, he argues, they abandoned what he calls the "cognitive" approach toward history, no longer desiring to know what had happened or why. Briefly, they tried out what he terms the "revolutionary" approach to history, trying to change history through protests, demonstrations, and civil disobedience. When they became disillusioned about the revolutionary approach, he says, they turned to the "transcendent" approach and tried to "get out of history and into eternity" through drugs or religion. Then, when none of these approaches sufficed, they turned toward "resignation to the fact that history exhausted all viable and generative possibilities" and concluded that "any historical action ... is an absurdity." As a result of this belief, Rueckert says, they adopted the "common modern decision to believe and act in and for only the immediate present" and, by doing so, they became "boxed in the present." In this box, he concludes, "Historical consciousness is refused, denied, ignored; and by acts of the will one does not think about the past or, especially, the future."

Rueckert's comments are exaggerated, of course. Try as we might, we never could have repudiated history to the extent he claims. Even present-tense fiction, after all, almost always incorporates some past events. But since present-tense narration appears to have arisen in part as a reaction to the eighteenth- and nineteenth-century idea of the novel as a kind of history, it seems likely that the obsession with present tense does stem to some extent from a change in our attitude toward history and, therefore, time. And that change is very obvious if we compare the literature of the first and second halves of the twentieth century.

The first half of the century—the modernist period—was the most time- and history-obsessed known to humankind. As Stephen Spender said back in 1941, "Modern literature is obsessed with problems of time. Writers who differ in everything else share this pre-occupation." Wyndham Lewis went so far as to label his contemporaries the "time-school" of modern fiction. This "school" includes such important writers as Joseph Conrad, John Dos Passos, William Faulkner, Ford Madox Ford, André Gide, Aldous Huxley,

James Joyce, Franz Kafka, D.H. Lawrence, Thomas Mann, Marcel Proust, Gertrude Stein, Thomas Wolfe, and Virginia Woolf. Given the work of these writers, it's no wonder that when Mendilow published his classic study *Time and the Novel* in 1952, he titled its opening chapter "The Time-Obsession of the Twentieth Century."

In the context of this time- and history-obsessed literature, present-tense narration—especially the first-person present-tense narration that is so common today—seemed a virtual impossibility. Indeed, Mendilow wrote that "A narrative in the first person and written throughout in the present tense would, if it were possible at all, appear so artificial as to make any identification [between reader and character] impossible. It would obviously be limited to sensations and thoughts and exclude all action." It's not surprising that Mendilow believed the technique was unfeasible since there were so few examples in all of literary history before this date. What is surprising is that, within a decade, this "impossible" technique would become common.

So why, given the modernists' obsession with time and history, did contemporary writers turn just as obsessively to the present? One possible answer is implicit in the question itself: They did so in part as a reaction against the literature that preceded theirs, as a way to overcome, in Harold Bloom's famous phrase, "the anxiety of influence." But a more accurate answer would have to be more complex because our obsession with the present is as much an *extension* of the modernists' attitude toward time and history as it is a *reaction* to it. With a few exceptions, the modernists limited their use of present tense to their characters' thoughts, reporting all actions in past tense. We, on the other hand, have extended the use of present tense to actions as well as thoughts. Our desire to escape the past, to live in the present—to "denude" ourselves of time, as Stein put it—is likewise a logical extension of the modernist belief that history is, as

Stephen Dedalus says in *Ulysses*, "a nightmare from which I am trying to awake." According to the scholar William T. Noon, "So traumatic has been the common experience of a loss of meaning in history, personal and collective, that a sense of the nightmare of time has become almost a staple of modern literature."

If history is a nightmare, many of us seem to have decided to deal with it by drastically subordinating the past to the present or even, in extreme cases, eliminating the past altogether. A considerable number of our stories and novels focus on present actions without examining in any significant detail their personal and social antecedents. But we don't have to look to our literature for evidence that this attitude toward history exists; we see it even in our everyday language. The word *history* has become a synonym for something worthless, discarded: trash. "You're history," the detective says as he slaps the handcuffs on the murderer.

What are the consequences of this subordination, even dismissal, of history? To the philosopher Mary Warnock, the principal consequence is the diminishment of the imagination. "The greatest enemy of imagination," she says, "is to be locked in the present," for the imagination's primary purpose is to make connections between past, present, and future. Joyce, too, warns us of the dangers of ignoring history. Although everyone remembers Stephen's claim that history is a nightmare, few seem to remember that he goes on to warn against turning our backs on it. "What if that nightmare gave you a back kick?" he asks. Those of us who focus more or less exclusively on the present in our fiction ought to ask ourselves the same question.

2. SEVEN ADVANTAGES OF PRESENT TENSE

Whatever the causes for the prevalence of the present tense in our fiction, it is important that we understand its advantages and disadvantages, so we can better decide when to use it. Our principal concern as writers ought to be to choose those techniques that best serve the particular story we're writing, and for some stories, present tense may be the exactly right choice. Here are seven major advantages the tense can offer us.

First, present tense has more "immediacy" than past. Past-tense narration is of course "immediate" in a way, since the events of the characters' past are happening in the reader's present. As Mendilow explains, the reader "translates all that happens ... into an imaginative present of his own," turning "he went" into "he goes" and so forth. Still, present tense is considerably more immediate than past, if only because no "translation" is required. It is the simplest solution to what Mendilow calls the most basic goal of writing: "to make the reader forget his own present and sink himself into the fictive present of the story."

Because the present tense is inherently more immediate, Ron Tanner says, fiction that employs it focuses on "the very difficult task of making sense of things as they happen," a focus that intensifies the character's situation. Without the "long view" provided by the past tense, characters don't have the leisure to analyze and elucidate the events of the narrative they're living through. And neither does the reader: As Tanner says, the present tense "is a way of shaking readers from a complacent reliance upon the authorial intelligence," and hence it requires "readerly participation" in a way that ruminative past-tense fiction doesn't. While we could argue that all good fiction, regardless of the tense it employs, requires such participation, Tanner's point does hold in many cases.

The immediacy of the present tense also allows us to convey a character's change *as it happens*, not after the fact. This advantage is perhaps most apparent in first-person narration. In a retrospective story, the narrator's change has occurred before he speaks the first word, and though we witness the process of his change throughout the story, we do so through the lens of his already-changed perceptions. In present tense, we are there with the narrator step by step as he changes, and hence the story's climax can be both more immediate and intense.

Second, the present tense allows us to extend the concept of realism into the realm of time. Virtually all fiction we call "realistic" portrays the passage of time *un*realistically, condensing a year to a sentence, for example, and expanding a moment into a chapter, and for this reason Sartre called for a kind of temporal realism, at least when we're portraying a character's stream of consciousness. If we are to "plunge the reader into a consciousness," he says, "then the time of this consciousness must be imposed upon him without abridgement." If a character thinks for ten minutes, in short, the reader should read for ten minutes.

The concept of temporal realism, the attempt to capture on the page the sense of actual time, resembles the "cinematic instantaneity" that Updike talks about, but we should not confuse the two concepts. Although we can see a moment in a film more instantaneously than in fiction, time is almost as malleable in film as in fiction, and no film I know actually conveys the experience of real time for more than brief moments. In 2001, the Fox network attempted to bring the concept of real time to television via a show called *24*, starring Kiefer Sutherland. Each season consists of twenty-four episodes, and each episode supposedly covers one hour of one day in "real time." At least that's what Fox, and the show's production company, Real Time Productions, claims, and that's what's implied by the relentlessly ticking digital clock that periodically appears on the screen. In fact, of course, the show is not filmed in real time. Far more happens during each episode than could possibly happen in an hour, much less in the forty-six minutes each episode actually runs. (Fourteen minutes are devoted to commercial breaks, during which real time is suspended.)

To live up to its claim of being in real time, the show would have to be filmed in one continuous shot. To date, there is only one feature-length film that has been filmed in this manner—Aleksandr Sokurov's *Russian Ark*—and despite this fact, it does not convey the experience of real time, nor does it even attempt to do so. Ironically, this ninety-five-minute nonstop slice of present time has as its subject the past. The film follows an off-camera contemporary Russian film director and a nineteenth-century French marquis famous for his scathing criticism of Russia as they tour St. Petersburg's Hermitage museum, and it compresses into that one continuous present three hundred years of Russian history, for as the director and the marquis walk through the museum in real time, they encounter such historical figures as Peter the Great, Catherine the Great, and Czar Nicholas and his family and they witness scenes from the Siege of Leningrad and other momentous events of Russia's past. The film is thus not about the present it records in real time but the past it compresses into that present.

Since both films and TV shows compress (and sometimes expand) time almost as much as fiction, presenting only relatively short moments of real-time action, Updike might have been wiser to compare the "instantaneity" he was after in *Rabbit, Run* to that found in drama rather than cinema. While it might seem that the scenes in both genres of necessity depict real time because they last precisely as long as it takes the actors to say and do what they say and do, the depiction of real time in film is compromised by the fact that each scene is composed of many fragments cut and spliced together—and those fragments may include flashbacks or even flashforwards. In fiction, of course, the depiction of real time is compromised not only by flashbacks and flashforwards but also by summaries, something that film can approximate only via montage. Although fiction writers can't match the ability of drama, or even film, to convey the passage of literal time realistically, we can certainly come closer to it if we use the present tense, since it discourages the use of these and other techniques that compress or expand time.

Third, narrating past events in the present tense helps us achieve originality and intensity through what the Russian formalist critic Viktor Shklovsky calls "defamiliarization." In his essay on this subject, Charles Baxter defines Shklovsky's term as "[making] the familiar strange, and the strange familiar" and suggests that defamiliarization is the principal way we can live up to Ezra Pound's injunction to "Make it new." Baxter discusses many ways to achieve defamiliarization, but there is one he doesn't mention (though several examples of it appear in his fiction): shifting to an unfamiliar, unexpected tense. When this kind of shift was less common, it was more defamiliarizing than it is now, of course, and more original. But even now, it can have a startling effect and increase the intensity of a scene. As Linda Schneider has pointed out, Baxter's abrupt shift to present tense in the story "Saul and Patsy Are Pregnant" serves "to highlight the material by forcing us to change gears while reading." Updike achieves a similar effect in *The Centaur*, the seventh chapter of which is the sole one in present tense. Other writers, from Tolstoy in "The Death of Ivan Ilych" to Bobbie Ann Mason in *In Country*, shift even more often into present-tense passages or chapters. In all of these cases, especially important and dramatic moments gain intensity from being presented in a defamiliarizing way. Janet Burroway acknowledges the value of shifting from past to present tense, but she wisely goes on to caution that this technique "needs both to be saved for those crucial moments and to be controlled so carefully in the transition that the reader is primarily aware of the intensity, rather than the tense."

Fourth, because the present tense can be defamiliarizing and, therefore, disorienting, it is an effective way to convey unfamiliar, disoriented states of minds. When we dream, the familiar becomes the strange, the strange the familiar, and time loses its normal meaning, so it makes sense that present tense works exceptionally well to convey dreams. Delmore Schwartz's "In Dreams Begin Responsibilities" is a marvelous example of this use of the present tense. The present tense also works superbly in Susan Dodd's "Potions," which reports the thoughts of a woman driven to the edge of insanity by grief, and in Victoria Redel's *Loverboy*, which takes us inside the mind of a woman lying comatose in a hospital.

Fifth, present tense can contribute to the characterization of a work's protagonist. As Joyce Cary said, he chose the present tense for his novel *Mister Johnson* because its title character lives in the present and he wanted his readers to be "carried unreflecting on the stream of events" just as Mister Johnson is. Cary acknowledged that the "restless movement" of the present tense "irritates many readers" by making them feel that "events are rushing them along before they have time to examine them, to judge them, and to find their own place among them." But, he explained, "as Johnson does not judge, so I did not want the reader to judge. And as Johnson swims gaily on the surface of life, so I wanted the reader to swim, as all of us swim, with more or less courage and skill, for our lives." Many of the most successful present-tense novels and stories deal with characters who, like Mister Johnson, are "boxed in the present."

One such character is Private Wesley Miller in Tobias Wolff's "The Other Miller." As Wolff has said, Miller "lives in the present, almost like an animal. So that was, it seemed to me, the natural tense for the story." For most of the story, Miller refuses to think about the future. "What lies ahead doesn't bear thinking about," he thinks, because "When you go from today to tomorrow you're walking into an ambush." But as the story approaches its end, it abruptly shifts its focus—and tense—to the future, and we see Miller ambushed by the fear he's been repressing all along, the fear that it is indeed his mother who has died, not the mother of the other W.P. Miller in his battalion. In future tense, he imagines, step by step, his long trip home, and then, in the story's final two paragraphs, Wolff shifts back to present tense—but not back to the story's present time. The final paragraphs describe in present tense his future arrival home, bearing flowers for his dead mother, and his warm reception by his stepfather, the man whose marriage to Miller's mother led Miller to leave home and refuse, for the past two years, to speak or write to her. This shift back to present tense has devastating implications, for it suggests that, by allowing his fears about the future into his present consciousness for the first time, Miller has finally realized that he has treated his mother cruelly and that he will now never be able to make amends to her. He will return home like the prodigal son, yes, and he will be forgiven by his stepfather and the other mourners, but he will never forgive himself. It's a harrowing realization, both for Miller and the reader, and its impact is due in large part to Wolff's superb handling of tense shifts.

Just as the present tense works well in fiction about characters who repress thoughts about the future, so it also works well in fiction about characters who repress thoughts about the past. An excellent example of this latter use of present tense is Abigail Thomas's "Sisters." Throughout this story, the narrator consciously tries to forget the past, both to diminish her sorrow over the loss of her father, who abandoned the family several years before, and to prevent her younger sister Janet from "taking him away from her" in a way. As she says, "I never discuss him with Janet. She will remember something I don't and another piece of him will belong to her." She also complains that Janet "acts as if the past belongs to her just because she remembers it better, as if I hadn't been there at all." In order to protect both her father and herself from further erasure, she, as she says, "specialize[s] in the present and the future." The story bears out her claim, relying almost solely on the present and, to a lesser extent, the future tenses. The past tense appears only rarely. And, importantly, most of the details about the past are relatively inessential ones—memories she can face without sorrow. Only one memory truly matters to her, and because she can't bear to remember it whole, she gives it to us in three brief fragments that we have to assemble: Once, when the narrator fell out of a pear tree and broke her wrist, her father carried her home in his arms. From this memory, and this memory alone, we sense the loss she's repressing by focusing on the present.

The present tense can also reflect the opposite characteristic: not the desire to forget the past but the inability to remember it. In the present-tense opening of Charles Baxter's *The Feast of Love*, a largely past-tense novel, the character Charlie Baxter awakens with what he calls "night amnesia" and in his disoriented state "cannot remember or recognize" himself. This causes him to lurch up in bed in a state of "mild sleepy terror." "There's a demon here," he says, "one of the unnamed ones, the demon of erasure and forgetting." The present tense is ideally suited to convey Charlie's terrifying feeling that the past, which gives us our identity, has been erased.

As these comments should suggest, a sixth virtue of the present tense is that it can reflect not only a character's nature but a work's theme. One major theme of Baxter's novel is "the presentness of the past" and therefore the use of the present tense when narrating past events makes excellent sense. Whereas Charlie fears the erasure of the past, his friend Bradley feels the present is, at times, *less* present than the past and therefore *more* subject to erasure. "The past soaks into you," he says, "because the present is missing almost entirely." In Bradley's view, the past is eternally present in memory. As he says, "that day was here and then it was gone, but I remember it, so it exists here somewhere, and somewhere all those events are still happening and still going on forever." Bradley does more than merely state his view that past events continue to happen in the present; he demonstrates it. At one point, after two young lovers, Chloé and Oscar, have been house-sitting for him, he hears the sounds of their lovemaking coming from the basement. He goes to investigate the source of the sounds, and once there, he says, "I felt the two of them passing by me, felt the memory of their having been physically present there …" And then the narrative, appropriately, shifts to present tense: "I follow them up the stairs. I watch them go into the kitchen and observe them making a dinner of hamburgers and potato chips. They recover their senses by talking and listening to the radio. I watch them feed each other. This is love in the present tense …"

There is at least one more advantage to present tense that must be acknowledged: It simplifies our handling of tenses. Whereas past-tense stories often contain the majority of our language's twelve tenses, most present-tense stories employ only four—the simple present, the present progressive, and a smattering of the simple past and the simple future—and many consist almost entirely of the simple present tense. (Diane Williams, for example, shifts away from the simple present tense only three times in "Here's Another Ending," each time for no more than a brief sentence.) Using fewer tenses reduces our ability to convey the full complexity of time relationships, of course, but there's something to be said for this kind of simplicity. One specific advantage is that it allows us to avoid what Monica Wood calls "the black hole of the past perfect." When we're writing in past tense, we need to shift into the past perfect in order to move into a flashback, and then we have to decide just how long to stay in the past perfect before shifting to the simple past for the bulk of the flashback, and then we have to decide at what point to shift back to the past perfect to signal the end of the flashback, so we can then return to the simple past to continue narrating our story's "present." Sound complicated? Well, often it is. When we're writing in present tense, however, we can simply shift into the simple past when a flashback starts and then return to the present when it's finished.

3. TEN DISADVANTAGES OF PRESENT TENSE

Our best writers almost always seem to know, either consciously or intuitively, when to use present tense. Many of us, however, do not. Perhaps because its advantages are so appealing, the present tense has become something of a fad, and we often use it even when past tense would serve the story better. If we become more aware of the tense's disadvantages, we should be able to avoid them and produce work as good as that which influenced us to use present tense in the first place. To that end, here is a brief discussion of the top ten hazards posed by the present tense. But before I begin the countdown, let me remind you that what is usually a disadvantage may in some stories be an advantage—and vice versa. To illustrate this point, at the end of the essay I will discuss a story that uses some of the disadvantages of the present tense to its advantage.

The first, and principal, problem posed by the present tense is that it restricts our ability to manipulate time, especially two of its most important elements, order and duration. Altering chronological order and varying duration both work against the primary purpose of present tense, which is to create the feeling that something's happening *now*. It seems natural to alter the chronology of events in past tense, when the narrator is looking back from an indeterminate present at many past times, but it seems unnatural to do it in present tense, when the narrator is speaking from and about a specific present. In his past-tense novel *Chronicle of a Death Foretold*, Gabriel García Márquez reports everything that led up to and resulted from a murder before he finally reports the murder itself. This reordering of chronology works beautifully to provide us with the fullest possible context in which to understand the act. If the novel were in present tense, however, the reordering of events would defeat any attempt to convey the feeling of presentness. A present-tense chapter which takes place chronologically *before* a previous present-tense chapter would feel "past" to the reader despite the tense used.

Ann Beattie's story "Waiting" provides a more specific example of how reordering chronology can undermine the sense of presentness; in it, the narrator tells us she's been fooled before she finds out she's been fooled. She says "Bobby calls" and "fools me with his imitation of a man with an English accent," but she doesn't actually discover until later in the conversation that the person she's talking to is Bobby. If the story were in past tense— if she had said, "Bobby called and fooled me with his imitation"— she'd be doing something quite natural: telling us now what she didn't know then. But in Beattie's story, the narrator tells us now what she doesn't know yet.

It's not only easier to alter chronology in past tense, it's considerably easier to vary duration, and therefore spotlight certain key moments and events. As the scholar Gérard Genette has noted, in *Remembrance of Things Past*, Proust devotes 190 pages to a three-hour-long party and dismisses an entire decade in one sentence, thus dramatically emphasizing the importance of those three hours. It's certainly possible to expand and compress time when using the present tense, but your options are far more limited. You can expand time by inserting exposition, flashbacks, and flashforwards, but these insertions, especially when they're extensive, suspend the forward momentum of the story. Whereas actual time would keep moving forward, the story's time stops. Again, Beattie provides an example when, in "Secrets and Surprises," she shoehorns five pages of background exposition into a present-tense scene that is a mere third of a page long, thus swamping the present with the past and eliminating any sense that the scene is happening "now." Alice Munro's "Labor Day Dinner" is another example of a story that, for all of its virtues, sacrifices presentness through the extensive use of exposition and flashbacks.

You can also compress time when using present tense, but again, your options are limited. Summaries and time shifts serve to compress time, but if they're not handled with great care, they can destroy the sense that the fiction is happening now by making time speed up unnaturally. Present-tense summaries make hours, days, or even years seem to happen in an instant. When Amy Hempel writes, in her story "Church Cancels Cow," "For days I see her car across the street," those days pass in a blink. And in the first sentence of Annie Proulx's "The Wer-Trout," an entire year whips by at warp speed. Time shifts in present tense are often unnatural and disconcerting also. In her story "You," for example, Joyce Carol Oates jumps, without so much as a section break or any other time transition, from one evening to the following afternoon—not to mention from one place (the narrator's apartment) to another (an airport). The effect of such abrupt shifts is to make the fiction seem as speeded-up and herky-jerky as a Keystone Kops movie.

Like overly abrupt time shifts, flashforwards can also create the feeling that time has sped up unnaturally, even as their insertion halts the flow of the story's "present" moment. But they defeat the purpose of the present tense in yet another way: They make the present seem like the past. In her story "Sometimes You Talk About Idaho," for example, Pam Houston interrupts her present-tense play-by-play of a blind date with this sentence: "When you look back on this date it's the cab ride you'll remember." This sentence lurches us forward in time to give us a retrospective look back at the very present we're supposed to be inhabiting.

Because flashbacks, flashforwards, summaries, and the other techniques that allow us to manipulate the order and duration of time often destroy the illusion of presentness, most writers of present-tense fiction use them sparingly. As a result, their fiction tends to focus on a very compressed period of time—a major reason that the tense generally works better in short stories than in novels. Also, their fiction tends to downplay or even omit temporal and causal context, the antecedents and consequences of the story's events, and this omission can diminish the work's complexity and meaning. As Vernon Lee says, the present tense does away with "the sense of cause and effect. For we cannot feel any causal connection without projecting ourselves into the past or the future. The present tense, constantly pushing us along, leaves no leisure for thinking about *why*; it hustles us into a new *how*." Christian Paul Casparis seconds this point, noting that present-tense narration "tends to be an additive account of separate, i.e., causally unlinked, events." One way our best writers have overcome this problem is through collage-like juxtaposition. Mansfield's "Spring Pictures" is an excellent example; by juxtaposing three "pictures" of spring, she suggests connections between the events depicted. Casparis comments, "The logic of cause and effect, as in a collage, has been replaced by artistic juxtaposition."

Second, while it is certainly possible to create complex characters in present-tense fiction, it's more difficult to do so without natural access to the basic techniques that allow us to manipulate order and duration. These techniques allow us to convey our character's subjective experience of time and thereby achieve more psychological depth and realism. They also help us complicate a character by placing her in a larger temporal context. The more we know about a character's past, for example, the more we can understand her present. Some present-tense works, like Porter's "Flowering Judas," do manage to convey a lot of a character's past, and the result is what Gass calls a "thick present," which he defines as "a present made up of a deep past." But in most present-tense works, he says, "one present follows hard upon another the way a hard rain falls, and all those things that thicken the present with their reflective weight … are omitted," and the result is a "thin present"—not to mention characters as thin as that present. In short, without the kind of context flashbacks provide, our characters tend to become relatively simple, even generic: types. Lorrie Moore is a master of the present-tense story, but even she is not immune to this problem. In her twenty-page story "How to Be an Other Woman," we learn only the following six facts about her character's past: When she was six she thought the word *mistress* meant "to put your shoes on the wrong feet"; her second-grade teacher once said, "Be glad you have legs"; in high school she was "runner-up at the Junior Prom"; she was a member of Phi Beta Kappa; she has had four previous lovers; and she once saw a Barbra Streisand movie. Good details, all. But I don't think they're enough to put sufficient flesh on her fictional bones. All too often, maintaining the illusion that the story is happening "now" keeps us from providing enough information about our characters' pasts to make them seem truly complex.

The difference between the complexity of characters in past-tense and present-tense fiction is most obvious when we consider the case of first-person narrators. A character who narrates in present tense is one person, whereas a character who narrates in past tense is, at the very least, *two* people: the person he was and the person he is now, as he looks back at his life. According to Mendilow, in this kind of narrative, "two characters are superimposed one upon the other, and the impression of the one who acts is coloured and distorted by the interpretation of the one who narrates." Thomas Mann was especially fascinated by the temporal complexity of such double portraits. Discussing his novel *Doctor Faustus*, he said, "this double time-reckoning arrests my attention. ... I am at pains to point out both ... the time in which the narrator moves and that in which the narrative does so. ... This is a quite extraordinary interweaving of time-units, destined, moreover, to include even a third: namely, the time which one day the courteous reader will take for the reading of what has been written; at which point he will be dealing with a threefold ordering of time: his own, that of the chronicler, and historic time." This particular way to complicate character, not to mention time, is simply not possible in present tense.

Third, because present-tense narrators do not know what is going to happen, they are unable to create the kind of suspense that arises from knowledge of upcoming events. The narrator of *Doctor Faustus* provides a good example of this kind of suspense: "The truth is simply that I fix my eye in advance with fear and dread, yes, with horror on certain things which I shall sooner or later have to tell ..." Carolyn Chute laments that we have to "sacrifice" this particular kind of suspense when we use present tense. What we gain in immediacy, she says, we lose in "tension." Present-tense fiction can create another kind of suspense, of course—the kind we feel when no one knows the outcome—but not this kind. And in many stories, this kind of suspense would be a plus.

Fourth, as Ursula K. Le Guin says, "The present tense, which some writers of narrative fiction currently employ because it is supposed to make the telling 'more actual,' actually ... takes the story out of time." It does so, she implies, because it resembles two specialized forms of the present tense, the "generalized" present and the "historical" present. We use the generalized present to talk about an act that is repeated throughout time, as in the sentence "I write every morning." The tense is present, but the events described are not. Hence they are unmoored from their actual places in time. The same thing happens in the historical present, in which we refer to an event from the past as if it were happening now. For an example of this you need look no farther than the beginning of this paragraph, where I preface my quotation from Le Guin's 1980 essay with the words "Le Guin *says*," not "Le Guin *said*."

There are times, of course, when taking a story "out of time" is appropriate. I think, for example, of García Márquez's story "Someone Has Been Disarranging These Roses," which uses the present tense to convey the eternal now in which the narrator, who is dead, exists. And I think of Beckett's *Molloy*, which uses the present tense in tandem with the past tense to convey Molloy's sense of time. "My life, my life," Molloy says, "now I speak of it as of something over, now as of a joke which still goes on, and it is neither, for at the same time it is over and it goes on, and is there any tense for that?" The implied answer, of course, is no, and hence the novel vacillates between past- and present-tense depictions of Molloy's past. But elsewhere Beckett suggests there's a brand of present tense that comes close to capturing the sense that time is both over and continuing. "I speak in the present tense … when speaking of the past," Molloy says. "It is the mythological present, don't mind it." But of course we do mind it. And as the novel proceeds, we see that Beckett's mythological present implies not only the presentness of the past, as the historical present does, but also the pastness of the present, and therefore this form of "present" tense takes us out of the realm of historical time and into the timeless realm of myth.

Despite these, and other, exceptions, I think Le Guin is right for the most part: Taking "the story out of time"—Stein's goal—contradicts the very nature of narrative, which "does not seek to triumph over or escape from time (as lyric poetry does)." Rather, narrative "asserts, affirms, [and] participates in directional time"; it "does not seek immortality" but is instead "a stratagem of mortality." She explains: "When the storyteller by the hearth starts out, 'Once upon a time, a long way from here, lived a king who had three sons,' that story will be telling us that things change; that events have consequences; that choices are to be made; that the king does not live forever." I think Le Guin is exaggerating the present tense's threat to narrative—many present-tense stories are just as narrative as any past-tense story—but I do believe that it can make narrative more difficult to achieve. At the very least, present tense reduces the span of time that can be adequately covered.

Fifth, as Le Guin says, the present tense tends to limit the speed of a narrative to "the pace of watch hand or heartbeat." As a result, it leads not only to a lack of complexity in the handling of time but also to a lack of variety in tempo. Whereas past-tense fiction can shift "from adagio through lento and andante to presto" (as Macauley and Lanning put it), everything in present-tense fiction seems to happen at the same pace—and that pace is *fast*. Many writers have turned to the present tense, I suspect, in order to create a sense of speed and urgency—Joyce Carol Oates's "August Evening" is a good example—but the more present tense dominates our fiction, the more that sense of speed and urgency dissipates. To quote Macauley and Lanning again: "No one seems to be going very fast when every car on the highway is traveling at seventy." Also, as I suggested earlier, it's more difficult to convey the relative importance of events if we cannot vary their duration sufficiently.

Sixth, as Casparis notes, the "watch hand" pace of present-tense narration leads us to focus on "perception" rather than on "cognition," on "a sequence of action" rather than on "recognition" of the events' meaning. Gass makes this same point, stating that one of the "principal perils" of the present tense is "its absence of mind"—the fiction's focus is on action and dialogue: the filmic scene rather than the mind experiencing it. Gass is of course ignoring the many present-tense interior monologues that populate contemporary fiction. Still, we see this "absence of mind" in many (but far from all) of the stories scholars tend to file under the heading "minimalist."

To make the minimal even more minimal, the present tense's focus on what L.D. Benson calls "the suggestion of *continuing action*" often causes us to put "vividness" on the back burner. The attempt to capture the *now-now-now* pace, in short, discourages us from pausing to describe the characters and settings, and as a result, present-tense stories often have little in the way of description. Ironically, by attempting to capture the immediacy and pace of film, we often sacrifice what is perhaps film's greatest quality, its vivid imagery. Raymond Carver's otherwise wonderful story "Fat" is typical in this regard. In it, we learn only that a couple seated in the diner are "old," that another customer is "fat," "neat-appearing and well dressed enough" and has "long, thick, creamy fingers," that Rita's fingers are "dainty," and that two people Rudy once knew were "really fat." These are the only descriptive details accorded the story's seventeen characters. And outside of occasional words like *chair*, *table*, and *bed*, there is no description of its three settings.

As all of this suggests, attempting to portray the immediacy and pace of film often leads to a style that is as impersonal and detached as a camera—and sometimes the camera doesn't seem to have any film in it. While there are numerous exceptions (one need think only of Joyce, Woolf, and Faulkner for superb examples), the style of present-tense stories tends to be quite basic, what one critic has called "Hemingway without the frills." The vocabulary is limited, the sentences short, the syntax uncomplicated, and metaphors are largely AWOL. Great works can be, and have been, written in this style, but I regret its dominance, in my own work as in others'. Significantly, many writers who use this rudimentary style in their present-tense works expand their vocabularies, complicate their syntax, and increase their use of metaphor when they write in past tense—evidence, I believe, that the present tense has contributed to the diminishment of stylistic experimentation in our time. Witness, for example, these two passages from Susan Minot, the first from her present-tense story "The Man Who Would Not Go Away," the second from her past-tense story "Île Sèche":

> The library is peaceful. I stack books under the lampshade, researching articles. Heads at other tables are bent over gently, pages rustle. Shoe clop by on the wooden floor. The heating vent hums in the drowsy air. Then I hear his voice behind me. It says my name.
>
> ...
>
> A white round thing bounced off some rocks and landed near the girl's feet. It was a seashell. In the almond-shaped opening was a red claw folding up. As she watched, the claw pulled itself in slowly, its joints ancient, creaking, furtive. You don't notice me, it seemed to say, you aren't seeing me at all. Nearby, tucked beneath a ledge, was another shell, smaller, then another beside that, all of them hiding their blue-edged fingers like reclusive old women drawing knuckles under shawls, tightening around a precious brooch. Some shells were chalk-white

with turret ends. Others were turban shells, swirled black and pearl, tipped like a meringue.

Seventh, although neither Gass nor Casparis mentions it, present-tense narration often has an effect diametrically opposed to the one they discuss: Rather than a focus on external events that leads to an "absence of mind" or "cognition," it often focuses so much on the character's inner life that the exterior world becomes only a bit player, an extra. In many present-tense stories little happens in the character's world but a lot happens in his mind. And much of it, alas, is expository summary rather than vivid scene. Since it is difficult to work exposition directly into present-tense narration, we frequently turn this task over to our characters, having them think the background information that we want to give the reader. And since it would be unnatural for a character to think for extended periods of time while doing something significant or dramatic, we tend to give our characters something trivial to do in order to make their expository reveries seem more plausible. Sometimes the action consists of nothing more dramatic than sitting, as in Updike's story "Lifeguard," in which the narrator never leaves his "white throne." Mary Robison's narrator in "The Nature of Almost Everything" at least changes location: First she sits in a car and thinks, then she sits on a park bench and thinks, and then she returns to the car and thinks some more. This so-called "action" is little more than a "clothesline" on which to hang relatively static exposition about her job, her relationship to her boss, and her alcoholism; it serves no plot function. The characters in Michael Cunningham's *The Hours* are only marginally more active: Following Woolf's example, he sends them out on uneventful walk after uneventful walk, moving their bodies through the world almost solely to reveal the contents of their minds. Even when this strategy is coupled with beautiful writing, as it certainly is in *The Hours*, it can significantly diminish the narrative's focus and momentum. In short, present tense too often encourages us to replace—in Mendilow's words—"causality on the plane of action" with "pure sequence on the plane of thought-feeling." Ideally, both our characters' actions and thoughts should be meaningful and essential to the plot.

Eighth, the use of present tense encourages us to include trivial events that serve no plot function simply because such events would actually happen in the naturalistic sequence of time. As a result, a present-tense story sometimes seems, in the words of Macauley and Lanning, "less the work of an author than an unedited film." This is true, I believe, of Kate McCorkle's slice-of-life story "The Last Parakeet," in which for no apparent reason we watch the *Today* show with the narrator while she eats a bowl of Rice Krispies. The principle of selection can be applied more readily, and ruthlessly, in past tense.

Ninth, because present tense makes first-person narrators simultaneously actors and observers, it creates an odd sense of detachment that often works against the very emotions the narrators are trying to convey. It is natural for past-tense narrators to be detached from their past selves—they are, after all, no longer who (or where) they were—but it seems unnatural for present-tense narrators to be detached from their *current* selves. At times, of course, this kind of detachment is appropriate, as in the opening section of Baxter's *The Feast of Love*, which aims to convey the dream-like sense of self-dissociation the narrator feels upon wakening. But all too often it merely seems odd, as if the narrator is doing a play-by-play broadcast of his own actions. (Imagine passing someone on the street and saying not "Hi" but "'Hi,' I say as I pass you on the street.") And the more dramatic the event the narrator's describing, the greater the sense of detachment that will result. Consequently, it's extremely difficult to narrate something like, say, a murder or rape in first-person present tense (though quite a few of my students have tried). Doing so often leads to unintentionally comic sentences like this one, which appeared in a story by one of my beginning students (who has graciously given me permission to quote his sentence): "'Take that!' he says, as he stabs me in the gut with a Ginsu knife." I don't know about you, but if someone were stabbing me in the stomach, I'd be paying more attention to the pain, shock, and fear I was feeling than to the brand of the knife.

In short, the sense of self-detachment created by first-person present-tense narration drains emotion from the story and therefore from the reader. If the narrator seems detached from what she's saying and doing and feeling, the reader will feel detached, too. Whether this kind of detachment is a cause or a symptom of the numb, shell-shocked, world-weary attitude that pervades many present-tense stories, I don't know. All I'm sure of is that it's in ample evidence.

Tenth, and last: As my "play-by-play" analogy suggests, first-person present-tense narration seems aimed at an audience, even when there's no audience there to hear it. This is the case in much past-tense fiction as well, of course, but there's an important difference: We usually don't know precisely where a past-tense narrator is in time or place, but we do know where and when the present-tense narrator is speaking. In past tense, the fact that the narrator addresses an audience detached from him in time and place seems natural because he is himself detached in time and place from the events he narrates. In present tense, however, addressing an audience who is not there seems unnatural because he *is* there. It's odd enough to be narrating your actions as you perform them, but it's odder still to announce them to the empty air. What's more, by transplanting into a present-tense story the past-tense technique of narrating to an absent audience, we make the story's "present" seem "past," something remembered, not something that's happening now—remembrances, in short, of things present. And by doing so, we compromise the very goal of the present tense.

4. VIRTUOUS VICES

These, then, are the principal virtues and vices of present-tense narration. But let me hasten to repeat that under certain circumstances a virtue may be a vice, just as a vice may be a virtue. The more we understand the perils and possibilities of present tense, the more we will be able to avoid the disadvantages or find a way to turn them to our advantage.

Lorrie Moore is one writer who, more often than not, has found ways to turn the present tense's vices into virtues. A marvelous example is "People Like That Are the Only People Here: Canonical Babbling in Peed Onk," a moving story about a mother whose infant son has cancer. Perhaps the main reason Moore is able to overcome so many of the vices of the present tense in this story is that she is, in an almost magical way, simultaneously writing in the past and the present.

The story begins with the narrator acknowledging the fact that, despite the use of present tense, she is looking back, not narrating something as it happens. "A beginning, an end: there seems to be neither," she says. "The whole thing is like a cloud that just lands and everywhere inside it is full of rain." After establishing that she is in this "cloud"—and has been in it long enough to experience "the whole thing," the entire experience the story will recount—she proceeds to tell us, in present tense, about the moment she first entered it: the day she found a blood clot in her son's diaper. Because the narrator overtly and self-consciously uses the present tense throughout the story to talk about the past, she is able to use summaries and flashbacks and flashforwards and exposition, all devices that normally seem alien to present-tense narration, in order to compress and expand time at strategic moments. By manipulating time in this way, Moore is able to convey the relative importance of various events, something that is virtually impossible when trying to maintain the watch-hand pace of actual time, and she is able to provide more characterization and description than we normally get in present-tense stories. And more "style," too. In addition, her narrative strategy allows her to cover a significantly longer period of time than we usually see in present-tense stories.

But Moore's narrator not only writes about her past in the present tense, she writes about herself in the third person, calling herself "the Mother." As a result, she's able to short-circuit some of the problems first-person present-tense narrators have, chiefly the sense of detachment from themselves during moments of intense drama. If "the Mother" were relating her highly dramatic emotions at the very moment she's feeling them, she would seem oddly detached from those emotions, and so the reader would be less able to share them. If, for example, the sentence "The Mother is hysterical" read "I am hysterical," she'd seem detached enough from her hysteria to narrate it calmly—and hence she wouldn't seem hysterical. But the use of third person eliminates this problem and allows Moore to take full advantage of present tense's immediacy and emotional intensity.

If Moore had invented this strangely dual narrative strategy— writing simultaneously in first and third person and in past and present tense—solely for the purpose of literary innovation, it would be far less impressive than it is. The chief value of this strategy is that it contributes so well to the story's themes and form. The fact that the story discusses the past in the present tense helps convey the idea that, as the narrator tells us, there is no real beginning or ending to her predicament, that she is, in a way, "out of time," stuck in an eternally present cloud of anxiety and terror. Also, the fact that the narrator vacillates between first and third person underscores the story's obsessive concern with the relationship between fiction and nonfiction. Like Moore, the narrator is a fiction writer living in the Midwest, and like her narrator, Moore is the mother of a child who was afflicted with cancer. Throughout the story, the narrator struggles against her husband's suggestion that she write a nonfiction article to pay for their child's treatment. "Take notes," he urges. "We are going to need the money." But the narrator answers, "I write fiction. This isn't fiction," and says she feels it would be immoral to make money from her son's illness. Eventually, she does write the notes, though we cannot know just how factual or fictional they are. "There are the notes," she says at the end of the story, then adds, with palpable bitterness, "Now where is the money?" Moore's ultimate purpose in using the present tense to write about the past, then, is formal: It helps convey the idea that the story is a collection of notes written as the events occurred.

The more aware we become of the dangers of present tense, the more we'll be able, like Moore, to circumvent them. But Moore is not the only author who has found ways to turn the disadvantages of the present tense to her advantage. There are hundreds of contemporary writers who write in the present tense, and many of them have found their own ways to turn the tense's vices into virtues. If we want to use present tense effectively, we need to study stories and novels that use it, looking for both successes and failures. But we should study the masterworks of past-tense narration as well, to see what we have lost by embracing the present tense so wholeheartedly. If we're lucky, those of us who are still boxed in the present tense, if not in the present, will discover ways out of it, and into a future full of the possibilities of the past.

V

SOME EPIPHANIES ABOUT EPIPHANIES

1. GOT EPIPHANY?

I'll spare you the math. Suffice it to say that, in thirty-four years of teaching creative writing and eleven years of editing literary journals, I have read approximately forty thousand unpublished short stories (not to mention several thousand published ones), and I would conservatively estimate that between a fourth and a third of them featured as their climax that blast-of-trumpets/choir-of-angels moment of sudden insight we call an epiphany. So I figure I have vicariously experienced eleven or twelve thousand brilliant, life-altering insights during my teaching and editing career. But am I even one whit wiser as a result? Well, maybe one whit—but not more. Mostly I'm just weary of all these revelations arriving right on schedule, like trains in a fascist state, and I confess I'm relieved and delighted when I encounter a story that refuses to allow its protagonist even a glimpse of Eternal Truth. But make no mistake: This is not a diatribe against epiphanies. I happen to love epiphanies, and I've written (and still write) them myself. But, as Flannery O'Connor might have said, a good epiphany is hard to find (and, as I can attest, even harder to write). So I've been thinking lately about what makes one epiphany successful and another one not. In this essay, I'll discuss the conclusions I've reached—my epiphanies, in short, about epiphanies.

But first, a definition of the term *epiphany* and a brief account of its history in fiction. In Christian doctrine, the Epiphany refers to the manifestation of God to the Magi in the form of the Christ child. In *Stephen Hero*, James Joyce adapted this term to secular and literary purposes. An epiphany is, his protagonist Stephen Dedalus informs us, "a sudden spiritual manifestation" of the essential nature of a person, situation, or object. Even the most ordinary of objects—Stephen's example is a mundane clock outside a Dublin office—can trigger an epiphany. When our "spiritual eye" adjusts its vision "to an exact focus," he says, the "soul of the commonest object," its "whatness" or essential significance, "leaps to us from the vestment of its appearance."

Though Joyce defined, and popularized, the epiphany as a literary technique, it, like the poor, has always been with us. The Bible contains not only the uppercase Epiphany but also numerous examples of this lowercase kind—most notably, perhaps, the blinding revelation on the road to Damascus that transforms Saul into Paul. And of course epiphanies appear throughout history in the religious texts of other cultures as well. But though epiphanies have long been staples of religious literature, they were slow to find their way into secular literature. Early fiction was primarily concerned with plot, not character—i.e., with changes of fortune, not changes of thought—and hence it paid little attention to the kinds of revelations that marked stories of personal salvation. But as the centuries passed and fiction became more and more concerned with the internal lives of its characters, stories began to borrow the concept of epiphany from religious literature and adapt it to secular matters. By the late nineteenth century, epiphanies were not only relatively common, they often played a dominant, even domineering, role. Kate Chopin's "The Story of an Hour," for example, is little more than an extended epiphany about the repressive nature of marriage hung like a hammock between two slender saplings of "plot."

And now, of course, epiphanies are as common as the common cold. As Charles Baxter argues in his brilliant essay "Against Epiphanies," contemporary fiction suffers from a "glut" of them. Ever since Joyce's *Dubliners*, he suggests, writers have aimed for "a climactic moment of brilliant transforming clarification," and now "The insight ending ... has become something of a weird norm in contemporary writing." "Suddenly, it seems, everyone is having insights," he laments. "Everyone is proclaiming and selling them. ... Radiance rules."

To say that the epiphany is the "norm," that it "rules" the fiction of our time, that "everyone" is writing them, is hyperbolic, of course. But there are indeed far too many epiphanies in American fiction these days, and as I've suggested, most of them are unearned and unconvincing, the literary equivalent of faked orgasms. There are many reasons for the popularity of epiphanies, not the least of which is Joyce's vast influence on writers, scholars, and literature professors. Another reason, Baxter notes, is that many editors consider them an essential element of a short story, what Francine Prose has derisively called the "cherry" on top of the "sundae." For example, Rust Hills, who for many years served as the fiction editor of *Esquire*, has claimed that epiphanies are "particularly appropriate to the modern short story," and his counterpart at *The Atlantic Monthly*, C. Michael Curtis, has touted one of his anthologies by saying that each story in it "achieves the sort of transforming moment one looks for in the short story form, a shift in understanding, a glimpse of unexpected wisdom." Given this kind of editorial emphasis on epiphanies, is there any wonder that so many writers employ them in their quest for the Holy Grail of Publication?

Despite the title of his essay, Baxter is not wholly "against" epiphanies. Though he clearly prefers stories that "arrive somewhere interesting without claiming any wisdom or clarification," he also has high praise for the epiphanies in *Dubliners*. In his opinion, however, subsequent writers have failed to live up to Joyce's standard. He argues that when fiction writers "discovered insight—revelation free of the obligations of organized religion—they made a serious investment in it, and the proportions so carefully watched over in *Dubliners* began, imperceptibly at first, … to be violated." And because writers are presenting banal, secular insights in the language of spiritual revelation, the very notion of revelation has been cheapened. As Baxter says, the typical contemporary epiphany is like the TV commercial in which a singer croons "Nobody Does It Like You" to a Hoover vacuum cleaner: "the feeling for proportion [is] off." Lisa Ventrella makes a similar point in her essay "Got Epiphany?," the title of which sardonically compares epiphanies to the boring, everyday staple featured in today's ubiquitous "Got Milk?" ads. What was once a life-altering spiritual revelation is now, she implies, just one more thing to check off on our fictive "grocery list."

The problem with contemporary epiphanies is not just a matter of "proportion," however. In the course of his essay, Baxter discusses four characteristics of epiphanies that, almost always, cause them to fail. (Let me stress that word *almost*, for Baxter wisely recognizes that these characteristics are not inevitably flaws.) Briefly, the four potential problems he discusses are:

1. *Discursiveness.* Baxter says that discursive insights are unrealistic because they are freakishly rare in life and that they are insufficiently dramatic because they convey

meaning through abstract statement rather than action or experience. Furthermore, they tend to make the events of a story "less important than what is made of them in the protagonist's consciousness."

2. *The Proclamation Effect.* Insights are too often presented incontrovertibly as true despite the fact that experience teaches us otherwise.

3. *Conclusiveness.* Whereas in life epiphanies are often fleeting and so change us only temporarily, if at all, in fiction epiphanies tend to alter characters' lives permanently.

4. *Rhetorical Inflation.* When describing epiphanies, writers tend to use language disproportionate to the insight conveyed, and in particular they tend to use religious language to torque up the significance of the insight.

What I would like to do now is, first, discuss two epiphanies that demonstrate some of these four potential pitfalls, plus three additional problems I'll describe shortly, then second, examine some successful epiphanies for ways to avoid these pitfalls. For though I agree with Baxter that epiphanies have become something like a plague of locusts in our fiction, I also believe that many writers, past and present, have had extremely valuable epiphanies about epiphanies that can teach us how to use them to superb effect in our fiction.

2. THE WORD NOT MADE FLESH

It would be both too easy and unhelpful to illustrate the common flaws of epiphanies by quoting selections from my introductory students' stories—all those grand mal seizures of insight beginning "And then I realized," "And then it dawned on her," and "Suddenly he understood"—so I'll use instead epiphanies from two manifestly great stories by acknowledged masters. And at the risk of committing sacrilege not only against Baxter, whose fiction and essays I revere, but also against the Überauthor himself, Mr. Joyce, I'll use as my first example the epiphany Baxter singles out for the most praise in his essay, the one that concludes Joyce's story "Araby." Baxter calls this epiphany "miraculous," but I don't share his enthusiasm for it. "Araby" is one of my favorite stories, but even great stories have flaws, and in my opinion the principal—maybe the only—flaw in "Araby" is the way its epiphany is handled. As I see it, "Araby" illustrates all four of the problems of epiphanies that Baxter discusses, especially the problem of discursiveness. The second story I'll discuss, Flannery O'Connor's "A Good Man Is Hard to Find," illustrates the mirror opposite of this problem, indirection and implication taken to the extreme of obscurity.

"Araby" is told by an unnamed protagonist who is looking back at his childhood, when he lived in a house whose previous tenant was a "very charitable priest" who left all his money to worthy institutions. Like the priest, the boy is generous—he promises to buy an older neighbor girl a gift at a bazaar called Araby—but his charity is self-serving, not religious in nature: His goal is to win the love of the otherwise unnamed "Mangan's sister." To make the point that he was no selfless priest serving God, but a selfish adolescent serving his own interests, the narrator ironically describes his youthful crush on Mangan's sister in religious terms. Walking through the busy streets of Dublin, listening to the "shrill litanies" of shop boys guarding barrels of pigs' cheeks, the boy imagines himself as a kind of priest, bearing the "chalice" of romantic love through the lowly throng. And when he spies on the girl from the window of the room where the priest died, he presses his palms together in the attitude of prayer and murmurs, "O love! O love!" We're also told that her name "sprang to [his] lips … in strange prayers and praises" and that what the boy feels for her is not mere infatuation but true "adoration." He even compares his body to that heavenly instrument, the harp, but this harp plays for her glory, not God's.

The boy is blind to the folly of his infatuation, though his adult self is not, and Joyce enforces the boy's metaphorical blindness by stressing in the story's first paragraph that his house was at the "blind" end of a "blind" street. (He later has the boy sneak a look at Mangan's sister from behind the parlor "blind.") Also, the story is dense with references to darkness and shadow, and the narrator remarks on the difficulty of seeing in the dark. That the boy was happy in his blindness is quite clear; as his adult self says, "I was thankful that I could see so little."

The final sentence of the story ends the boy's blindness and begins what has apparently been a life of self-awareness. After traveling to the false temple of Araby, like the faithful to Mecca, the boy discovers that his pilgrimage has been for naught: Everything is so expensive that he cannot possibly buy a gift for Mangan's sister. He arrives just as the bazaar is closing, and when all the lights have been turned out in the upper part of the hall, he stands there, suddenly no longer blind, looking up into the darkness of both the hall and himself. The last sentence of the story, the sentence Baxter calls "miraculous," reads, "Gazing up into the darkness I saw myself as a creature driven and derided by vanity; and my eyes burned with anguish and anger."

Though this sentence by no means ruins the story—it would take a good deal more than one imperfect sentence to ruin such a masterpiece—it does diminish its power, I believe. Baxter says, "The insight follows the images but is not secondary: It balances them." But I'm not convinced. In my opinion, the final sentence knocks the story off balance. Even though the insight occupies only one relatively brief sentence, it significantly outweighs in importance all the imagery and action that has preceded it. To borrow Baxter's own criticism of another story, this epiphany makes the images and events of the story "less important than what is made of them in the protagonist's consciousness."

Furthermore, the boy's epiphany is precisely the kind of "discursive insight" that Baxter criticizes as being "so rare" in life that it seems "freakish." What has been so subtly conveyed through the story's imagery is now spelled out for us in abstract terms. It's possible, I suppose, to argue that in this particular case the sudden shift from subtle implication to discursive statement is an effective way to suggest the boy's abrupt awareness of his essential, "unpriestlike" character, but even if this were true, this discursive kind of insight is uncomfortably akin to those old-fashioned "morals" in which the author steps in and tells the reader his "point." It relies on assertion, not implication; on statement, not presentation. Since an epiphany is supposed to be a *manifestation*—the Word is supposed to be made Flesh, the idea made action—a discursive epiphany is by definition not so much an epiphany as a *summary* of one. In my opinion, the best epiphanies approach their revelations indirectly, through imagery, metaphor, and symbol rather than through direct statement. In short, they arrive with some elusiveness, like insight itself. And by suggesting more than they state, they allow readers into the story, where they can actively participate in the discovery of the revelation's meaning.

In addition to discursiveness, the last sentence of "Araby" also illustrates the other characteristics Baxter complains about in contemporary epiphanies. It is presented as a "proclamation," something that is incontrovertibly true. It is also presented as something "conclusive," an insight that permanently alters the character's life. (The character seems to have never lost his anguish and anger at his childish vanity; even now, as he narrates the story, he rails against his "foolish blood" and judges his romantic feelings to be "innumerable follies" that "laid waste" to his youth.) And finally, the epiphany employs the inflated rhetoric of religious revelation; indeed, the narrator's judgment upon himself sounds uncannily like an Old Testament prophet's judgment on deluded, depraved humankind. As I noted earlier, these characteristics are not necessarily flaws, though more often than not they are. In this case, I believe the religious rhetoric is appropriate, given the ironic analogy drawn throughout between the boy and the priest. But I am not convinced the epiphany is incontrovertibly true, much less permanently life altering. Nothing in the story's plot—the boy promises Mangan's sister he will buy her a gift, he overcomes a variety of obstacles to reach the bazaar just as it's closing, and then he discovers he's too poor to buy the promised gift—persuasively motivates the boy's epiphany. Why do these events make him feel anguish and anger at his vanity? Wouldn't they be more likely to make him feel anguish and anger at his poverty and bad luck? In short, the narrator's epiphany does not arise naturally out of the story's events and so it seems imposed on the story, willed into being.

In my opinion, Joyce's epiphany illustrates a problem that Baxter doesn't discuss, the problem of *insufficient causation*. Because the epiphany is presented as an intuitive understanding that simply comes to the boy, like an instance of grace, it seems largely unmotivated, unearned, and thereby makes the actions of the story seem relatively inessential. The best epiphanies do not arrive like an instance of grace, I believe; instead, they arrive step by causal step. As William Olsen has said, "Recognition … doesn't come as an epiphanic burst of light but *over time*, so slowly and unconsciously—so blended to who we are—that it almost cannot be safely termed recognition."

The epiphany in "Araby" also reveals a second problem that Baxter doesn't discuss, the problem of *self-congratulation*.

This problem is less obvious in "Araby" than in many other first-person stories containing epiphanies but it is nonetheless worthy of mention. The epiphanies of a first-person narrator often seem a bit self-praising, as if the narrator is saying, "See how perceptive I've become?" And when the epiphany involves the narrator's recognition of his own flaws, as it does in this case, the narrator can seem to be congratulating himself not only on how perceptive he is but also on how honest he can be about himself. There is, in short, a tinge of vanity in the narrator's revelation that he was vain. His self-excoriations seem at least partly self-congratulatory, and therefore to an extent they're self-defeating.

There is at least one other problem that afflicts some epiphanies that Baxter doesn't discuss. This problem is the diametric opposite of discursiveness; it is *indirection and implication taken to the extreme of obscurity*. It, too, prevents the Word from becoming Flesh, the revelation from becoming experience. My example of such an epiphany is the one that concludes another of my favorite stories, Flannery O'Connor's "A Good Man Is Hard to Find." Whereas the epiphany in "Araby" is too overt, the epiphany in "A Good Man Is Hard to Find" is too obscure—so obscure, in fact, that I suspect few readers would even notice it, much less understand it, if O'Connor hadn't explained her intentions. Before reading the story at Hollins College in October 1963, O'Connor instructed her audience to look beyond the story's surface plot, the murder of a family by an escaped convict and his gang. "Be on the lookout," she tells her listeners, "for such things as the action of grace in the Grandmother's soul, and not for the dead bodies." She finds it necessary to say this, she says, because "Our age … does not have a very sharp eye for the almost imperceptible intrusions of grace." I think there is another reason she had to tell her audience to look for "the action of grace in the Grandmother's soul": She has not fully captured on the page the epiphany she wished to present.

In the story's concluding scene, The Misfit, who is wearing the shirt of the grandmother's now-murdered son, is holding her at gunpoint while his cohorts kill her grandchildren and daughter-in-law in the woods nearby. He has just concluded a history of his misdeeds and the reasons for them by telling her that Jesus shouldn't have raised the dead because doing so has "thown everything off balance."

> "Maybe He didn't raise the dead," the old lady mumbled, not knowing what she was saying and feeling so dizzy that she sank down in the ditch with her legs twisted under her.
>
> "I wasn't there so I can't say He didn't," The Misfit said. "I wisht I had of been there," he said, hitting the ground with his fist. "It ain't right I wasn't there because if I had of been there I would of known and I wouldn't be like I am now." His voice seemed about to crack and the grandmother's head cleared for an instant. She saw the man's face twisted close to her own as if he were going to cry and she murmured, "Why you're one of my babies. You're one of my own children!" She reached out and touched him on the shoulder. The Misfit sprang back as if a snake had bitten him and shot her three times through the chest.

O'Connor told her Hollins College audience that at this moment the grandmother realizes that "she is responsible for the man before her and joined to him by ties of kinship which have their roots deep in the mystery she has been merely prattling about so far." What mystery has she been prattling about? The mystery of human goodness, which, in O'Connor's view, is inextricable from the mystery of God's grace. Five times the grandmother tells The Misfit that he is "a good man at heart," someone who "could be honest" if he'd "only try," and four times she tells him to pray for Christ's help. This is "prattle," at first, because the grandmother doesn't really believe it and is saying it only to save her own skin. But just before her death, she realizes, thanks to one of those "almost imperceptible intrusions of grace," that The Misfit actually is, at bottom, a good man, someone who is capable, with God's grace, of redemption. A good man may be hard to find, as the title says, but she finds one in The Misfit. And finding God's goodness even in this man's murderous heart leads to her spiritual transformation and redemption.

Well, all of this sounds pretty nifty, but is it actually in the story? Judging from her comments, O'Connor believed the story's final scene conveys her intentions. I'm not so sure. It is difficult to see the grandmother's last words and gesture as sufficient to redeem her, especially since O'Connor has spent so many pages delineating her sins like a prosecuting attorney. Also, although she tells us that "the grandmother's head cleared for an instant," it is hard to recognize the old lady's statement that The Misfit is "one of her children" as a "clear-headed" thought, much less as an epiphanic and soul-saving recognition that she, like her fellow sinner The Misfit, is a good person at heart and thus capable of redemption. The grandmother's mind appears to be anything but "clear"; hence, the claim that her head "cleared for an instant" seems—and this wouldn't be unusual for an O'Connor story, of course—simply, and darkly, ironic. And since the act that accompanies the grandmother's words involves touching The Misfit's shirt, it seems reasonable for the reader to assume that, in the delirium of her fear, she thinks The Misfit is her son Bailey merely because he's wearing his shirt.

Furthermore, the grandmother's supposedly soul-saving words follow closely on the heels of her most un-Christian utterance, the statement "Maybe He didn't raise the dead." O'Connor is attempting to elevate the grandmother from the depths of disbelief to the heights of spiritual faith in one whoopjamboreehoo of an epiphanic moment, and that is just too enormous a change to attribute to her last words and gesture. As Baxter might say, the sense of proportion is off.

But the story contains—or was intended to contain—not just one epiphany, but two. O'Connor intended The Misfit to have a transformative epiphany of his own, one that rides "piggyback" on the grandmother's. Referring to Christ's parable in Mark 4:30-31, she told her audience that she imagines the old lady's final gesture will "like the mustard-seed … grow to be a great crow-filled tree in the Misfit's heart, and … be enough of a pain to him there to turn him into the prophet he was meant to become." There are three clues in the story, all quite subtle, that The Misfit has had an epiphany of his own. First, immediately after killing the old woman, he takes off his glasses and begins to clean them, an act I suspect O'Connor intended to suggest that he will "see more clearly" from now on. But before an act can work symbolically, it must work literally, and on a literal level The Misfit's act seems to suggest the opposite of what O'Connor apparently intended. Symbolically, the act suggests that he's been utterly changed by his encounter with the grandmother, but literally, it suggests that he's so unaffected by her, and by his murder of her, that his thoughts turn immediately to something as banal as cleaning his glasses. Second, he says, "She would of been a good woman … if it had been somebody there to shoot her every minute of her life"—a statement that may imply he believes she did in fact become a good woman in her final moments. And third, he recants his belief, which he expressed just seconds before he shot her, that there's "No pleasure but meanness," saying, in the story's final words, "It's no real pleasure in life." Evidently, O'Connor intended these three passages to imply that The Misfit has had a revelation that will transform him into "the prophet he was meant to become." But

I don't believe she sufficiently motivated or conveyed his epiphany any more than she did the grandmother's.

If, as O'Connor says, "intrusions of grace" are "almost imperceptible" and require a "very sharp eye" to be noticed, The Misfit must have one of the sharpest eyes ever granted to a literary character, not to mention to a sociopath, for he sees something that I suspect few, if any, readers could: the grandmother's transformation from sinner to saint. If readers cannot *experience* the character's epiphany, as we do in the best examples, or at least *understand* it, as we do in "Araby," the epiphany inevitably fails. But let me hasten to add that I'm *glad* that O'Connor's epiphanies failed. For my money, "A Good Man Is Hard to Find" is a great story in large part because she didn't achieve her intentions. If the epiphanies were more successfully conveyed, the story would become more religious tract than story, and its significance and power would dwindle.

3. SOME MODEL EPIPHANIES

As I've said, the best epiphanies are those that allow us to experience them, rather than simply understand them. Such epiphanies are presented indirectly, via imagery, metaphor, and symbol, rather than directly, via discursive statement, and they arise causally out of the story's events. A splendid example of this kind of epiphany is the one that concludes Joyce's "The Dead." That story gradually builds up to Gabriel's epiphany, tracing a series of increasingly intense threats to his self-image during and immediately after a holiday dinner at his aunts' house. First, Lily, the caretaker's daughter, embarrasses him when she responds bitterly to his condescending teasing; next, his wife Gretta makes fun of him for insisting she wear "goloshes," to the great enjoyment of all listening; then, Miss Ivors upbraids him for being a

"West Briton," an Irishman who affects the ways of the English. And finally, at their hotel room after the dinner, Gretta destroys Gabriel's sense of self-importance by telling him that she has not been thinking of him, much less feeling "impetuous desire" for him, as he had believed, but has been remembering with great sadness a boy she loved when she was a girl, a boy named Michael Furey who died because he left his sickbed in the rain for one last chance to see her before she left home for the convent. These events soften Gabriel up, prepare him for his revelation in a way that the pilgrimage to the bazaar doesn't prepare the narrator of "Araby" for his. And "The Dead" culminates not in a discursive summary of Gabriel's devastating discovery but in imagery that conveys its effect on him, imagery of snow falling both literally outside the window and in imagination throughout the entire universe.

> A few light taps upon the pane made him turn to the window. It had begun to snow again. He watched sleepily the flakes, silver and dark, falling obliquely against the lamplight. The time had come for him to set out on his journey westward. Yes, the newspapers were right: snow was general all over Ireland. It was falling on every part of the dark central plain, on the treeless hills, falling softly upon the Bog of Allen and, farther westward, softly falling into the dark mutinous Shannon waves. It was falling, too, upon every part of the lonely churchyard where Michael Furey lay buried. It lay thickly drifted on the crooked crosses and headstones, on the spears of the little gate, on the barren thorns. His soul swooned slowly as he heard the snow falling faintly through the universe and faintly falling, like the descent of their last end, upon all the living and the dead.

Now, this may be the most magnificent epiphany ever written, not to mention one of the most beautiful passages of prose in the English language, so how are we mere mortals to match it? The answer is, we can't—or at least *I* can't. But we can find ways to handle epiphanies in our fiction without succumbing to the various pitfalls we've been discussing. In the space that remains, I'd like to look at a number of other epiphanies that strike me as successful and extrapolate from them some additional techniques we can use to write more effective epiphanies.

I'll start with a couple of examples from the writer I believe has most influenced those who share Baxter's (and my) suspicions about epiphanies: Anton Chekhov. Often, a Chekhov protagonist will have an epiphany and then swiftly relapse into old habits and beliefs. By revealing that epiphanies are not always life-altering events, Chekhov avoids the problem of "conclusiveness." "A Gentleman Friend" is a good example of his belief in the fleeting nature of enlightenment. In it, a prostitute who goes by the name of Vanda (her actual name is Nastasya) has just been released from the hospital, and after paying her medical bills she is too poor to afford the fancy clothes she needs to go to nightclubs and ply her trade. To solve this problem, she decides to ask one of her "gentlemen friends," a dentist named Finkel, for some money. While she waits in the hall to be let into Finkel's office, she looks at herself in the mirror and is "ashamed" of looking poor, "like a seamstress or a washerwoman." Indeed, she thinks that she looks like "Nastasya"—i.e., her real self—not "charming Vanda." Although she is confident that Finkel will give her the money she needs, when she enters his office, he fails to recognize her. Embarrassed, she pretends to be there because she has a toothache, and so Finkel unnecessarily pulls out one of her teeth—and then charges her for it. When she leaves his office, she is in pain and poorer than when she arrived. As a result of this humiliating experience, she sees herself, her "whatness," clearly for the first time. Chekhov writes:

> When she came into the street she felt still more ashamed than
> before, but she was not ashamed of her poverty anymore. Nor
> did she notice anymore that she hadn't an elaborate hat or a
> modish jacket. She walked along the street spitting blood and
> each red spittle told her about her life, a bad, hard life; about
> the insults she had suffered and had still to suffer—tomorrow, a
> week, a year hence—her whole life, till death ...
>   "Oh, how terrible it is!" she whispered. "My God, how terrible!"

The climax of this story, then, is the main character's realization that she has misspent her life, that she has been more concerned with material matters than spiritual, and that she's lost her true self as a result. Reading this passage, we expect that Vanda will become Nastasya again and remain her true self for the rest of her life. If the story had indeed ended with this implication, it would have been false and preachy. But Chekhov knew that epiphanies don't often change us or our lives very much, if at all, so instead of ending the story with the epiphany, he goes on, in the next and final scene, to show his character back to her old ways the following day at a club ironically named the Renaissance, the epiphany and her good intentions already forgotten.

> But the next day she was at the Renaissance and she danced
> there. She wore a new, immense red hat, a new jacket *à la
> mode*, and a pair of brown shoes. She was treated to supper
> by a young merchant from Kazan.

"The Kiss" is another of Chekhov's stories whose epiphany nicely avoids the problem of conclusiveness, but it does so in a different way. Like Vanda, Ryabovich, the protagonist of this story, suddenly sees the error of his ways, but instead of ignoring his insight and relapsing into his old habits and beliefs, he *overreacts* to it and thereby squelches any chance he might have of profiting from it.

At the end of "The Kiss," Ryabovich returns to the site of a party he attended several months before, fully expecting to meet the woman who, mistaking him for someone else, kissed him in a dark room that night. In the months between visits to the general's home where the party took place, he has given in to fantasies about the woman, about whom he knows nothing, and he has concocted not only a composite image of her but also a future marriage and family. When he returns to the place, her absence and the contrast between reality and his fantasy cause him to see "the incident of the kiss, his impatience, his vague hopes and disappointment … in a clear light. It no longer seemed to him strange that … he would never see the girl who had accidentally kissed him instead of someone else; on the contrary, it would have been strange if he had seen her."

When we read this passage, we're relieved that Ryabovich has recognized the truth. But Chekhov makes sure our relief is short-lived, for Ryabovich immediately overreacts to his insight. "And the whole world, the whole of life, seemed to Ryabovich an unintelligible, aimless jest," Chekhov writes. And a few sentences later, when Ryabovich learns he and his fellow officers have been invited to a party at the home of another general, his disillusionment leads him to refuse the invitation, and therefore his chance at a real romance: "For an instant there was a flash of joy in Ryabovich's heart, but he quenched it at once, got into bed, and in his wrath with his fate, as though to spite it, did not go to the general's."

In "A Gentleman Friend," we're disappointed that Vanda's epiphany isn't conclusive—we'd like her to stay true to her epiphany—but Chekhov wisely denies us the easy assurance that insight leads to positive change. But in "The Kiss," we're disappointed that Ryabovich's epiphany *is* conclusive—or rather, that Ryabovich responds to it as if it were conclusive. While we're glad that he's finally "faced reality," we're appalled that he overreacts to the point of dooming himself to a miserable, lonely life. We're glad he's seen the truth but sad that he can't see beyond it. Chekhov turns the story, and our attitudes throughout, on their head, and we now lament that Ryabovich has finally learned what all along we've been wanting him to learn.

Like Chekhov, Baxter knows that epiphanies are not necessarily conclusive. Indeed, he argues that their effect may be fleeting at best. His story "Saul and Patsy Are Pregnant" provides a perfect example of this. Throughout the story, Baxter seems to be winding up to deliver his protagonist, Saul, a cosmic bolo punch of an epiphany. After having his sense of himself and his life challenged by a car accident, then a disturbing meeting with a former student, an equally disturbing dream, and a startling, nearly surreal encounter with an albino deer that seems "a sign of some kind," Saul finally has the revelation he's desired all along: Suddenly, Baxter writes, "he understood it all. He understood everything, the secret of the universe." But his epiphany is so evanescent, it evaporates a "split second" after he has it. Baxter ends the story with these stunning words:

> After an instant, he lost it. Having lost the secret, forgotten it, he felt the usual onset of the ordinary, of everything else, with patsy around him, the two of them in their own familiar rhythms. He would not admit to anyone that he had known the secret of the universe for a split second. That part of his life was hidden away and would always be: the part that makes a person draw in the breath quickly, in surprise, and stare at the curtains in the morning, upon awakening.

Whereas Chekhov and Baxter counter the notion that epiphanies are inevitably conclusive by showing what happens *after* them—the character relapses into old beliefs and behavior, overreacts in a way that cancels the value of the epiphany, or simply forgets what he realized—Raymond Carver often counters it by ending *before* his protagonist has an epiphany. However, he rarely ends a story without letting the *reader* have the epiphany. "Fat" is an excellent example. In it, the main character, the narrator, is making love with her boyfriend Rudy when suddenly she feels as fat as the lonely man she served that night at the diner where she works. She says,

> I get into bed and move clear over to the edge and lie there on my stomach. But right away, as soon as he turns off the light and gets into bed, Rudy begins. I turn on my back and relax some, though it is against my will. But here is the thing. When he gets on me, I suddenly feel I am fat. I feel I am terrifically fat, so fat that Rudy is a tiny thing and hardly there at all.

Her epiphany comes in the form of imagery solely; there is no discursive explanation tagging along. Disturbed and confused by this image of herself, she tells her friend Rita about it, but Rita is unable to understand its significance any more than she is. Carver ends the story before the narrator's intuition can become insight. The story concludes, "My life is going to change. I feel it." She can *feel* the change is coming, but she doesn't yet know what it will be or why it will happen. She merely senses it coming the same way we sense, just by smelling the air, that it's going to rain.

But though she may not have an epiphany, at least not "onstage," *we* do: Her sudden feeling that she's as fat as the man at the diner tells us not only how her life is going to change (she's going to leave Rudy) but also why (she's as lonely as the fat man, and as hungry for love as he is for food). We are forced to do the interpretive work that the narrator—and Rita—are unable to do. Hence we have the insight they fail to achieve. This is a brilliant way to handle epiphany, especially if you have a first-person narrator, because it allows you not only to draw the reader into the story more fully but to avoid three of the major problems that can plague epiphanies: discursiveness, conclusiveness, and self-congratulation.

Unlike the narrator of "Fat," the narrator of Carver's story "Cathedral" does have his epiphany onstage, but he is unable to articulate it. His epiphany occurs as he attempts to describe a cathedral to a blind man by drawing one on a paper sack while the man rests his hand on top of his. The closest he can come to "explaining" what he realizes in that moment is the statement "It's really something." Like "Fat," this story demonstrates that the absence of an articulated, discursive epiphany makes us participate in the discovery of the story's meaning. We have to determine what "It's really something" means. The epiphany sends us back into the story, to explore the implications of its imagery and events, leading us to discover that what the intolerant, self-absorbed narrator "sees" through the blind man's "eyes" is the cathedral of friendship, the holiness of human communion.

"It's really something"; "My life is going to change. I feel it": Both of these "epiphanies" illustrate another way to make epiphanies work—by using ordinary, even understated, language. Carver does not hype up his characters' epiphanies by using the inflated language of religious revelation, even in a story whose primary image is a cathedral. The use of ordinary language downplays the grandiosity that taints so many epiphanies—and as a bonus, it implies that an epiphany is an ordinary event, one that can be prompted by something as minor as drawing a cathedral on a grocery bag or serving a fat man in a diner.

Baxter also avoids torqued-up, religious rhetoric in the epiphany in his story "Prowlers," even though the story is about a minister and the epiphany is religious in nature. The epiphany occurs as Robinson, the minister, watches a man who has loved Robinson's wife for years give her a "plain, neutralized kiss." Baxter writes:

> At this moment the thought occurs to him that God is no better
> and no worse than the sum of everything that happens and
> has happened on earth.

The matter-of-fact way Baxter expresses this potentially life-altering thought does much to counter the pomposity that is every epiphany's special peril. The fact that the epiphany is not conclusive, that it *doesn't* change Robinson's life, also helps make it a successful one. Like Chekhov, Baxter knows that epiphanies don't necessarily change us. Indeed, we often *resist* the epiphanies that might change our lives. If Robinson didn't resist his, he might have to resign his position as minister. But Robinson turns his back on his own insight. The very next sentence reads, "As soon as he has thought of this idea, he tries to shove it out of his mind." And he succeeds at shoving it out of his mind: Neither this thought nor anything similar to it is mentioned again in the remaining eight pages of the story. However, the reader never forgets it nor what it reveals about how essential repression is to the minister's fragile sense of himself.

This epiphany is successful not merely because it, like the examples from Carver, avoids the problems of conclusiveness and highfalutin rhetoric, but also because it occurs well before the story's climax. In virtually all cases, epiphanies appear at the end of the story—hence the common belief that culminating insights are the raison d'être for fiction, the "payoff," as Baxter calls it, for our reading—but Baxter places Robinson's epiphany about midway through the story, so there's nothing in the least climactic about it.

The placement of the epiphany in Sheila M. Schwartz's "Afterbirth" is even less climactic and conclusive, and more innovative. Schwartz actually *begins* her story with the epiphany, then proceeds to explore, for the rest of the story, her protagonist's intricate, complex response to it. In a sense, the story is itself the "afterbirth," for it tells us what happens after the epiphany that constitutes the rebirth of the protagonist. The story opens with its main character, Donna, calmly flying home from a conference when suddenly the pilot of the plane announces that they're having a problem with the landing gear. Donna's immediate reaction is to feel "almost glad." This surprising reaction causes "a sudden ching! of recognition" to course through her; what she recognizes is that her children's safety is more important to her than her own. She may be about to die, but her three children are "safe on the ground." That she is capable of feeling "so selfless" comes as a major revelation to her because she had felt so burdened by the responsibility of caring for them that she'd been "eager" and "happy" to leave them, and while she was gone, she enjoyed feeling free of her duties as a wife and mother so much she had an affair with a stranger. As Schwartz has said, "I began the story with this idea—that a woman could feel lucky to be dying as long as her children weren't. I hadn't realized until then that it was possible to *begin* a story with a revelation as well as end with one."

Alice Munro's "Miles City, Montana" is a story that both begins *and* ends with an epiphany. Or, to put it more precisely, it begins and ends with the same epiphany, though the narrator experiences it in different ways at different times in her life. The epiphany first occurs when, as a child, she looks at her parents while attending the funeral of a boy who drowned and thinks she is "understanding something about them for the first time." This nascent, intuitive understanding makes her feel a sudden "furious and sickening disgust" and "anger" at her parents. Her reaction, she says, "could not be understood or expressed" and eventually "died down … into a heaviness, then just a taste, an occasional taste—a thin, familiar misgiving." Like the narrator of "Fat," she has had an epiphany but hasn't yet understood it. The story then jumps ahead twenty years to the day her own daughter almost drowns and the narrator finally understands her original insight. She realizes that, as she watched her parents at the boy's funeral, she was "understanding that they were implicated." Munro's narrator explains:

> Their big, stiff, dressed-up bodies did not stand between me and sudden death, or any kind of death. They gave consent. So it seemed. They gave consent to the death of children and to my death not by anything they said or thought but by the very fact that they had made children—they had made me. They had made me, and for that reason my death—however grieved they were, however they carried on—would seem to them anything but impossible or unnatural.

By presenting an epiphany that ends twenty years after it began, Munro's story beautifully illustrates William Olsen's belief that epiphanies don't come in a "burst of light" but gradually, "over time."

Unlike the epiphanies in "Afterbirth" and "Miles City, Montana," the principal epiphany of *The Great Gatsby* does not appear at the beginning of the narrative—it appears at the end of chapter six, three chapters before the novel's end—but it *chronologically* precedes, and motivates, virtually all of the events of the novel. In the following passage, Fitzgerald's narrator, Nick Carraway, describes Gatsby's seminal epiphany:

> He talked a lot about the past, and I gathered that he wanted to recover something, some idea of himself perhaps, that had gone into loving Daisy. His life had been confused and disordered since then, but if he could once return to a certain starting place and go over it all slowly, he could find out what that thing was …
>
> … One autumn night, five years before, they had been walking down the street when the leaves were falling, and they

came to a place where there were no trees and the sidewalk was white with moonlight. They stopped here and turned toward each other. Now it was a cool night with that mysterious excitement in it which comes at the two changes of the year. The quiet lights in the houses were humming out into the darkness and there was a stir and bustle among the stars. Out of the corner of his eye Gatsby saw that the blocks of the sidewalks really formed a ladder and mounted to a secret place above the trees—he could climb to it, if he climbed alone, and once there he could suck on the pap of life, gulp down the incomparable milk of wonder.

His heart beat faster and faster as Daisy's white face came up to his own. He knew that when he kissed this girl, and forever wed his unutterable visions to her perishable breath, his mind would never romp again like the mind of God. So he waited, listening for a moment longer to the tuning-fork that had been struck upon a star. Then he kissed her. At his lips' touch she blossomed for him like a flower and the incarnation was complete.

This is the sort of epiphany that often concludes a story or novel, but in this work it's a given, not a culmination; a premise, not a conclusion. And Gatsby spends the entire novel trying, and failing, to recapture this epiphanic sense of wonder. Imagine how different the novel would have been if this were its culminating insight rather than its originating one.

And, worse, imagine how corny this insight would be if it were narrated by Gatsby himself, swooning with wonder at his transcendent vision. But Fitzgerald has Carraway narrate it. What's more, he strongly implies that the epiphany is at least partly the product of Nick's imagination, a reflection of his own romantic notions. Carraway admits that he didn't know what Gatsby was trying to "recover" by talking about the past, nor, he believes, did

Gatsby himself. The epiphany, therefore, is just what Carraway "gathered," what he assembled from fact and imagination, not a recounting of what Gatsby actually told him. As a result, the passage tells us as much, or more, about Nick than it does about Gatsby. Presenting the epiphany secondhand downplays the insight and up-plays the characterization of the two men involved.

Thus, another way to avoid the pitfalls of your standard-issue epiphany is to have your first-person narrator report *someone else's* epiphany. Doing this can help distance us from the experience of the epiphany and thereby keep it from seeming portentous and melodramatic. Imagine Gatsby saying, "I knew that when I kissed this girl, and forever wed my unutterable visions to her perishable breath, my mind would never romp again like the mind of God," and you'll get some idea of how strained and pretentious this passage would be if Gatsby narrated it. (And, worse, imagine Kurtz in Joseph Conrad's *Heart of Darkness* expostulating in melodramatic, breast-beating detail about his recognition of "The horror! The horror!") Furthermore, having a first-person narrator report someone else's epiphany allows us the same advantage we see in such third-person epiphanies as the one that concludes "The Dead": The character can have an epiphany without seeming to be congratulating himself on his perceptiveness and honesty. If Gatsby were narrating his own epiphany, we would think him even more self-deluded than he already is.

This passage from *The Great Gatsby* also illustrates a way to avoid another major pitfall of epiphanies, the proclamation effect. Sometimes our insights are true, but sometimes they're not. As Baxter says, "most of my own large-scale insights have turned out to be completely false. They have arrived with a powerful soul-altering force; and they have all been dead wrong." One way to counter the proclamation effect, then, is to present an epiphany that is manifestly false, and that's exactly what Fitzgerald does. Gatsby's epiphany is the height of self-delusion. He not only believes his mind is capable of romping "like the mind of God," but that Daisy is the "incarnation" of his "unutterable visions" of transcendence and wonder when in fact his feelings for her result primarily from his fascination with her wealth and class. Whereas Ryabovich's epiphany is true but leads to false conclusions, Gatsby's is false from the very beginning. It's no wonder, Fitzgerald implies, that its consequences are so tragic for Gatsby.

John Updike's "Pigeon Feathers" illustrates yet another way to skirt the proclamation effect: by making the truth or falsehood of its culminating insight impossible to ascertain. In this story, a young boy named David happens upon the passage in H.G. Wells's *The Outline of History* that states that Christ was "an obscure political agitator, a kind of hobo" upon whom a religion was founded because he "survived his own crucifixion," though he "presumably died a few weeks later." After reading this, David begins not only to question his faith but also to think obsessively about dying. At one point he is "visited by an exact vision of death: a long hole in the ground, no wider than your body, down which you are drawn while the white faces above recede … There you will be forever" while "the earth tumbles on, and the sun expires, and unaltering darkness reigns where once there were stars." After eons of being buried in continually shifting strata of rock, all that will remain of him, he imagines, is his teeth "distended sideways in a great underground grimace indistinguishable from a strip of chalk." At the end of the story, David regains his faith after an epiphanic response to the beauty and order of the feathers of some pigeons he has killed.

> He dug the hole, in a spot where there were no strawberry
> plants, before he studied the pigeons. He had never seen a

bird this close before. The feathers were more wonderful than dog's hair, for each filament was shaped within the shape of the feather, and the feathers in turn were trimmed to fit a pattern that flowed without error across the bird's body. He lost himself in the geometrical tides as the feathers now broadened and stiffened to make an edge for flight, now softened and constricted to cup warmth around the mute flesh. And across the surface of the infinitely adjusted yet somehow effortless mechanics of the feathers played idle designs of color, no two alike, designs executed, it seemed, in a controlled rapture, with a joy that hung level in the air above and behind him. Yet these birds bred in the millions and were exterminated as pests. Into the fragrant open earth he dropped one broadly banded in slate shades of blue, and on top of it another, mottled all over in rhythms of lilac and gray. The next was almost wholly white, but for a salmon glaze at its throat. As he fitted the last two, still pliant, on the top, and stood up, crusty coverings were lifted from him, and with a feminine slipping sensation along his nerves that seemed to give the air hands, he was robed in this certainty: that the God who had lavished such craft upon these worthless birds would not destroy His whole Creation by refusing to let David live forever.

This epiphany is nothing if not ambiguous. If we take "live forever" to refer to mortal life, David's epiphany is obviously false, a repression of his overwhelming fear of death. But if we interpret that phrase to mean that David recognizes that his *soul*, not his body, is immortal, then the epiphany may be true. Let me stress the words *may be*, for the way Updike describes David's "revelation" suggests that it might be the result of self-love and, therefore, self-delusion. With what seems to be incredible vanity, David believes that God's "refusing" to grant him immortality would be tantamount to "destroying His whole Creation." Rather than being overwhelmed with gratitude and love for God, who has granted him the *opportunity* for eternal life, he appears to feel that God is merely giving him his due. In the ambiguity of this ending, Updike, like all of the other writers we've been discussing, has discovered a way to circumvent some of the dangers inherent in epiphanies.

4. TO EPIPHANIZE OR NOT TO EPIPHANIZE

Baxter begins his essay by saying that the words "I've just had a major revelation" typically fill him "with dread." I have the same reaction to them, and to all the other words that announce an orgasmic insight is imminent, because they are so often followed by the kinds of problems we've been discussing. But just because epiphanies are problematic doesn't mean we should forgo writing them altogether, as Baxter seems to suggest in his essay (though not necessarily in his work). I believe he is right to lament the banalization of insight, and I also agree that there's a place in literature—a noble place—for fiction that eschews epiphanies, but I believe we should acknowledge, and learn from, the inventive and valuable ways writers have developed to avoid the problems that usually accompany them. Epiphanies have grown tiresome, I agree, but let's not overreact and banish them as a result. Instead, let's do what some of the best writers of the past hundred years have done: explore ways to save this problematic fictional technique from itself. If we do this, we'll have epiphanies about epiphanies that will enrich not only our own fiction but also that of future generations of writers.

VI

STACKING STONES:
BUILDING A UNIFIED SHORT STORY COLLECTION

1. MEA CULPA

I have a confession to make. While I know from my own experience how carefully, even obsessively, a writer will assemble the stories in a collection into their optimal order, until recently I rarely read a collection's stories in the order they were printed. Unless it was misleadingly marketed as a novel, à la Louise Erdrich's *Love Medicine* and David Mitchell's *Cloud Atlas*, or a "novel in stories," à la Gloria Naylor's *The Women of Brewster Place*, I almost always treated it more or less as a literary journal or anthology, something to sample in whatever order I wished. I was one of those people, in short, that Stuart Dybek was referring to when he said, "People read around in books ... without realizing they're redesigning them." Then, in the summer of 2003, I served as judge for *Shenandoah*'s Glasgow Prize for Emerging Writers, and reading six exceptional story collections from beginning to end made me realize just how much I'd been missing by reading stories out of order all these years. I'd thought I'd read a lot of story collections in my life, but in a way, I realized, I hadn't read more than a few. I'd read the *stories*, sure, but I hadn't read the *books*.

The 2003 Glasgow Prize honored the best first collection of stories by an author who had not yet published a second one, and Rod Smith, the editor of *Shenandoah,* chose the finalists from more than fifty books. All but one of the six had already won significant prizes, including the Flannery O'Connor Award for Short Fiction, the Iowa Short Fiction Award, the John Simmons Short Fiction Award, the Mid-List Press First Series Award for Short Fiction, and the Katharine Bakeless Nason Fiction Prize, so clearly they were the cream of the cream of the crop. Reading these books made me feel viscerally what I had previously only known intellectually—that a story collection, when it's really good, is a unified whole, one whose parts cannot be rearranged without doing damage to its unity. What Pascal said about syntax is true also of story collections: "Words differently arranged have a different meaning, and meanings differently arranged have different effects." The placement of a story in a collection can alter both its meaning and its effects. Even in a collection that aims to be nothing more than a Whitman's Sampler of sorts, a selection of the author's recent work in the genre, the placement inevitably alters the reader's response. Sometimes the alteration is slight, but other times it can be substantial. As the film editor Walter Murch has said, "When I watch a scene in the context of the whole work, it may appear just the opposite of how it seemed when I saw it in isolation."

In short, while it is true that a story is a discrete thing, a unity unto itself, it is also true that, as Hortense Calisher has said, "The presence of neighbors changes it. Worlds meant to be compacted only to themselves, bump. Their very sequence can do them violence." But if the stories are placed in an optimal sequence, they not only don't "bump," they connect in ways that, in the words of the scholar Robert M. Luscher, "expand and elaborate the contexts, characters, symbols, or themes developed by the others." If the collection is well constructed, reading the stories out of sequence is like listening to the movements of a symphony out of order—we do violence both to the parts and the whole.

And when we structure our collections without sufficient concern about how one story "bumps" up next to another, we do violence to our own stories. Like doctors, writers should follow the Hippocratic proscription "First, do no harm." But we have to do more than avoid doing violence to our stories; we need to find a way to order them so that they "expand and elaborate" each other and, ultimately, become one unified work. Robert Frost said, "If you have a book of twenty-four poems, the book itself should be the twenty-fifth poem." The same is true, I believe, for story collections. And I'm not talking only about those collections that are dubbed "novels in stories," collections that, in Dybek's words, "mimic the novel's sense of unity but arrive at that unity in a different way." When a collection of disparate stories is well ordered, it, too, is a whole made up of wholes. This is not the same kind of unity we find in a novel, of course; rather, it is, as Luscher has said, a "loose unity," something akin to that of a sonnet sequence, and discovering this unity requires that "our pattern-making faculties bristle with attention and seek to pull together material which might initially seem disparate."

Essentially, a successful short story collection is an elaborate system of parallels, contrasts, repetitions, and variations that creates unity out of diversity. (The same could also be said of an individual short story, of course; hence Susan Neville's observation that "A collection comes together in the same way that a story comes together.") When we begin to assemble a collection, we're faced with the same sort of problem a person trying to build a house out of fieldstone faces: We've got a pile of stories, all of different sizes, shapes, textures, and colorations, and we have to find a way to assemble them that's both functional and aesthetically pleasing. The stories aren't uniform, like bricks, so one wouldn't work as well as another in a given location. Hence we have to find the right place for each story, a task that requires us to discover the relationships already inherent in our stories. Let me stress the word *discover*. Because our choices of words, characters, and plots arise from our own obsessive concerns and themes, from our own individual selves, it is inevitable that there be unifying relationships between the stories. But we must discover them and then, to heighten their effects, strategically add connecting details, parallels, contrasts, repetitions, and variations to mortar the stories together and turn our piles of stones into well-structured houses the reader can live in.

The finalists for the 2003 Glasgow Prize are just such well-structured houses. The finalists were Leslee Becker's *The Sincere Cafe*, K.A. Longstreet's *Night-Blooming Cereus*, Elizabeth Oness's *Articles of Faith*, Ann Pancake's *Given Ground*, Paul Rawlins's *No Lie Like Love*, and Enid Shomer's *Imaginary Men*. Ann Pancake's collection received the prize, but we could all live happily in the houses these writers have built for us.

Ultimately, organizing stories, like everything else in art, is largely a matter of intuition: what feels right. Still, there are some techniques and principles that can help guide our decisions. In this essay, I will look at the techniques and principles some of our best storywriters have used to turn their piles of stones into well-structured houses. These include such techniques as liaisons and motifs; recurring characters, settings, and subject matter; parallels, contrasts, mirrors, and frames; and such structural principles as aesthetic quality, variety, the order of composition, theme, chronology, configuration, and mimesis. I will discuss each of these techniques and principles in turn, showing how they can be used to link and unify individual stories, groups of stories, and ultimately the collection as a whole, and while I will take many of my examples from the Glasgow Prize finalists, I will also discuss collections by numerous other contemporary short story writers.

2. UNIFYING TECHNIQUES

Liaisons

Liaisons are the principal cement that mortars our stories together into a unified collection. In his superb book *Shakespearean Design*, the scholar Mark Rose defines a liaison as a key word or image whose repetition links two seemingly divergent scenes in a play and thereby reveals their underlying connection and unity. Such words and images perform the same functions in story collections and, in my opinion, so do repeated actions. Most of the time, liaisons do their work subliminally. The reader isn't really conscious of them—and often the writer isn't either, at least initially. Liaisons tend to occur naturally because they relate to the author's obsessive concerns—they are his "totem" words and images. But whether they work subliminally or overtly, they serve to create a unifying sense of connection between stories.

Ann Pancake's *Given Ground* contains an excellent example. Her story "Wappatomaka" concludes with the sentence "I drop my shovel because I am tired, heavy with this dirt in our veins," and the next story, "Dirt," repeats, in its very title, that sentence's key word. These two stories also illustrate the fact that liaisons are especially valuable when—to adapt Rose's comment about Shakespeare's scenes—"the connection between [stories] is conceptual rather than narrative." Their shared reference to dirt helps convey the fact that both stories, however different they may be, deal with the same theme—the "dirt in the veins" of those raised in Appalachian mountain country, the sense of place that they carry with them even to Vietnam and the tunnels of Cu Chi.

But, as I've noted, a liaison doesn't have to be verbal. In *Night-Blooming Cereus*, K.A. Longstreet links two stories set in different times and countries with an image: Near the end of "Clove Hitch," she refers to a "cord of blood" on the chin of one of the characters, and on the opening page of the next story, "The Visiting Room," she mentions a character who has "one thin red razor scratch" on his chin. And a repeated action can also serve as a liaison. Enid Shomer's *Imaginary Men* provides a fine example. In the climactic scene of her story "Stony Limits," a young boy touches a girl's breast, and in the opening scene of the next story, "The Problem With Yosi," we learn that a young man has been touching a woman's breast against her will. This liaison helps connect two stories that are otherwise very different: The first deals with a sixteen-year-old girl and is set in an American high school for "exceptional children," and the second deals with a thirty-two-year-old man and takes place in an Israeli kibbutz.

Liaisons not only take different forms—words, images, actions—they occur in different places in the stories, not just, as in the examples above, at the beginnings and ends. In *The Sincere Cafe*, Leslee Becker links two adjacent stories by repeating, eight pages apart, the words "something's missing." Similarly, in *Night-Blooming Cereus*, Longstreet links two stories by repeating the question "What am I to do?" nine pages apart. And in *Articles of Faith*, Elizabeth Oness repeats the title of her story "Momentum" seventeen pages later in the body of the following story, "Theodolite." When such "long-distance liaisons" are handled well, as they are in these examples, the sense of connection between the stories is particularly subtle, and subliminal: We feel the connection more than notice it.

Liaisons can also link stories that are not adjacent. Often, to mute the connection, an author will place a third story between two stories linked by liaisons. Frequently that story will bear some thematic relationship to the linked stories that frame it, and hence the liaison serves to connect and unify a group of stories, not just two adjacent ones. For example, Becker links the second and fourth stories of her collection, "Wicked" and "The Musical Lady," by repeating, thirty-eight pages apart, references to sadness and hope: the phrase "sad human hopes" in the former and the phrase "sad but hopeful" in the latter. Furthermore, these two stories are also linked by several other liaisons—references to prisons, letters written under false names, books about birds, and stars.

Motifs

When a liaison appears throughout a work, not just in adjacent stories or in a small group of stories, it has become a motif. A motif is nothing more, or less, than an extended, expanded liaison—a liaison on steroids—and what I've been saying about liaisons applies to them as well, only in larger terms. As one might guess from its title, a principal motif of Shomer's collection is imaginary men. Throughout the book, we encounter men who are literally imagined, men whom women imagine to be other than they are, men who imagine themselves to be other than they are, and men who, because they are no longer alive, have become imaginary characters through the fiction of memory. Likewise, ghosts function as a major motif in Pancake's book; though the title of its first story is "Ghostless," the book is anything but. And Oness's book is unified by its repeated use of the words *restraint* and *order*, one or both of which occur in every one of its stories. As these examples should suggest, motifs are more than just extended liaisons. Whereas liaisons usually do little more than serve as "trailer hitches" to link stories, motifs generally have a thematic component and hence can "expand and elaborate" the stories' meaning.

Recurring Characters, Settings, and Subject Matter

Recurring characters, settings, and subject matter are also motifs in a way since, like recurring words, images, and actions, they help unify diverse stories and "expand and elaborate" their significance. As Andrea Barrett has said, in a review of Mary Swan's *The Deep and Other Stories*, "Each time a character reappears, doors open between the stories, enlarging the view ..." This is certainly true of Shomer's stories about the Stern and Goldring families. Similarly, the use of recurring settings in Pancake's stories—which take place in the Appalachian mountain country of West Virginia and explore their characters' relationship to their "given ground"—also "open doors" between stories and "enlarge the view." Unlike the motifs we discussed earlier, however, these recurring elements are usually found only in those collections that are designed, either from the beginning or fairly early in the process of composition, as unified wholes, so they are not much help to writers who are trying to make a coherent collection out of stories about different characters, places, and subjects. Nonetheless, they are perhaps the most unifying "motifs" possible.

In addition to Shomer's *Imaginary Men* and Pancake's *Given Ground*, we see the use of recurring characters and/or recurring settings in such collections as James Joyce's *Dubliners*, Sherwood Anderson's *Winesburg, Ohio*, Eudora Welty's *The Golden Apples*, Frederick Busch's *Domestic Particulars*, Russell Banks's *Trailerpark*, Annie Proulx's *Close Range: Wyoming Stories*, Rosellen Brown's *Street Games*, Pam Houston's *Waltzing the Cat*, Stuart Dybek's *I Sailed with Magellan*, John Edgar Wideman's

Damballah, Louise Erdrich's *Love Medicine*, Tim O'Brien's *The Things They Carried*, Gloria Naylor's *The Women of Brewster Place*, Julia Alvarez's *How the García Girls Lost Their Accents*, Edward P. Jones's *Lost in the City*, and Alice Mattison's *In Case We're Separated* (which is appropriately subtitled *Connected Stories*). Rosellen Brown's collection is an excellent example of how a recurring setting can help unify stories with a variety of characters. Outside of the fact that they live on George Street in Brooklyn, there is little else to link, say, the Puerto Rican male grocery store owner lamenting the dissolution of his family and his business in "I Am Not Luis Beech-Nut" and the white female social worker pleading her case to God in "Questionnaire to Determine Eligibility for Heaven." Similarly, O'Brien's book is an excellent example of how recurring characters can help unify stories with a variety of settings—in this case, Vietnam, Massachusetts, Iowa, and Minnesota.

Excellent examples of collections whose diverse stories are unified by recurring subject matter include A.S. Byatt's *The Matisse Stories* and Dennis Vannatta's *Lives of the Artists*, both of which are devoted to stories that deal with paintings and painters, and David Quammen's *Blood Line*, whose stories examine the relationships of fathers and sons. Vannatta's collection is an especially good example of how subject matter can help unify a collection whose stories differ in style, form, tone, setting, theme, and so forth. Indeed, the collection's unity and diversity are integrally connected. The unity comes from the fact that each of Vannatta's seventeen stories is "about" a particular painting, and the diversity comes from the fact that exploring the meaning of paintings as diverse as the cave drawings at Lascaux, Piero della Francesca's "The Flagellation of Christ," and Jackson Pollock's "Lavender Mist" inevitably requires different narrative strategies and techniques.

Parallels

Another way we can help unify our story collections is by making one story parallel another. In a sense, a parallel of this sort is an extended, expanded form of liaison, one that incorporates such smaller liaisons as recurring words, images, actions, characters, and settings to parallel the plot or "compositional pattern" of another story. Rose refers to such parallels as "alliterating" and says that they "produce an effect of intensification through repetition." Two adjacent stories in Becker's book illustrate this technique well. Both "Correspondence" and "The Sincere Cafe" have protagonists who think about a loved one who died young—in "Correspondence," it's the protagonist's friend, and in "The Sincere Cafe," it's the protagonist's son. Also, both stories end with lost animals being returned to the protagonists—in "Correspondence," it's a lost chicken that has "miraculously returned," if only in a story the protagonist writes to comfort herself, and in "The Sincere Cafe," it's the protagonist's lost dog. Furthermore, in both cases, the returned animal is conflated in the protagonist's mind with the lost loved one: In the first, the chicken is named "Betty," after the protagonist's dead friend, and in the second, the dog is so connected in the protagonist's mind with his dead son that when his wife says "They found him!" he feels for an instant almost as if his son is about to be returned to him. Because these two stories are placed back to back, their parallel compositional patterns are emphasized, and so is the feeling that one plus one equals not two but a larger One. Also, as Rose suggests, the emotion of the second story is intensified because of the repetition. When we reach the end of the second story, we are, in effect, simultaneously (though to different degrees) experiencing the anguish and false elation of the protagonists of *both* stories.

Parallels can be used to link more than two stories, of course. The first three stories of Paul Rawlins's *No Lie Like Love* function as parallels, and they also reveal how paralleling can not only unify a group of stories but intensify our reactions to each. Both the first story, "No Lie Like Love," and the second story, "Big Texas," are narrated by a man who loses the woman he loves to someone else. In the first story, the young narrator loses his girlfriend to someone he doesn't know, and in the second, the narrator loses his girlfriend to his best friend. The third story, "The Matter of These Hours," varies this compositional pattern by dealing with a young boy facing the inevitable loss of his only friend to AIDS. Our response to this story is intensified by the fact that we have just read two stories about men who have lost the person they love.

Sometimes, a parallel is so subtle that we might not even notice it if the author had not called attention to it by placing the stories side by side. Flaubert's *Three Tales* contains perhaps the most famous example. We would have been much less likely to recognize that he intended "A Simple Heart" to be, as he said, a "modern saint's legend" if he had not placed it alongside "The Legend of St. Julian Hospitator," his retelling of an actual saint's legend. As this example suggests, paralleling can be a subtle and powerful way to reveal thematic intention.

Contrasts and Mirrors

Parallels are closely related to another structural technique, contrasts. Obviously, unless we first establish a parallel, we cannot establish a contrast. But how do we tell one from the other? I don't think it's merely a matter of whether the focus is predominantly on similarities or differences; I think it's a matter of the effect the author intends. Both parallels and contrasts involve repetition with variation, but in the former, the purpose is to intensify the reader's response, to build on the emotion of the previous story, and in the latter, the purpose is to complicate, even *reverse*, the reader's response to the previous story. For an example of such a contrast, let's look at two stories Longstreet juxtaposes, each of which is about a character who deals with the trauma of his World War II experiences through imaginative submersion in art.

In "Travels in Arabia Deserta," a young Jewish boy, who has lost his parents to the Holocaust and is hiding from the Nazis in an Amsterdam cellar, escapes both his torturous present and his memories by entering, imaginatively, into the nineteenth-century book that provides the story's title, Charles M. Doughty's memoir *Travels in Arabia Deserta*, and does this to such an extent that, by the end, he says he wouldn't recognize his mother and father if they passed him on the street in broad daylight, though he would recognize Doughty in the "dead of night" if he saw nothing more than "his shadow." And in "Wheat Field at Auvers," an older man deals with the fact that he collaborated with the Nazis during the war by submerging himself in the work of Vincent van Gogh to the point that he gradually "becomes" the artist, dying his hair and even cutting off his earlobe to resemble him.

The second story repeats with variation the first, but instead of reinforcing or intensifying our response to the first story, it complicates and alters that response. Before reading "Wheat Field at Auvers," we are likely to see the young boy's imaginative entrance into the world of Doughty's book as a positive, even life-saving act, and his belief that he would recognize Doughty merely by seeing his shadow as a testament to the "reality" that characters in books can assume, a reality that can surpass, and outlast, that of actual people. Indeed, the story may seem to be a paean to the power of art and the imagination to help us survive the horrors of reality. But "Wheat Field at Auvers" presents the negative side of that theme; it shows us that sometimes the imagination crosses the border into delusion and that therefore we transcend the trauma of our lives at the risk of losing our selves. As a result, our reaction to "Travels in Arabia Deserta" darkens. We now see the boy's inability to remember his parents as vividly as a character in a book as a frightening disconnection from reality, a step toward madness. What's more, we now see his loss of memory as a *second*, and perhaps even more devastating, loss of his parents, one caused not by Nazis but by his own imagination. As I noted earlier, what Walter Murch said about scenes in a film applies to stories in a collection: When we read a story in context rather than in isolation, its meaning may seem the opposite of what we originally thought. And it's not just context that alters our understanding, it's also placement. If we read "Travels in Arabia Deserta" *after* "Wheat Field at Auvers" rather than before, we would not feel the same retroactive shock we feel when we discover its darker implications, for the latter story's shadow would darken our response to it from the very beginning.

Both stories illustrate the point made in "Wheat Field at Auvers," that for these characters "Life and art have become one," but because one presents that point via a sane victim with whom we sympathize and the other via an insane victimizer with whom we do not sympathize, the point is complicated and enriched by the contrast, and so are the two stories and our responses to them. By the time we finish these stories, we respond to the victimizer with some of the sympathy we felt for the victim, and we respond to the victim with some of the horror we felt for the victimizer.

As these stories might suggest, contrasts often function much like "mirrors." Just as a literal mirror reverses the image it reflects, so a story that functions as a mirror reverses another story's situation, plot, characters, and/or theme. Even something as small as an inverted liaison can make one story mirror another. For example, in Paul Rawlins's adjacent stories "Home and Family" and "Good for What Ails You," the contrasting use of water makes the two protagonists, and the two stories, mirror each other. Both characters are unemployed men, but one responds to his unemployment by turning off the water to his house and the other responds by watering his lawn obsessively, five to six hours at a time.

Longstreet's "Travels in Arabia Deserta" and "Wheat Field at Auvers" are good examples of mirrors, especially in their use of inverted characters (a victim and a victimizer, a young boy and an old man) and themes (the power of the imagination to overcome adversity, the danger of succumbing to the imagination). But her stories "Don't Thank Me" and "Clove Hitch" are perhaps even better examples. In "Don't Thank Me" a young person accidentally kills an old person, and in "Clove Hitch" an old person accidentally kills a young person. Also, in the former an old man talks to a live young girl as if she's his dead wife, and in the latter an old woman talks to a dead young girl as if she is her dead daughter. But these stories do not reverse only characters, actions, and plots; they also reverse tones and themes. Whereas "Don't Thank Me" is darkly humorous, "Clove Hitch" is deadly (literally) serious. And whereas the former presents a character's denial of death as poignantly funny, the latter presents its darker side: a form of madness that can be murderous.

Frames

As with liaisons, parallels and contrasts need not be adjacent. They, too, are sometimes separated by another story, or even stories, in order to mute the parallel or contrast and/or to suggest a thematic relationship with the story or stories that appear between them. Parallels and contrasts are used to further yet another unifying technique, then, the technique of framing. Just as putting a frame around a painting focuses our attention on the painting, so the framing technique focuses our attention on the story that is framed. Rose compares this kind of structure to that of Renaissance triptychs, three-panel paintings in which the two frame panels are clearly related in content but the central one at first glance appears unrelated, though it is in fact connected to the others, even "emblematic" of them and their concerns. By framing a seemingly unrelated story, then, the other stories call attention to its subtle connections to them.

Becker's *The Sincere Cafe* provides a superb example. Its second and fourth stories, "Wicked" and "The Musical Lady," function much like the outer panels in a triptych. As I mentioned earlier, these stories are linked by repeated references to sadness and hope, prisons, letters written under false names, books about birds, and stars. The story which these stories frame, "Twilight on the El Camino," does not contain any of these liaisons, however. Nonetheless, the story is intimately connected with the two that surround it, though this connection would be far less noticeable were it not framed by two such clearly related stories. It, too, is a story about sad hopes, one in which the protagonist is, metaphorically, imprisoned by his deceptions of others and himself. And though he wants to take a journey back to the town of his origin, he is no more able to fly away than those birds that are confined to books. But instead of the sad "stars of loss" in "Wicked" or the hopeful star made of light bulbs in "The Musical Lady," a star associated with the protagonist's home and the renewed life she is returning to, "Twilight on the El Camino" gives us—as the title suggests—something between the dark of "Wicked" and the light of "The Musical Lady." This story about two lies—one that results in sadness and another born of hope—ends with a long "spine" of stoplights on El Camino, all of them at the story's final moment glowing yellow, the color of caution that lives halfway between the colors of stopping and going, of despair and hope. By framing this seemingly unrelated story with two overtly related stories, Becker brings its images and themes into focus in a way that would be impossible if the story appeared anywhere else in her collection.

Parallels can be used to frame more than one story, of course, and even an entire book. Framing a collection with stories that parallel each other not only conveys the sense that all the stories are related, part of one thing, but also a sense of symmetry, of the collection coming full circle. Symmetry almost inevitably creates a sense of closure, so it shouldn't be surprising that it is a common structural device in story collections. We see a good example of it in Shomer's *Imaginary Men*, the last story of which returns to the themes and images of the first story. Indeed, the final story, "On the Boil," ends precisely where the first story, "Street Signs," begins: with a sentence about a character literally or symbolically leaving his or her old name, and old self, behind. "Street Signs" opens with Beryl changing his name to Barry, thus breaking his connection to his great uncle, the family hero who is his namesake, and to his family and his roots. Similarly, "On the Boil" ends with the protagonist identifying with a dog who ran away, choosing wildness over domesticity (as Beryl/Barry chooses "adventure" over family), and saying, "I know what it would feel like to run that hard, the pulse in your head so loud that it drowns out any name you might once have answered to."

Longstreet's stories "Don't Thank Me" and "Clove Hitch" are good examples of contrasts that serve as frames. As we've noted, in the former, a young person accidentally kills an old person, and in the latter, an old person accidentally kills a young person. Also, in the former, an old man talks to a live young girl as if she's his dead wife, and in the latter, an old woman talks to a dead young girl as if she is her dead daughter. As typically happens, the story these two stories frame, "On the Night," parallels each of the contrasting stories in different ways. "On the Night" parallels "Don't Thank Me" in that it, too, deals with the death of an old woman confined to a wheelchair and contains a man who, shortly before he dies, thinks his dead wife has returned to him. And it parallels "Clove Hitch" in that it also deals with a woman coming to terms with the death of a family member. Because the story parallels the contrasting stories that frame it, it provides a natural segue between them. But more importantly, the frame stories call our attention to the fact that it also explores the theme of the imagination's role in helping us transcend trauma. This theme is presented much more subtly and indirectly in "On the Night" than in "Don't Thank Me" and "Clove Hitch," so without the frame we would be less likely to see the connection between the three stories.

As with parallels, contrasts may frame not only a single story but also a group of stories or even an entire book. In the latter case, they sometimes function much like a prologue and epilogue in a novel. Gloria Naylor's *The Women of Brewster Place*, for example, begins with a sketch called "Dawn" and ends with one called "Dusk," and as the contrasting titles suggest, these two sketches are mirror opposites of each other, one dealing with the rise of Brewster Place and the other with its decline. This kind of frame can seem more like scaffolding than a part of the fictional house, however, so the use of mirroring stories to frame collections generally works best when there are subtler, more integral relationships between the stories. Pancake's book supplies a good example. Its opening story deals with a contemporary character who has lost his connection to his past and laments the fact that he has become "ghostless," and the closing story moves the reader into the past that narrator has lost and, in telling us about the lives of characters living in the same place a century earlier, brings back the lost ghosts.

3. STRUCTURAL PRINCIPLES

So far, I have talked about techniques that primarily link individual stories and groups of stories. Now I will turn to principles that guide the overall structure of a collection. I will start with three principles of organization that rarely, if ever, transform a pile of stones into a well-structured house but are nonetheless important because they take into account the reader's experience of the work, then I will turn to principles that, to varying degrees, can help us assemble collections whose sequence serves to create unity.

Aesthetic Quality

Judging from my conversations with other writers, aesthetic quality is a, if not *the*, major consideration during the construction of a story collection. Usually, writers who order their collections according to this principle put their best story first, and they do so in part for pragmatic reasons. The opening story is, after all, the one that has to sell the book, first to the editor and then to the reader. And often, writers will put a story they consider almost as successful at the end of the collection, to leave the reader with a good impression. But some writers take this principle even farther. A writer I know has confessed (with enough embarrassment to want to remain anonymous) that he structures his story collections according to a strict mathematical formula. The formula ensures that the book opens and closes with its two strongest stories while maintaining in between a relative balance of quality. Here is the formula he used for his second collection, which contains seven stories: *1-3-5-7-6-4-2*. As this formula indicates, three of the five highest-ranked stories appear at the beginning, in descending order, and three of the six highest-ranked stories appear at the end, in ascending order. Nestled in between is the story he judged least successful. This sort of arrangement may help sell a book, and keep a reader reading—both very important practical concerns of any writer, of course—but if the collection that results from it becomes a unified whole, it is largely an accident, a matter of serendipity. Still, we would be wrong to ignore the issue of aesthetic quality entirely when arranging our stories, for doing so would amount to ignoring the reader's response to our work.

Variety

The principle of variety provides another reader-centered approach to organization. Philip Larkin once said he treated his poetry collections "like a music-hall bill: you know, contrast, difference in length, the comic, the Irish tenor, bring on the girls." Likewise, some fiction writers intentionally order their stories so there is continual variety of tone, style, point of view, gender, time, setting, subject matter, and length. Hortense Calisher argues for this principle when she says that story collections should be structured with "the natural rhythms of an audience" in mind: "the rise and fall of interest, the need to go from frivol to gloom, from dark to light, from female to male to the general, and from an untrustworthy reality to a joyously recognizable fantasy." While this kind of variety may be pleasing to readers—or at least some readers—it is not necessarily conducive to unity. (Calisher's practice is only partly guided by this principle: When it came time to structure her *Collected Stories*, she divided them into four sections of stories related in content and theme.) Still, like aesthetic quality, variety is something the writer should take into account. To give just one example, varying the length of stories can improve the rhythmic quality of a collection. In the same way that a variety of sentence length makes for flowing prose, so a variety of story lengths makes for a flowing collection. If six stories of similar length appear in succession, they can have the same stultifying effect that six consecutive simple sentences in a paragraph have. Also, the rhythm of a collection is part of its meaning, a way of conveying musically the ideas and emotions that define it. An important part of constructing a collection, then, is discovering its appropriate "syntax," what Walter Murch calls the work's "rhythmic signature."

Night-Blooming Cereus is a good example of a collection that, though highly unified, contains considerable variety. Its eleven stories range from eight to twenty-four pages in length; from the Greek Islands, Amsterdam, and rural Virginia to Zurich, Paris, and Minneapolis in setting; and from World War II to the present in time. Six employ the first person and five the third person; and six focus on the point of view of females, three on the point of view of males, and two alternate between female and male points of view. Finally, eight of the stories are in past tense, two in present, and one uses both past and present tense (and uses the present tense for the past and the past tense for the "present"!).

Order of Composition

Another principle of order that does not necessarily create unity but still deserves our consideration is the order of the stories' composition. Two excellent collections that employ this principle, according to their prefatory remarks, are Tillie Olsen's *Tell Me a Riddle* and William H. Gass's *In the Heart of the Heart of the Country*. Behind this principle, I believe, is the assumption that the creative process is inherently orderly, that the chronology of the stories' creation constitutes a sort of narrative history of the author's mind and heart and soul. A collection that adheres to this principle is therefore a form of indirect autobiography, and what unifies it is the author's very self. For some writers, compositional order may lead to unity and wholeness, but I believe that, for most writers, this principle would establish an arbitrary, artificial structure, not a meaningful, unifying one. Still, we ought to look carefully at the order in which we composed our stories and examine it for clues to the connections between the stories that will help us organize them into a whole.

Theme

Since one of the premises behind the use of compositional order is that it reveals the author's developing ideas and beliefs, it is related to the principle of thematic structure. Organizing stories according to theme is perhaps the most common method of creating unity in a collection, and it may also be the oldest. We see this principle of organization in the earliest known story collection, the Egyptian *Tales of the Magicians*. Written between 1500 and 2000 B.C.E., this collection contains three stories framed by King Khufu's request for stories about the deeds of magicians, and each of its otherwise very diverse tales deals with the restoration of social order through magic. We also see this principle of structure in Boccaccio's vastly influential *The Decameron*, which divides its one hundred stories into ten groups of ten, each group devoted to one theme. For example, one group is devoted to tales that treat, in varied ways, the theme of failed love. (The adjoining group, devoted to tales of successful love, mirrors this one.) Oness's *Articles of Faith* is a contemporary example of a collection structured around such "variations on a theme" since, as I suggested earlier, its stories address, in different and complementary ways, the related themes of "restraint" and "order." To borrow a metaphor from Laura Miller, who was discussing another collection of thematically related stories, Joan Silber's *Ideas of Heaven*, Oness's collection "resembles the color separation process used by printers, each sheet with a partial image in a single color, the full picture only emerging when the sheets are layered."

Other recent collections designed as "variations on a theme" include David Quammen's *Blood Line: Stories of Fathers and Sons* and Dan Chaon's *Among the Missing*. As Quammen's title and subtitle suggest, *Blood Line* examines the relationships between fathers and sons—including, in the final novella-length retelling/reinvention of Faulkner's *Absalom, Absalom!*, the relationship between literary fathers and sons. And as Chaon's title suggests, the stories of *Among the Missing* parse the omnipresence of absence in our lives. Among the missing in these stories are: a brother-in-law imprisoned for serial rape; the children of a lonely sperm donor; a family mysteriously drowned in a car; a runaway mother; a lost son; a dead husband; a stillborn daughter; the million imaginary inhabitants of Beck, Nebraska; and, most importantly, the many missing persons that comprise a self, those versions of ourselves that "we abandon over the years" and that "end up nearly forgotten, mumbling and gasping for air in some tenement room of our consciousness."

Presenting variations on a theme is not the only way to structure a collection thematically, however; we can also arrange our stories so they comprise a thematic narrative which follows something akin to the plot structure of an individual story. A collection of this kind begins with a story that introduces the book's thematic conflict, the "issue" to be resolved; follows that with stories that complicate that conflict by questioning, redefining, modifying, or clarifying it; and then concludes with a story that brings the thematic conflict to a climax and resolution. Longstreet's book is a superb example. Despite their wide variety of characters, settings, and times, her stories are thematically unified by their concern with the roles memory and imagination play in our attempts to deal with the traumas of our lives. As the narrator of "Wheat Field at Auvers" says, "Everyone does something to defend against the mirror"—i.e., against seeing the reality of both the world and the self—but, as the book's stories demonstrate, sometimes that defense is justifiable and healthy and sometimes it leads to delusion and madness. The collection begins and ends with stories that show the positive side of dealing with trauma through memory and imagination, and in between, her stories explore the borderline between healthy and unhealthy uses of memory and imagination. In the first story, "Envoi," an old woman in a hospital finds solace from her present pain and suffering by half-remembering, half-imagining a journey through the Greek Islands at the beginning of World War II, a journey on which she met her now-dead husband. And in the final story, "Night-Blooming Cereus," which deals with a child who turns to the imagination not to replace memory or reality but to clarify and understand it, the conflict between painful memory and comforting imagination that constitutes the book is resolved. Even Mary Catton, the story's champion of reason and memory, realizes this at the end, when she awakens and her "half-dreaming mind" sees the world with a clarity that startles her. "The world seemed distilled as though passed through some clear and necessary lens of crystal," the narrator tells us, and we realize, with Mary, that it is the lens of the imagination that clarifies what the lens of memory only begins to allow us to see.

My own collection *Black Maps* is also—or is at least intended to be—a thematic narrative, and I offer it as an example of how titles and epigraphs can serve to announce the thematic unity of the stories to follow. The book has two epigraphs, one of which supplies the book's title and both of which point to its unifying concern, the crossing of various kinds of borders. The first epigraph is from Milan Kundera's *The Book of Laughter and Forgetting*, and it reads: "It takes so little, so infinitely little, for a person to cross the border beyond which everything loses meaning: love, convictions, faith, history. Human life—and herein lies its secret—takes place in the immediate proximity of that border, even in direct contact with it; it is not miles away, but a fraction of an inch." The second epigraph, drawn from James Galvin's poem "Cartography," reads: "Three things about the border are known: / It's real, it doesn't exist, it's on all the black maps." As these epigraphs suggest, the stories in the collection attempt to map this border by showing various characters crossing it in one way or another. I hasten to add that I did not *begin* the collection with the epigraphs, title, or thematic structure in mind: What I did was discover, in the process of assembling the collection, a unifying pattern and concern in many of the stories I'd written over a period of years. I chose to include only these thematically related stories, rejecting all of the other stories I'd written, even if I liked them as much, or more than, some of the stories I included, and I tried to arrange the stories so they told one overall "story." The first four stories deal with characters who cross some metaphorical border so utterly that, as Kundera's epigraph suggests, all meaning is lost and their selves are essentially dissolved; the central two focus on characters who begin, if tentatively and temporarily, the process of returning from the other side of the border; and the final three deal with characters who, to differing extents, cross back over the border and regain their selves. The book, then, moves thematically from negation to affirmation, from the blackest of maps to one that shows the possibility of light.

Chronology

The next principle of structure I'd like to discuss is chronology. In a sense, both thematic narratives and compositionally ordered collections are structured chronologically, even if the stories themselves are not presented in chronological order. In the case of compositionally ordered collections, the chronology is the author's, for the stories, regardless of their temporal settings, move the reader chronologically through the history of the author's developing self. And in a thematic narrative, the chronology is the reader's, for no matter how much the stories move backward and forward in time, the reader (at least the reader who reads the stories in their published order) experiences the thematic "plot" in a linear, chronological fashion. But other collections are structured according to more literal kind of chronology. As rudimentary as it may seem, placing stories in the order in which their events occur is a very effective way to give disparate stories a sense of unity. Not surprisingly, this principle of structure is most often found in collections that contain recurring characters and, in that regard, resemble novels. (Indeed, they are often marketed as novels—misleadingly, in my opinion, since their "chapters" can stand alone in a way that a novel's chapters cannot.) One example is David Michael Kaplan's *Skating in the Dark*, whose twelve stories convey the life of his protagonist from 1951 to 1990, frequently with large gaps of time in between. (Ten years pass between the second and third stories, for example.) But not all collections that employ the principle of chronology adhere to it strictly. Take Frederick Busch's *Domestic Particulars*, for example. Its opening story chronicles the years 1919 to 1951 and its second story backtracks to 1939, and then, beginning with the third story, which takes place in 1953, the remaining eleven stories proceed in chronological order to

1976. Louise Erdrich's *Love Medicine* is another collection that departs slightly from chronological order. It opens with a story set in 1981, then presents ten stories that progress from 1934 to 1980, and then returns, in the collection's twelfth story, to 1981. By framing these ten stories, Erdrich calls attention to their thematic relationship. She also calls attention to the story that follows the frame, a story that—not coincidentally, I believe—is the collection's title story and thematic centerpiece. In a sense, the collection "starts over" with its thirteenth story, which takes place in 1982, and progresses chronologically to 1984 in the five stories that follow. What we see in Erdrich's collection, then, is the principle of chronology modified by the technique of framing.

In Edward P. Jones's *Lost in the City*, we see yet another modification of the principle of chronology. Instead of arranging his stories in the order in which their events occur, Jones arranges them according to the ages of their protagonists. The collection begins with a story about a young girl and concludes with a story about a woman near the end of her life, and in between Jones's diverse protagonists progress chronologically through adolescence and middle age to old age. The result is a collection of disparate stories that come together to form a single chronological narrative of an entire community's passage from childhood to death.

Configuration

My earlier discussion of frames, triptychs, and mirrors anticipated the principle I would like to turn to now, that of configurational structure. Frames, triptychs, and mirrors are all metaphors that help us recognize the configuration of the stories, their arrangement into a "shape." David Mitchell, Alice Mattison, Diane Lefer, John Barth, E.M. Forster, and other fiction writers and scholars have described many such configurations. What follows is a quick survey of eight of them: the mirror, the double sestina, the ring, the Möbius strip, the hourglass, the mosaic, musical improvisation, and the instant replay.

As its name suggests, the "mirror" configuration is essentially a larger-scale version of the mirror technique we discussed earlier: Instead of two stories serving as inverted reflections of each other, in this kind of configuration the two halves of a collection mirror each other. David Mitchell's *Cloud Atlas* is the only collection I'm aware of that uses this particular structure, although Mitchell doesn't use the mirror analogy to describe it. (His analogy is much more elaborate and arresting: As he told his editor, the collection is structured like a series of nesting Russian dolls, and the reader is "on the tip of a drill bit that's going through the navels" of the dolls "and out through the base of the spine"!) In many ways, *Cloud Atlas* is one of the most diverse collections imaginable: The stories cover a vast range of time (from the mid-nineteenth century to the distant future) and a large variety of settings (New Zealand, California, London, Korea, and Hawaii), and they are written in widely divergent styles. Despite this diversity, the collection is almost obsessively unified, thanks chiefly to the mirroring effect created by the fact that the protagonist of each of the last five stories reads (or views a film) about the life of the protagonist of one of the first five stories. What's more, the second half of the book revisits the stories of the first half in inverted order, as in a mirror. The stories appear in this order: *1, 2, 3, 4, 5, 6, 5, 4, 3, 2, 1.* Of the collection's eleven stories, only one—its literal (and thematic) centerpiece—doesn't contain and reflect another story.

Although Edward P. Jones doesn't use the mirror configuration in either his first collection, *Lost in the City*, or his second, *All Aunt Hagar's Children*, the two collections, taken together, do mirror each other in a way similar to that of the two halves of

Cloud Atlas. As Wyatt Mason has noted, the fourteen stories of *All Aunt Hagar's Children* "revisit not merely the city of Washington but the fourteen stories of *Lost in the City*. Each new story ... is connected, as if umbilically, to the corresponding story in the first book" through the use of recurring characters and images. The first story of *All Aunt Hagar's Children*, for example, revisits, fifty-six years earlier, a character we previously met in the first story of *Lost in the City*. As a result of this kind of mirroring, the two books create what Mason calls "fourteen distant marriages." These marriages give birth to "a suite of 'third things' that extend beyond the ... stories themselves" and form, in essence, a third book, one composed, like *Cloud Atlas*, of two mirroring halves. We can't find this third book on a bookshelf, however; it exists solely in the mind of the reader who looks in the mirror of one book and sees reflected and refracted there the stories of the other.

For the structure of her collection *In Case We're Separated: Connected Stories*, Alice Mattison borrowed a configuration from poetry—that of the double sestina. A traditional sestina consists of six six-line stanzas followed by a three-line envoi. The stanzas turn not on terminal rhymes but on the repetition, in an elaborate, constantly changing order, of six end-words. If, for example, the end-words of the first stanza are *one, two, three, four, five, six*, the next five stanzas would follow this pattern: *six, one, five, two, four, three* // *three, six, four, one, two, five* // *five, three, two, six, one, four* // *four, five, one, three, six, two* // *two, four, six, five, three, one*. And in the concluding envoi, each of the three lines would contain two of the end-words, in this order: *one, two / three, four / five, six*. The poem thus comes full circle, ending with the same order—albeit compressed in fewer lines—as that of the opening stanza. (This example isn't hypothetical, by the way; I've just described James Merrill's witty

"Tomorrows," which playfully substitutes homophones for some of the end-words—for instance, *one* transforms into *won* and *two* into *to, Timbuktu,* and the Spanish *tu*. And Merrill even creates a single homophone out of two words, when he repeats *five* by writing *belief I've.*) A double sestina would repeat this pattern twice, and thus would consist of thirteen six-line stanzas. As Mattison says in a note at the conclusion of her collection, "This book's thirteen stories imitate in prose the thirteen stanzas of a double sestina, using repeated topics or tropes in something like the way a sestina … uses repeated words. In the changing order prescribed by the sestina pattern, each story includes a glass of water, a sharp point, a cord, a mouth, an exchange, and a map that may be wrong." These are all motifs, of course, but Mattison doesn't just repeat them to link her stories; she uses them to create a larger, all-encompassing pattern, one that shows a harmonious order broken and rearranged in many different ways before being restored. The double sestina form is a superb choice for this collection, for as its title suggests, the book is about family members who are separated, both literally and emotionally, but nonetheless remain integrally connected.

Joan Silber's *Ideas of Heaven: A Ring of Stories* is also about family members who are separated but nonetheless connected, but in her case the family is the family of humankind. On the surface, her collection would seem to be far more various than unified: Its stories range widely in time and place (from sixteenth-century Italy to nineteenth-century China to twentieth-century America, France, England, Greece, Slovenia, Thailand, and various other countries). Despite this diversity, the stories are linked by the reappearance of characters in an ingenious pattern: Throughout the collection, a minor—sometimes even incidental—character in one story reappears as the protagonist of the next (or vice versa). For example, the protagonist of the first story is a dancer named Alice who takes lessons from a man named Duncan. Duncan, in turn, is the protagonist of the second story, which deals with his love for a man whose favorite writer is the sixteenth-century Italian poet Gaspara Stampa. Stampa is the protagonist of the third story, and she also reappears in the fourth story, whose protagonist, Tom, reads about her in Rilke's *Duino Elegies* and *The Notebooks of Malte Laurids Brigge* and compares his own lost loves to hers. Tom is married to Mattina, whose great-great-grandmother is the protagonist of the fifth story. This pattern of one character "passing the baton" to another continues until the final story, whose protagonist is a secondary character in the first story—Alice's lover Giles. Thus Silber brings her interlocking stories full circle to form, as her subtitle notes, "a ring of stories." To further stress the interconnections between the stories in this ring, the final story also refers to people and places that appear in the previous stories. Formally, then, the book may seem to illustrate the idea that, as one of Silber's characters puts it, "the earth [is] linked by a great net of glorious strands." But any reader who takes these "glorious" linkages as a sign that the earth is Silber's "idea of heaven," or who takes the ring her stories form as a symbol of the spiritual "marriage" of all humankind, would be mistaken. Despite their surface calm, her stories, like Stampa's poems, are about unhappy loves— loves that may be glorious for a time but eventually collapse into anguish and regret—and they're less about the connections between people than they are about the heartrending loss of those connections. It is fitting, then, that another of Silber's characters finds the interconnections of the world more frightening than glorious: "The whole world's going to blow up," a woman says after her daughter is killed by a terrorist's bomb. "It's going to be nothing. Now that it's all tied together." The more we're all tied together, she implies, the more the world shrinks, and the more the world shrinks, the greater the danger it will disappear entirely. The ultimate ring, then, Silber seems to suggest, just may be the hellish ring of fire formed by a nuclear blast.

In his foreword to *Lost in the Funhouse*, John Barth describes the collection as a thematic narrative that takes the form of a Möbius strip. His aim, he says, was to assemble a series of stories that "would be strung together on a few echoed and developed themes and would circle back upon itself: not to close a simple circuit like that of Joyce's *Finnegans Wake*, emblematic of Viconian eternal return, but to make a circuit with a twist to it, like a Möbius strip." Indeed, the very first story is, literally, a Möbius strip: "Frame-Tale" consists of an inch-wide strip that contains the words "ONCE UPON A TIME THERE" on one side and "WAS A STORY THAT BEGAN" on the other. If we follow Barth's instructions to "cut on the dotted line," then twist the strip and attach its two ends, the result is a Möbius strip that is, as Barth notes, simultaneously "the shortest short story in the English language" and "endless." It is also an "overture" of sorts to the symphony that follows, preparing us for both the book's structure and its thematic focus on the nature of narrative.

In his *Aspects of the Novel*, E.M. Forster defines an hourglass structure as one in which the characters and/or themes gradually change until they reverse themselves in the middle and go in the opposite direction for the remainder of the work. He also points out that, given that the bottom half of an hourglass mirrors the top half, a work with an hourglass structure generally ends by returning, in some inverted way, to its opening concerns. Forster's examples are novels—Anatole France's *Thaïs* and Henry James's *The Ambassadors*—but story collections can employ this configuration as well, as I hope my previous comments on both Longstreet's *Night-Blooming Cereus* and my *Black Maps* demonstrate.

Diane Lefer's essay "Breaking the 'Rules' of Story Structure" provides definitions of the other three configurations I mentioned above. Her essay focuses on the structure of individual stories, but what she says about them can apply to collections as well. According to Lefer, a mosaic story—her example is Amy Hempel's "In the Cemetery Where Al Jolson Is Buried"—is composed of brief, fragmentary, discontinuous sections that may seem relatively unrelated until, eventually, the reader is able to assemble them and "the whole picture comes together." This sort of structure, she notes, is especially well suited to portray "the complexities of a world marked by ambiguity and dislocations, chaos and incongruities, where answers are suspect and bizarre juxtapositions a part of daily life." An example of a story collection that follows the mosaic pattern is Lydia Davis's *Almost No Memory*. It consists of fifty-one very brief stories (they average about three pages, and many are less than a page and one a mere forty-six words) whose jagged intersections and inter-relationships allow Davis, as Jeffrey Eugenides says in a jacket blurb, to "render the fractured nature of contemporary life while imposing order on her material." As Eugenides' comment suggests, the mosaic form tends to be thematically mimetic—i.e., it embodies, in its very structure, the author's meaning. The danger of such a form is that it can easily devolve into the formal equivalent of the "imitative fallacy," the notion that a story about boredom should be boring, and a story about meaninglessness should be meaningless. Students often make the mistake of assuming that a mosaic story is easier to write than a more conventionally structured story, but if anything, it's far more difficult. And creating a mosaic structure for an entire story collection is geometrically more difficult. David Shields has put his finger on the essence of this form's difficulty. "Literary mosaic is a fascinating form, but a difficult one to execute," he has said, for "momentum derives not from narrative but the subtle, progressive buildup of thematic resonances."

Sandra Cisneros's *Woman Hollering Creek and Other Stories* demonstrates how the form musical improvisations take can be used to shape a collection. Lefer aptly describes the book as "a series of Mexican-American vernacular solos of ... spilling-forth immediacy." In each story, she says, "Cisneros states an idea or image in the first sentence, flies away with it and returns to the same image (the way a musician returns to a chord) to ground the story in the end." Some of the stories read like ballads, she says, another like a "*ranchera*-style love song," and the overall effect of the collection is like "attending a concert."

Lefer's example of an instant replay is Tim O'Brien's "How to Tell a True War Story," which describes, "again and again, differently each time," the death of a man who stepped on a land mine. *The Things They Carried*, the collection that contains this story, employs a similar structure. Several of its stories obsessively retell—and, often, revise—the events of earlier stories. Just as instant replays in baseball might invite the viewer to reexamine an umpire's call from various angles, the instant replay structure in fiction invites the reader to reconsider an event, scrutinize it from different perspectives, in an attempt to discover its true meaning.

These are just eight of the configurational structures available to writers. An in-depth study of the geometry of story collections would undoubtedly reveal many others.

Mimesis

The final principle I will discuss, mimetic structure, is essentially a combination of configurational structure and thematic narrative. In mimetic structure, the form of the book imitates its theme. Perhaps the finest example of this kind of structure is the book we just discussed—O'Brien's *The Things They Carried*. Both within individual stories and within the collection as a whole, O'Brien's characters continually replay events that have traumatized them. In the title story and "Speaking of Courage," for example, the protagonists—Jimmy Cross in the former and Norman Bowker in the latter—repeatedly return in memory to a death for which they feel partially responsible. And throughout the book stories replay the events of previous stories. Three stories—"Speaking of Courage," "In the Field," and "Field Trip"—deal with the death of Kiowa, each time approaching the event from a different perspective. And the character Tim O'Brien, the protagonist of many of the stories and of the book as a whole, tells the story of "the man he killed" three times—in "The Man I Killed," "Ambush," and "Good Form." The collection's stories are not arranged chronologically; rather, they move in two opposite directions almost simultaneously, some stories looping back to the past—as in "On the Rainy River," which deals with the months before O'Brien decided to go to Vietnam—and others approaching a time close to the present—as in "Field Trip," which deals with O'Brien's return to Vietnam twenty years after ending his tour of duty. The stories' continual looping back and moving forward in time imitates one of the book's principal themes: that continually returning to the past is the only way to move into the future. The way back, the book tells us in content and form, is the way forward; the recovery of the past, the way to recover from it. This theme culminates in the book's final story, "The Lives of the Dead," in which O'Brien goes farther back in time than in any previous story—all the way back to his protagonist's original trauma, the death of Linda, a girl he loved when he and she were both nine—and moves that past into the present, in order to deal with it. In the final paragraph, he takes us into his character's present: It is 1990, he says, and "I'm forty-three years old, and a writer now, still dreaming Linda alive." O'Brien concludes the story, and the book, with his statement about the purpose of returning to the past: This story, and all of the others, he suggests, is about "Tim trying to save Timmy's life with a story." To save our lives in the present, to make moving into the future possible, we have to continually loop back to the past, as both the stories and the book as a whole do. For stories, O'Brien tells us, in form as well as in words, "are for joining the past to the future."

4. A RESOLUTION

O'Brien joins the past and the future so superbly in *The Things They Carried* that the book is truly, as the title page says, "A Work"—note the singular—"of Fiction." His collection is not only the finest example I know of mimetic structure but also of virtually all of the methods of creating unity that we have discussed (the sole exceptions being compositional and chronological order). It illustrates the use of liaisons and motifs; recurring characters, settings, and subject matter; parallels, contrasts, mirrors, and frames; and the principles of aesthetic quality, variety, and thematic, configurational, and mimetic structure. Because it uses so many of these methods, and uses them so masterfully, it has more than the loose unity we find in most story collections; it has a tight unity, one that approaches that of the finest novels.

Anyone interested in learning how to build a fictional house out of a pile of variously sized and shaped stories would be well served to turn from this essay to O'Brien's book, and to the six finalists for the 2003 Glasgow Prize and the other collections I've mentioned here, and read and reread and re-reread them. And anyone interested in discovering the full artistry and meaning of any short story collection should do what I have resolved to do from here on out: read the stories in the order their author intended.

VII

LEVER OF TRANSCENDENCE:
CONTRADICTION AND
THE PHYSICS OF CREATIVITY

1. NAMES AND ALIASES

For years now, I have given the students in my introductory writing classes a two-part exercise that I tell them, only half-facetiously, will teach them virtually all they need to know about the creative process. Here's the exercise: First I ask them to write their names on a piece of paper, then I ask them to make up an alias. That's it. The entire exercise takes only thirty to forty seconds, but it usually provokes a long discussion about what transpired during those seconds. What this little exercise reveals is that the creative process requires a mode of thought that is diametrically opposed to our usual way of thinking. When I ask my students to write their actual names, there is only one correct response and an infinite number of incorrect ones, but when I ask them to make up aliases, there are an infinite number of correct responses and only one incorrect one. The first mode of thought is called "convergent," since it requires us to converge on the sole correct answer, and the second is called "divergent," since it requires us to diverge from the one incorrect answer—the fact—and consider a range of possible correct answers.

When we use the divergent mode of thought, we're like the narrator of William H. Gass's "The Pedersen Kid," who describes himself as being "alone with all that could happen": We have the entire panorama of possibility at our disposal. And the best writers, as Dickinson noted, "dwell in Possibility," not in the prosaic realm of fact.

All of us use both the convergent and divergent modes of thought, of course, but the convergent mode dominates our thinking to the point of being reflexive. My students don't hesitate when I ask them to write their actual names, but they do when I ask them to make up fictitious ones. The creative process, I tell them, resides in that hesitation, that moment of uncertainty. For without uncertainty, the imagination simply does not come into play. As Donald Barthelme has said, "Not-knowing is crucial to art, is what permits art to be made. Without the scanning process engendered by not-knowing, without the possibility of having the mind move in unanticipated directions, there would be no invention." And, according to Gaston Bachelard, there would also be no discovery of new or larger truths. "Not-knowing is not a form of ignorance," he says, "but a difficult transcendence of knowledge." As Bachelard's words suggest, not-knowing is far from being a passive state; resisting the mind's tendency to converge on a comfortable certainty requires an arduous, active effort. Those who can resist this tendency possess what Keats called "Negative Capability," the ability to remain "in uncertainties, mysteries, doubts, without any irritable reaching after fact and reason." And that ability, I tell my students, is the most valuable talent a writer can possess.

I believe what I tell my students—I am nothing if not certain about the need for uncertainty—but I also believe that merely encouraging them to embrace uncertainty doesn't help them learn how to write. Uncertainty is, well, too uncertain a subject for us to grasp. And in any case, once we have accepted the idea that creativity begins where certainty leaves off, what do we do next? Facing the blank page, not knowing what will happen in the story or poem, or what its ultimate meaning will be, is exhilarating for those students who intuitively know how to walk on the water of the imagination, but there are many otherwise very talented students who find themselves stuck at the edge of uncertainty, unable to proceed. Generally, these writers do one of two things—they revert to convergent thinking and create a DOA paint-by-numbers story or poem, or they edit their every thought back into the silence from which it came and write nothing at all. More and more I think what Bertrand Russell said about teaching philosophy is also true about teaching creative writing: Our principal goal should be "to teach how to live without certainty and yet without being paralyzed by hesitation." Hesitation is an essential part of the creative process—without it, divergent thinking is impossible—but we need to find a way to move through and beyond it or we risk being paralyzed by the very uncertainty that makes creativity possible. In my opinion, the key to avoiding this sort of creative paralysis lies in the cultivation of contradiction.

Beginning writers, however, almost universally equate contradiction with error and failure and so work strenuously to avoid it. And, obviously, many contradictions *are* errors. As the philosopher Graham Priest has said, "it is irrational to believe that I am both a fried egg and not a fried egg." But some contradictions, he maintains, are not only "rationally possible" but also "rationally obligatory." In this view, Priest is the descendent of such philosophers as Heraclitus, Plotinus, Nicholas of Cusa, Hume, Engels, and Hegel. Of these, Hegel goes the farthest in endorsing the rational obligation to accept contradictions. "According to Kant," he said, "thought has a natural tendency to issue in contradictions or antinomies, whenever it seeks to apprehend the infinite. But Kant … never penetrated to the discovery of what the antimonies really and positively mean. The true and positive meaning of the antinomies is this: that every actual thing involves a coexistence of opposed elements." For Hegel, then, contradiction leads us *to* truth, not *away* from it.

Simone Weil agrees. "Contradiction," she tells us, "is the lever of transcendence." Like a lever, it allows us to lift what we otherwise could not, and the act of lifting allows us to transcend what we already know. In other words, contradiction allows us to transcend the convergent mode of thought, what Weil calls the mere "discursive intelligence," and the false certainty it inspires. "We are only certain," she says, "about what we do not understand." The way to understanding, then, is through uncertainty, and the way to leave false certainty behind and enter the realm of uncertainty is through the use of contradiction: "As soon as we have thought something," she advises, "try to see in what way the contrary is true." Importantly, the purpose of investigating ideas dialectically is not to eradicate one or the other idea, for contradiction, she argues, is an essential element of both truth and beauty: "In all beauty we find contradiction," she says, and "all truth contains a contradiction." Behind the dialectic method Weil proposes is the belief that something can be true on one level, its opposite can be true on another, and when they are synthesized, both of them can be simultaneously true on a higher level. Jean Cocteau seconds this belief: "All creation," he has said, "is the spirit of contradiction in its highest form." And in its highest form, contradiction transcends the "either-or" mentality of simple negation—"This is true, that isn't"—and achieves the complex affirmation of what Cleanth Brooks calls the "both-and" mode of thought. According to Amy Hempel, this is the mode of thought that initiates her fiction. "A story happens," she says, "when two equally appealing forces, or characters, or ideas try to occupy the same place at the same time, and they're both right."

Given the role the "both-and" mode of thought plays in the creative process, it's not surprising to find it also in the act of dreaming, which is of course the kissin' cousin of the creative process. As Freud has said, "Dreams show a special tendency to reduce two opposites to a unity or to represent them as one thing" and hence "anything in a dream may mean its opposite." Freud also notes that this same tendency characterizes primal languages such as ancient Egyptian, in which, according to the philologist Karl Abel, there are many words "which at one and the same time denoted a thing and the opposite of this thing" (the same word denoted "strong" and "weak," for example) as well as compound words in which two "contrary meaning[s] are united into a whole" (Abel's examples include "oldyoung," "farnear," and "outsideinside"). Remnants of this primal, contradictory mode of thought are evident in our own language: Witness the words *cleave*, which means both to part and to cling together, and *sanction*, which conveys both approval and condemnation. It is this mode of thought, this form of meaningful contradiction, that Weil advises we adopt in our search for truth and beauty.

Weil's advice is especially helpful to writers because the creative process not only involves contradiction but is itself inherently contradictory. After all, the very first step in the creative process is destruction. To invent an alias, to diverge from the factual and scan through the possible, we first have to destroy our actual names, reject that convergent thought. And to create something new, we have to destroy not only many facts but also the first thoughts and expressions that occur to us. If, for example, we write the words *flat as a*, our first thought will most likely be to add the word *pancake*, but if we choose that word, we have succumbed to cliché and failed to create anything new. The same principle applies to all other aspects of literature: If we do not destroy our first, convergent thoughts, we will end up with red-haired characters with fiery tempers; plots in which boy meets girl, boy loses girl, and boy gets girl again; rhymes like *love / dove* and *June / moon*; and potted themes like "love conquers all" and "beating your wife is not nice." If we want to write originally, we must do what Robert Venturi, an advocate of contradiction in architecture, recommends: "Use convention unconventionally." And that requires destruction as well as creation, and destruction requires rejection, negation, and contradiction.

But once we have destroyed the cliché, the stereotype, the formulaic plot, the predictable rhyme, the potted theme, and so forth, how do we go about creating something new? The answer, as I have suggested, is to court contradiction. We need to take Keats's notion of Negative Capability one small but important step further: Our goal as writers should be not only to persist in uncertainty but to seek it out, even intentionally create it, through contradiction. For, paradoxically, the best way to avoid being paralyzed by uncertainty is to intensify it, and the most intense form of uncertainty possible is contradiction.

2. THE SCIENCE OF CONTRADICTION

When I tell my beginning students that contradiction can function as a lever of transcendence in the creative process, they almost invariably mutiny. Contradictions are evidence of "fuzzy" thinking, they say, and if our goal is to tell the truth about "reality," we should avoid contradictions, not seek them out. I've tried to convince them otherwise by barraging them with testimonials from such writers as William Blake ("Without Contraries is no progression"), Oscar Wilde ("A Truth in art is that whose contradictory is also true"), Robert Graves ("Poetry is the fusion of contradictory ideas"), and Federico García Lorca ("The light of any poet is contradiction"), but my students tend not to trust writers to know, much less tell, the truth about their own art. However, they do tend to trust scientists, so I have taken to calling them to my defense. Here is a quick survey of what scientists of various stripes have taught us about contradiction and the role it plays in our understanding of ourselves and the world.

According to neurologists, human beings are biologically hardwired for contradiction. In their essay "Creativity and the Bisected Brain," Joseph E. Bogen and Glenda M. Bogen say, "One of the most obvious and fundamental features of the cerebrum is that it is double. Various kinds of evidence, especially from hemispherectomy, have made it clear that one hemisphere is sufficient to sustain a personality or mind. We may then conclude that the individual with two intact hemispheres has the capacity for two distinct minds." Furthermore, these two minds have contradictory functions, the left hemisphere dealing with what the Bogens call "propositional" thought and the right dealing with "appositional" thought. Whereas the left, propositional hemisphere is logical and analytic, the right, appositional hemisphere is perceptual and synthetic—in other words, it juxtaposes perceptions without analysis or judgment. In the right hemisphere, then, opposites are not differentiated and the concept of contradiction does not exist. Anton Ehrenzweig, in his book on the psychology of artistic imagination, calls this mode of thought "dedifferentiation" and notes that its principal characteristic is "freedom from having to make a choice." As a result, he says, dedifferentiated perception "can grasp in a single undivided act of comprehension data that to conscious perception would be incompatible." (André Breton would second this assertion; in his "Second Manifesto of Surrealism," he says, "there exists a certain point in the mind at which life and death, the real and the imagined, past and future, the communicable and the incommunicable, high and low, cease to be perceived as contradictions.") This ability to bring together incompatible perceptions is, Ehrenzweig suggests, a crucial characteristic of the creative process. This may account for the fact there are so many manic-depressives among the great writers in literary history, for as Kay Redfield Jamison has noted, manic-depressives exhibit a pronounced tendency toward "combinatory thinking," a mode of thinking characterized by the bringing together of "seemingly contradictory moods, observations, and perceptions."

But this doesn't mean that in order to improve our creativity we need to be bipolar, have our left hemispheres removed, or—maybe worse—follow the advice of those ubiquitous "writing with the right brain" books. Creativity is not a mental illness, nor is it a function of one hemisphere. According to the Bogens, creativity requires "interhemispheric communication," the dialogue between the two opposing parts of the brain. This communication is made possible by the corpus callosum, the brain fiber structure that connects the two hemispheres. If the corpus callosum is severed or removed, the Bogens discovered, the creative process is rendered impossible. Creativity, therefore, requires the fusion of the contradictory functions of both hemispheres. The very nature of art supports this conclusion; as the psychiatrist Albert Rothenberg notes, the fact that art integrates "abstract ideas with concrete forms" proves that art requires the "capacity to maintain opposite cognitive orientations simultaneously." In essence, then, art is nothing more—or less—than the product of the contradictions implicit in the biological structure of our brains.

Rothenberg has conducted extensive research, both clinical and experimental, on the psychology of creativity, and his principal conclusion is that the creative process requires "the capacity to conceive and utilize two or more opposite or contradictory ideas, concepts, or images *simultaneously*." He calls the "both-and" form of cognition that makes this possible "Janusian thinking." Janus was the Roman god of doorways—and, significantly, of communication—whose two faces simultaneously looked in opposite directions. According to Rothenberg, a writer using Janusian thinking is likewise looking in opposite directions at the same time and, as a result, is able to create symbols that "connote logical contradiction and basic truth simultaneously" and thus achieve "the integration of opposites" that is the defining characteristic of art. Rothenberg goes on to say that "this form of thinking, the simultaneous conceptualization of opposites, produces artistic products which appear to embody unconscious material because opposites are equal in the unconscious." However, he emphasizes that Janusian thinking is a conscious, not unconscious, thought process. As such, it is one that can be practiced and developed.

Janusian contradiction is not only evident in the structure of the brain, and in the artistic creations that result from that structure, it is also evident in the structure of the physical universe. In the words of the physicist J. Robert Oppenheimer,

> One of the first things the student of atomic structure must come to understand is the rather deep and subtle principle which has turned out to be a clue to unraveling the whole domain of physical experience. This is the principle of complementarity, which recognizes that various ways of talking about physical experience may each have validity and may each be necessary for adequate description of the physical world, and may yet stand in a mutually contradictory relationship to each other.

The theory of complementarity that Oppenheimer describes was introduced in 1927 by the physicist Niels Bohr, who asserted that two mutually exclusive explanations of the nature of light (as a wave and as a particle) were both true and that we can achieve a complete understanding of light only by recognizing their "complementary" relations. "There are the trivial truths and the great truths," he said. "The opposite of a trivial truth is plainly false. The opposite of a great truth is also true." Clearly, in Bohr's view, contradiction is a lever of transcendence. And his theory of complementarity doesn't apply only to light, or even only to quantum physics; in his opinion, it is an "all-pervasive principle," one that applies to all of nature, both human and physical. That all of life is paradoxical and complementary is not a new theory, of course. As revolutionary as Bohr's theory was, and remains, its philosophical roots are ancient, a fact that Bohr acknowledged when he chose for his coat of arms the symbol for yin and yang. Bohr's contribution was in revealing that this ancient concept of unity as the marriage of opposites was not just a mystical notion but a matter of literal physical, subatomic reality.

Perhaps the ultimate expression of physicists' faith in the complementary relationship of contradictions can be found in contemporary chaos theory. According to the scholar Brian Ward, at the center of chaos theory is the scientific concept of "deterministic chaos," the "paradoxical co-existence of randomness and determinism." Hence chaos is, as his fellow scholar N. Katherine Hayles has defined it, "Orderly Disorder." What's more, chaos not only does not repudiate order, she says, it "makes order possible." Though not a scientist, Henry Adams saw in the discoveries of modern science the same paradoxical unity of order and chaos described by today's chaos theorists. Confronted with the kinetic theory of gases, which he called "an assertion of ultimate chaos," he said that science had proved that "in the last synthesis, order and anarchy were one." This realization led him to predict that "the new universe would know no law that could not be proved by its anti-law" and therefore "the new American would need to think in contradictions."

To think in contradictions is, in my opinion, the essence of the creative process in both art and science, at least when the contradictions involve the "great truths" that Bohr talks about. According to his fellow physicists, Bohr habitually "looked for and fastened with greatest energy on a contradiction, heating it to its utmost before he could crystallize the pure metal out of the dispute." And the pure metal, as we have seen, consists of the Janusian fusion of opposing truths. It is precisely this pure metal that we find in the greatest works of literature.

3. MODES OF JANUSIAN CONTRADICTION

Janusian contradiction manifests itself in virtually every aspect of successful works of literature, from such large, all-encompassing issues as theme and structure to such small elements as metaphor, oxymoron, and synesthesia—from the universe of the work, so to speak, to its very atoms. But it manifests itself most overtly, perhaps, on the level of theme. Robert Hass has said that the greatest works of art are those that "come very close to saying the opposite of what they mean," and I agree. But some of the greatest works come more than close; they actually assert opposing meanings simultaneously. *The Brothers Karamazov* is a prime example of this sort of complementary thematic contradiction. At the heart of the novel is a religious debate between the saint-like Alyosha and his atheistic brother Ivan. A lesser writer who shared Dostoevsky's conviction that "Christianity alone" was "the salvation" of humankind would have made Ivan's arguments weak enough to refute without breaking a sweat. But Dostoevsky enters fully into the spirit of Janusian contradiction and writes so passionately and persuasively from Ivan's perspective that many readers have believed he agrees with the opinions expressed in Ivan's tale of the Grand Inquisitor. D.H. Lawrence, for example, asserts that "we cannot doubt that the Inquisitor speaks Dostoevsky's own final opinion about Jesus. The opinion is, baldly, this: Jesus, you are inadequate. Men must correct you." But Lawrence makes the mistake of assuming that half of Dostoevsky's truth is all of it. In a letter, Dostoevsky clearly reveals the complementary nature of his thinking, saying Ivan's argument is "irrefutable" but his novel is nonetheless a "refutation" of it. And in his private notebook, he writes, "Ivan is deep; he is not one of your present-day atheists whose unbelief demonstrates no more than the narrowness of their point of view and the obtuseness of their small minds. ... Those thickheads never dreamt of so powerful a negation of God." Unlike Lawrence, the scholar Edward Wasiolek recognizes the complementary nature of the novel's theme, saying that, for Dostoevsky, "the truth of Christ ... does not demolish the Grand Inquisitor's truth any more than the Grand Inquisitor's truth demolishes Christ's truth." The fact that one of the most ardently Christian novels ever written contains perhaps the most powerful argument against religious belief ever written is a major reason *The Brothers Karamazov* is a masterpiece.

Sometimes the thematic opposition takes place not in an argument between two characters but in an argument within a single character. In such cases, we witness the process of the dialectic struggle with contradictory beliefs or feelings. An excellent example of this is Emily Dickinson's Poem 501. It opens with a strong assertion of faith—so strong that Dickinson ends it with one of the few periods in all of her work: "This World is not Conclusion." But as the poem proceeds, she begins to question the concept of an afterlife, the belief that "A Species stands beyond."

"Faith slips," she says, "Plucks at a twig of Evidence— / And asks a Vane, the way." And by the poem's end she asserts not certainty but doubt, calling the assurances of religion "Narcotics" that "cannot still the Tooth / That nibbles at the soul—." Elizabeth Bishop's poem "Roosters" follows a similar pattern: It opens by presenting the roosters as emblems of cruelty and violence, but by the end, the roosters have "come to mean forgiveness." Both of these poems begin with one assertion and end with an opposing one, but sometimes poems examine opposing assertions throughout and build up to a concluding statement that joins them into a Janusian whole. For example, Marianne Moore's "What Are Years?" builds up to the lines "This is mortality, / this is eternity," which equate two contradictory conceptions of time. Similarly, Sylvia Plath's "Medusa" concludes its speaker's exploration of her conflicting feelings toward her mother with the line "There is nothing between us," which in the context of the poem simultaneously means both "nothing connects us" and "nothing separates us." All of these poems provide superb support for Jane Hirshfield's contention that "a good poem is able both to answer uncertainty and contain it."

Of course, there is no reason that the number of contradictory characters or themes in a work need be limited to one or two. When it is used as a lever of transcendence, contradiction is a *both-and*, not an *either-or*, matter—and often the *and*s proliferate. As this suggests, another way contradiction manifests itself in a work of literature is through the presentation of a multiplicity of perspectives, the totality of which comprises its author's most complete vision of truth. We tend to associate the use of multiple perspectives with such twentieth-century works as *Ulysses* and *As I Lay Dying*, but in fact it has a long pedigree: Witness Boccaccio's *The Decameron*, each section of which consists of ten stories offering different perspectives on one theme. The assumption behind the use of multiple perspectives, then and now, is that no single perspective can possibly encompass the full complexity of truth. Conrad's *Lord Jim* illustrates this point better, perhaps, than any other novel. Essentially, it is a mosaic composed of thirty characters' conflicting views on Jim, as told to its primary narrator, Conrad's alter ego Charlie Marlow. Taken separately, each of these views is illusory. But to a writer whose vision of the world is Janusian, to define a perspective as an illusion is not to dismiss it. As Marlow says, illusions are "visions of remote, unattainable truth, dimly seen." Illusions don't blind us to the truth, Conrad suggests; rather, they offer us dim glimpses of it. What *does* blind us to the truth is convergent thinking, which leads us to assume that only one perspective can be true and the others are false. If we want to understand Jim and the meaning of his life, then, we need to take into account the complementary relations of all of these perspectives.

Conrad's approach to truth in *Lord Jim* is essentially a literary manifestation of the scientific principle of parallax. Just as the location of a star seems to change when it is observed from different vantage points, so, too, the nature of a character or event or situation changes when observed from different vantage points. Clearly, this is the principle upon which Joyce structured *Ulysses* and its eighteen separate points of view on the events of Bloomsday—hence the novel's recurring use of the word *parallax*—and it is a principle that underlies many other works of modern and contemporary literature and art, perhaps most vividly cubist painting, in which various front, back, and side perspectives on a subject are often combined into a single uniplanar image. By combining a variety of parallactic perspectives into a complementary whole, an artist in any genre can achieve what Robert Venturi says should be the aim of art: "the difficult unity of inclusion rather than the easy unity of exclusion."

In his own quest for this difficult kind of unity, Fernando Pessoa took the principle of complementary parallax farther than perhaps any other writer before or since. He rejected the "dogma of artistic individuality," saying that "no artist should have just one personality," and called for the "Synthesis-of-Humanity Man," the man who can say, "I am all others" and who can write "in the most genres with the most contradictions and discrepancies." And he answered his own call, filling his work with contradictions. Walt Whitman could have been speaking for Pessoa when he said, in defense of his own contradictions, "I am large, I contain multitudes." But Pessoa not only contained multitudes, he let those multitudes write their own works. His principal contradictory heteronyms were Álvaro de Campos, Alberto Caeiro, and Ricardo Reis, all of whom collaborated, criticized, and even translated one another, but he also wrote under more than seventy other names. Furthermore, he wrote in three different languages (Portuguese, English, and French) and in an astonishing variety of genres—poetry, fiction, drama, philosophy, literary criticism, linguistic theory, political commentary, social criticism, translations, horoscopes, diaries, and even jokes. As the number of his heteronyms suggests, he possessed, and in abundance, the ability to "other himself," which is perhaps the essential characteristic of Negative Capability. Hence if we want to know what Pessoa himself thought and believed, we must take all seventy-some of his parallactic perspectives into account. We need not go to Pessoa's extremes to make use of the principle of parallax in our own work, of course. But if we wish to create literature that does justice to the beautiful complexity of truth, I believe we must adopt his willing acceptance of complementary contradictions.

Another way contradiction manifests itself in literature is through paradox. Paradox is such an integral part of poetry in particular that Cleanth Brooks has flatly stated that "the language of poetry is the language of paradox." He argues that paradox is "inevitable" in poetry because the imagination works by welding together—i.e., making a complementary whole of—"the discordant and the contradictory." Paradox is not the sole property of poetry, however; it is an important element of all literary genres, and—as we have seen—even philosophy and the sciences. But paradox is certainly predominant in poetry. A few examples should suffice. In "Holy Sonnet 14," John Donne asks God to "overthrow" him so he "may rise and stand," and pleads "Take me to you, imprison me, for I / Except you enthrall me, never shall be free, / Nor ever chaste, except you ravish me." In "Brahma," Ralph Waldo Emerson proclaims that "Far or forgot to me is near; / Shadow and sunlight are the same; / The vanished gods to me appear; / And one to me are shame and fame." Wallace Stevens, too, views unity as the integration of complementary opposites. In "Connoisseur of Chaos," he says, "A violent order is disorder" and "A great disorder is an order," and concludes, "These / Two things are one."

The paradoxical conjoining of opposites is achieved not only through direct statement, as in the examples I've just cited, but also, I would argue, through what we could call Janusian lineation. Consider these lines from Stephen Dunn's poem "The Soul's Agents": "Trust us, your secrets differentiate you / from no one." Taken as a sentence, this statement is not paradoxical. But Dunn's strategic line break makes the reader pause and momentarily think the thought "our secrets *do* differentiate us," a thought the next line contradicts. Hence the reader must think, if only for an instant, two diametrically opposed thoughts.

Importantly, paradox does not manifest itself in poetry only through direct statement or Janusian lineation. It can also reside, as Brooks notes, in an unstated premise that under-lies—and perhaps initiates—an entire poem. Discussing Words-worth's sonnet, "Composed Upon Westminster Bridge, September 3, 1802," which consists entirely of straightforward, unpara-doxical assertions about the beauty of London in the morning light, Brooks points out that the poem gets its power from the unstated paradox that "the common was really uncommon, the prosaic was really poetic."

Irony is yet another manifestation of contradiction in liter-ature, for it, at least in its verbal form, consists of stating one meaning in order to imply its opposite. When Jane Austen opens *Pride and Prejudice* with the assertion, "It is a truth universally acknowledged, that a single man in possession of a good fortune, must be in want of a wife," it is clear that she is mocking, not af-firming, the assumption of the good ladies of Elizabeth Bennet's neighborhood. And when Elizabeth Bishop says, in "One Art," that "The art of losing's not too hard to master / though it may look like ... disaster," we know that in truth the loss of her lover is actually a great disaster, one that is impossible to master. In its simplest form, as in these examples, verbal irony is not com-plementary since only one of its contradictory meanings—the unstated one—is meant to be taken as true. There is a more complex form of verbal irony, however, in which both of the contradictory meanings *are* meant to be taken as true. Accord-ing to William Van O'Connor, we find this paradoxical form of irony especially in the work of such German Romantics as Lud-wig Tieck, Friedrich Schlegel, and Heinrich Heine, all of whom were trying to convey "the polarities ... which post-Kantian phi-losophy found everywhere in experience." Typically, O'Connor says, a writer using this sort of irony will create one mood, then abruptly destroy it "by a change of tone ... or a violently contra-dictory sentiment." The contradiction does not serve to reject what preceded it, however; rather, it complements it. James Wright's "Lying in a Hammock at William Duffy's Farm in Pine Island, Minnesota" is a contemporary example of this form of irony. In this poem, Wright creates a peaceful, pastoral mood by describing in beautiful terms even the ugliest objects that surround the speaker (including horse droppings, which "blaze up" in the sunlight "into golden stones") and then he jars us with the final line: "I have wasted my life." While this line may at first seem to negate the affirmative lines that precede it, in fact it ironically complements them. For what the speaker has realized is the very irony on which the poem is built: that only when he is lying in a hammock, lazily "wasting time," is he *not* wasting his life. And this irony implies a further irony, one that is even more richly paradoxical: Because he has realized he has wasted his life, he has not wasted his life. The final line, then, simultaneously conveys two contradictory but nonetheless true meanings.

Symbols, too, simultaneously convey complementary contradictions. Coleridge makes this point when he says, "except in geometry, all symbols of necessity involve an apparent contradiction." Contemporary geometers would disagree with Coleridge's exception—after all, they define a circle as a round polygon composed of very short straight lines—but even if Coleridge were right, nothing would preclude writers from using geometrical symbols in the same Janusian way they use other symbols. And at least one writer has done just that: Witness the mystical geometry of *A Vision*, in which Yeats uses double cones, gyres, and spheres to portray human history as a cyclical pattern generated by the conflict of opposites. Yeats clearly saw these symbols in Janusian terms, for he said, "They have helped me hold in a single thought" the contradictory ideas of "reality and justice."

Rothenberg uses the iceman in Eugene O'Neill's *The Iceman Cometh* to illustrate the role of Janusian thinking in creating a symbol. In the play, O'Neill overtly compares the iceman to death, but he also implicitly compares the iceman to Christ and an adulterer, since the title alludes both to the phrase "the bridegroom cometh" from Christ's parable about his second coming in Matthew 25:6 and to a joke current at the time, in which a husband, home early from work, calls upstairs to his wife, "Has the iceman come yet?" and she responds, "No, but he's breathing hard!" As a result of these conflicting connotations, the iceman symbol fuses numerous pairs of oppositions into equations, including the equation of the adulterer with Christ, the paragon of celibacy; of sex, which begins life, with death, which ends it; and of Christ, the bringer of eternal life, with death.

An example of another, even more complexly contradictory symbol would be Melville's white whale, which is subject to at least nine conflicting interpretations, one during each of the gams that take place between the Pequod and other ships in the course of *Moby-Dick*, but I'll content myself with a simpler example from that novel, one which I believe conveys the essence of a Janusian symbol with oxymoron-like simplicity: the "coffin life-buoy" that rescues Ishmael from drowning. Hemingway's *A Farewell to Arms* provides another simple yet effective example: In it, rain, the traditional symbol of life and rebirth, is allied with death, both directly when Catherine says, "I'm afraid of the rain because sometimes I see me dead in it," and indirectly when, after Catherine has died while giving birth, Frederic Henry walks back to the hotel in the rain.

Whereas Hemingway links an image associated with life to death, Li-Young Lee links an image associated with death to life. Discussing his use of the word *night* in his poetry, Lee not only reveals the Janusian nature of his thinking but defines what I believe is, or should be, the primary goal of all art:

I'm not sure what it means, life or death. It's always double for me, in that all the associations of that word bring out that place in me where the meeting of opposites happens. And I do think that the practice of poetry is a way to find a path of negotiation between all of our opposing tendencies: good and bad, the demonic and the angelic, the spiritual and the material ... to find exactly that center and suffer right there all of the contradictions of our human nature.

Since symbols are essentially recurring and/or expanded metaphors, it should be no surprise that metaphors are also manifestations of Janusian thinking. Indeed, Monroe C. Beardsley finds it necessary to use a Janusian paradox to define a metaphor: It is, he says, a "logical absurdity," a "significant self-contradiction" that asserts that something is what it is not. Rothenberg defines metaphors similarly, saying they are "manifestations of the integration of mild oppositions." Despite his claim, those oppositions are by no means always "mild." Take, for example, Donne's "The Flea," in which he compares the commingling of two lovers' blood in a flea that has bitten them to the coupling of the lovers themselves on their "marriage bed." And if those oppositions seem mild to you, consider the oppositions in the classic metaphor (variously attributed to Plato, Giordano Bruno, Marsilio Ficino, and Sir Thomas Browne), "Light is the shadow of God," or in Franz Wright's line, "Thirst is my water." In both of these examples, we see the strongest of antitheses—light and darkness, thirst and what quenches it—integrated, made one.

The metaphorical integration of oppositions, whether mild or strong, results not just in a new way of seeing something but in something new. Karsten Harries summarizes this view, saying a metaphor "joins dissimilar things not so much to let us perceive in them some previously hidden similarity, but to create something altogether new." And that something new must by definition transcend what already exists. Not all metaphors are created equal, however; some are more transcendent than others. When we join things that are merely dissimilar, such as a flea and a marriage bed, one plus one adds up to three. But when we join things that are truly antithetical, like light and shadow, one plus one adds up to far more. If "a command of metaphor ... is the mark of genius," as Aristotle said, the Janusian integration of opposites is the primary source of that genius.

Oxymorons are yet another manifestation of Janusian opposition in literature. As Frank J. Warnke and Alex Preminger have said, oxymorons reveal "a compulsion to fuse all experience into a unity"—and since what they fuse are contradictory ideas or attributes, they reveal a compulsion to see all experience as complementary. It is no accident, then, that the proponents of chaos theory use the oxymoron "orderly disorder" to convey their paradoxical vision of physical phenomena.

Essentially, an oxymoron is a condensed paradox. Rendered as oxymorons, the paradoxes that end Donne's "Holy Sonnet 14," for example, would be "imprisoned freedom" and "chaste ravishment." The classic examples of oxymoron come from *Romeo and Juliet*, in which Shakespeare refers to "loving hate," "heavy lightness," "feather of lead," "bright smoke," "cold fire," "sick health," and "still-waking sleep." Other examples include Milton's "living death," Robert Herrick's "wild civility," Donne's "unkindly kind," Melville's "sane madness," and Faulkner's "peaceful despair." Clearly, writers have—as Samuel Beckett wryly commented—"a strong weakness for oxymoron."

Since synesthesia involves the oxymoron-like fusion of mutually exclusive senses, it too is Janusian, and so it is not surprising that a study by the psychologist Peter Grossenbacher concludes that there is a significant link between synesthesia and creativity. His survey of eighty-four synesthetes—people who literally see sounds and hear colors, etc.—revealed that 31 percent of them were professional artists, writers, or musicians and an additional 52 percent were "serious amateurs." So do we have to be synesthetes to be creative? Hardly. We merely need the ability to see one sense as analogous to another, and as psychologists have determined, this ability is a result of neural coding and thus is hardwired into our brains. At least six independent studies by developmental psychologists have demonstrated that children under the age of one perceive loudness and brightness as equivalents. In the words of the philosopher Maurice Merleau-Ponty, "Synaesthetic perception is the rule, and we are unaware of it only because ... we unlearn how to see, hear, and generally speaking, feel." But, as this comment implies, we can relearn what we have unlearned.

In any case, we have not completely unlearned synesthetic perception; if we had, we would not commonly refer to "warm" colors, "bitter" cold, "heavy" heat, "cool" jazz, "dark" looks, "white" noise, "purple" prose, and so forth. In our literature, we seem particularly inclined toward what the French call *audition colourée*, "colored hearing." Among the many literary examples of colored hearing are Dickinson's "blue ... buzz," Fitzgerald's "yellow cocktail music," and Hart Crane's "white echo." And of course there are also numerous examples of what we could call "sonic vision," as in Poe's "the murmur of the grey twilight" and Dylan Thomas's "the sun roars."

Sight and sound are not the only senses we use synesthetically, of course. When A.S. Byatt compares scarlet to "the scream of someone falling through a skylight," she is comparing the color not only to a sound but also to the physical sensation of falling and crashing through glass. Similarly, when W.S. Merwin describes the coming darkness of night as "cold and like thunder," he conveys what he can only see in terms of something he can hear and feel. And when Federico García Lorca says "green wind," he conveys what he can only feel in terms of something he can see.

Vladimir Nabokov, who was a synesthete, offers a smorgasbord of synesthetic combinations in his work. Just flipping through his story "The Potato Elf," I find these examples: "silvery voice," "warm whiffs," "soft hollow notes," "humid light," and "wobbly" music. Baudelaire, who may also have been a synesthete, offers similar smorgasbords. For example, in "Correspondences," a poem that did much to popularize the use of synesthesia in poetry, he mingles smell, taste, and hearing when he refers to "Perfumes … as sweet as the oboe's sound." The poem also asserts that, in nature, "All scents and sounds and colors meet as one" and, what's more, they correspond to each other—i.e., their apparent contradictions are complementary, not exclusionary.

If contradiction is an essential part of both the creative process and the work of literature that results—and I am convinced it is—it stands to reason that it is also a significant part of the reader's response to that work. Aristotle acknowledged this fact, I believe, when he said that the ultimate goal of a tragedy is to effect "through pity and fear … the proper purgation of these emotions" in the spectator. Aristotle never explained what the proper purgation, or catharsis, of these emotions involves, but it is clear that it requires the experience of contradictory emotions, for he says "through pity *and* fear," not "through pity *or* fear." Clearly, Aristotle believes that for a tragedy to be successful we must feel both drawn toward *and* repelled away from the protagonist. Feeling only pity, as we might in a melodrama, or only fear, as in a thriller, would not lead to catharsis, Aristotle's formulation suggests, since catharsis involves feeling both emotions simultaneously. Furthermore, it involves more than just vomiting up those emotions—if it didn't, *Love Story* and *The Texas Chain*

Saw Massacre would be more cathartic than *Oedipus Rex*. As I see it, through the cathartic combination of pity and fear, tragedy purges us of falsely simple emotions—pity *or* fear—by making us experience the complex true emotion their fusion creates.

I believe that Aristotle's principle also applies to other combinations of contradictory emotions—for instance, approval and disapproval, attraction and repulsion, love and hate, belief and doubt, pride and shame—and therefore it applies to many other kinds of literature besides tragic drama. Whether Aristotle would agree, I obviously cannot say, but I do believe that Janusian contradiction is part of his conception of catharsis. And I further believe that the Janusian contradiction underlying catharsis also accounts for much of the sense of discovery and transcendence we feel when we read a truly great work of literature.

4. ARGUING WITH OURSELVES

If Janusian thinking is indeed the key to the creative process, the question remains, how do we develop the ability to think, and write, in this manner? To an extent, simply practicing the literary techniques we have discussed—thematic complementarity, parallactic structure, paradox, irony, symbol, metaphor, oxymoron, and synesthesia—will start us on our way. But no matter how proficient we become at these techniques, I don't believe practicing them is nearly enough. If we want our work to be infused with "the spirit of contradiction in its highest form," we need to change the very way we think. Janusian thinking is ultimately a matter of the moral, intellectual, and emotional stance we take toward experience, not a matter of technique. So if we don't already intuitively follow the dialectic mode of thought Weil recommends—and most of us don't, since our religious and secular educations have instilled in us an uncomplementary view of truth—we need to practice it, to work against our first, convergent thoughts and feelings, until our writing process becomes an extended argument with ourselves. Stephen Dunn describes his writing process in precisely these terms. "I … have learned to argue with myself as I go," he says, "to assert then doubt a claim, to compose dialectically. … In short, I think I've learned how to 'find' the poem I'm writing by resisting where it wants to go and/or resisting my initial impulses for it." Now, he suggests, that method is habitual, involuntary: "When I say or assert something, I almost immediately hear and start to entertain its opposite." Adrienne Rich concurs: "If the imagination is to transcend and transform experience, it has to question, to challenge, to conceive of alternatives … You have to be free to play around with the notion that day might be night, love might be hate; nothing can be too sacred for the imagination to turn into its opposite."

Robert Lowell is yet another poet who often found his poems by resisting his initial, convergent impulses. According to Jonathan Raban, Lowell's "favorite method of revision was simply to introduce a negative into a line, which absolutely reversed its meaning." Such reversal is perhaps the most drastic form of divergent thinking, for it severs us completely from the familiar, comfortable certainty that results from convergent thinking, and by doing so, it establishes a vital tension between the two poles of our original thought and our negation of it, a tension that can lead to further divergence and, ultimately, to the sort of fusion of contradictory impulses and ideas we have been talking about. It is in the tension between these two poles that meaning resides; as Leonard Bernstein said, "A work of art does not answer questions, it provokes them; and its essential meaning is in the tension between the contradictory answers."

Mark Cox's poem "After Rain" reveals how Lowell's technique of dialectic reversal can create poles between which truth may be sought. In it, Cox's speaker finds himself "opened some-how" by all he sees during a quiet night after a rainstorm, and in this open state, he feels "what's real [soak] in further." And what's real is both the transitory and the eternal, the "sparks" from our "psychic fire" that will disappear with our death and the stars that will continue forever. Considering these opposites, Cox writes, "The journey is long. / The journey is not long." What he discovers in the tension between these two contradictory an-swers to the question of time is a state of mind that integrates them both, a state of "worship" in which his eternal longing finds a momentary peace like that of "the calm after rain / and before the slate's clearing." "The journey is not long" is thus not a *cor-rection* of the thought "The journey is long"; rather, it is a *com-pletion* of it.

Like Lowell and Cox, Dunn often discovers the meaning of a poem through the use of dialectic reversal. We see examples of this in certain of his lines—as in "The Past," where he says, "Nothing in nature is a metaphor. / Everything is."—but he also uses this technique on a larger scale. When a poem isn't work-ing, he says, he will sometimes "write a poem against it, tak-ing a different point of view." One thing we can do when we are blocked by uncertainty, then, is to write against our work. If we practice this sort of self-contradiction, we may find a line or sentence—or even an entire poem or story—in the tension be-tween our original conception and its opposite. And, if we're lucky, we may also find ourselves transcending the previous limits of our thought and talent.

5. A PLACE TO STAND

For the metaphor that conveys her view of the role contradiction plays in transcendence, Simone Weil turned to physics, and I have done likewise in my attempt to elucidate her brilliant insight. But I have not yet mentioned the physicist who provided Weil with her metaphor: Archimedes. "Give me a lever and a place to stand," he famously said, "and I will lift the world." For a writer, I believe, the place to stand is uncertainty, and the lever is contradiction. While we can practice the various techniques through which contradiction manifests itself in literature, we cannot truly find the right place to stand or the right lever to use until we learn to argue with ourselves, to think dialectically, to look, like Janus, in opposite directions at the same time. The more we develop this mode of thought, the more we will increase our Negative Capability and clear a space in our imaginations for poems, stories, novels, and plays that transcend our quotidian understanding and convey a larger, more complementary vision of the world and ourselves. And the more we use contradiction as a lever of transcendence, the more we will increase our chances of becoming true physicists of the language, capable of lifting the world.

NOTES ON THE ESSAYS

AUTOBIOGRAPHOBIA: WRITING AND THE SECRET LIFE

Anderson, Sherwood, cited in *Writers on Writing*, 3rd ed., edited by Jon Winokur (Philadelphia: Running Press, 1990), 349.

Borges, Jorge Luis. "Epilogue." In *Dreamtigers*, translated by Harold Morland (Austin: University of Texas Press, 1978), 93.

Butler, Robert Olen. *From Where You Dream: The Process of Writing Fiction*, edited by Janet Burroway (New York: Grove Press, 2005), 23.

Cavafy, C.P. "Hidden Things." In *Collected Poems*, edited by George Savidis, translated by Edmund Keeley and Philip Sherrard (Princeton: Princeton University Press, 1992), 195.

Chekhov, Anton. Letter to Grigori Rossolimo, October 11, 1899. In *The Selected Letters of Anton Chekhov*, edited by Lillian Hellman, translated by Sidonie Lederer (New York: Farrar, Straus and Giroux, 1955), 251.

_____. "The Bishop" and "The Lady With the Pet Dog." In *A Doctor's Visit: Short Stories by Anton Chekhov*, edited by Tobias Wolff (New York: Bantam Classics, 1988), 72-73, 77, 157-158.

Dickinson, Emily. Poem 1129. In *The Poems of Emily Dickinson*, edited by Thomas H. Johnson (Cambridge: Harvard University Press, 1955), 506.

Dunn, Stephen. Lecture at Lyon College, Batesville, Arkansas, April 1995.

Eliot, T.S. "The Love Song of J. Alfred Prufrock." In *The Complete Poems and Plays*, *1909-1950* (New York: Harcourt, Brace and World, 1971), 6.

Flaubert, Gustave, cited in Albert Thibaudet, *Gustave Flaubert* (Paris: Gallimard, 1935), 92.

_____. Letter to Louise Colet, December 23, 1853. In *Madame Bovary*, edited by Paul de Man (New York: Norton, 1965), 317.

Graham, Jorie. "Noli Me Tangere." In *The End of Beauty* (New York: Ecco Press, 1987), 41.

Greene, Graham, cited in Robert Olen Butler, *From Where You Dream: The Process of Writing Fiction* (New York: Grove Press, 2005), 23.

Hall, Donald. "Goatfoot, Milktongue, Twinbird: The Psychic Origins of Poetic Form." In *Claims for Poetry*, edited by Donald Hall (Ann Arbor: University of Michigan Press, 1982), 142.

_____. "Interview With Peter Stitt." In *Death to the Death of Poetry* (Ann Arbor: University of Michigan Press, 1994), 153.

_____. *Their Ancient Glittering Eyes: Remembering Poets and More Poets* (New York: Ticknor and Fields, 1992), 38.

Hughes, Ted. "The Art of Poetry LXXI," *The Paris Review* 134 (spring 1992): 75.

Jauss, David. "Cyrano." In *Improvising Rivers* (Cleveland: Cleveland State University Press, 1995), 50-51.

Johnson, Edgar. *Charles Dickens: His Tragedy and Triumph* (New York: Simon & Schuster, 1952), 34-46.

Kunitz, Stanley. *Next-to-Last Things: New Poems and Essays* (Boston: Atlantic Monthly Press, 1985), 28-29.

Machado, Antonio, cited in Tom Hansen, "The New Old Imagination," *Willow Springs* 27 (winter 1991): 64.

O'Brien, Tim. *The Things They Carried* (New York: Penguin, 1990).

Paley, Grace. Interview with Kay Bonetti in American Audio Prose Library (June 1, 1987).

Schmidt, Elizabeth. "Imagining Emily," *The New York Times Book Review*, 102 (March 2, 1997): 31.

Shakespeare, William. *As You Like It*, Act III, scene iii.

Simic, Charles. Introduction to *The Best American Poetry 1992* (New York: Scribner, 1992), xiv.

Trilling, Lionel. "Art and Neurosis." In *The Liberal Imagination* (New York: Scribner, 1950), 169.

Walters, Mark Jerome. *The Dance of Life: Courtship in the Animal Kingdom* (New York: Arbor House, 1988), 9.

Wilde, Oscar. "L'Envoi" to *Rose-leaf and Apple-leaf*. In *The Works of Oscar Wilde*, vol. 9 (New York: Lamb Publishing Co., 1972), 74.

_____. "The Critic as Artist." In *The Artist as Critic: Critical Writings of Oscar Wilde*, edited by Richard Ellmann (New York: Random House, 1969), 389.

__Note:__ The "autobiographical" section titled "Zorro's Servant" is in fact fictional.

FROM LONG SHOTS TO X-RAYS: DISTANCE AND POINT OF VIEW IN FICTION

Baxter, Charles. "Media Event." In *Through the Safety Net* (New York: Penguin, 1986).

Booth, Wayne C. *The Rhetoric of Fiction* (Chicago: The University of Chicago Press, 1961), 151, 161.

Bowen, Elizabeth. "The Demon Lover." In *The Collected Stories of Elizabeth Bowen* (New York: Vintage, 1982), 665.

Brockmeier, Kevin. "These Hands." In *Things That Fall From the Sky* (New York: Vintage, 2002), 3.

Burroway, Janet. *Writing Fiction: A Guide to Narrative Craft*, 5th ed. (New York: Longman, 2000), 209.

Casparis, Christian Paul. *Tense Without Time: The Present Tense in Narration* (Bern: A. Francke, 1975), 39.

Chekov, Anton. "A Trifle From Real Life." In *Russian Silhouettes: More Stories of Russian Life by Anton Tchekoff*, translated by Marian Fell (New York: Scribner, 1915), 27-28.

Cohen, Richard. *Writer's Mind: Crafting Fiction* (Lincolnwood, IL: NTC Publishing Group, 1995), 93.

Cohn, Dorrit. *Transparent Minds: Narrative Modes for Presenting Consciousness in Fiction* (Princeton: Princeton University Press, 1978), 65.

Conrad, Joseph. "Heart of Darkness." In *The Portable Conrad*, edited by Morton Dawen Zabel (New York: Penguin, 1978), 481, 496, 500, 518.

Dostoevsky, Fyodor. *Crime and Punishment*, translated by Constance Garnett (New York: Modern Library, 1950), 99.

Eliot, T.S. "Hamlet and His Problems." In *The Sacred Wood: Essays on Poetry and Criticism* (London: Methuen, 1983), 100.

Eugenides, Jeffrey. *Middlesex* (New York: Picador, 2002), 442.

Faulkner, William. *Light in August* (New York: Random House, 1959), 130.

_____. *The Sound and the Fury*, edited by David Minter (New York: Norton, 1987), 59.

Fitzgerald, F. Scott. *The Great Gatsby* (New York: Collier Books, 1986), 112.

Flaubert, Gustave. *Madame Bovary*, translated by Mildred Marmur (New York: Signet, 2001), 85-86, 131, 272.

Grass, Günter. *The Tin Drum*, translated by Ralph Manheim (New York: Vintage International, 1990), 25.

Hemingway, Ernest. *A Farewell to Arms* (New York: Scribner, 1995), 258.

_____. "Hills Like White Elephants" and "The Light of the World." In *The Short Stories of Ernest Hemingway* (New York: Scribner, 1966), 275-278, 384.

James, Henry. "Preface to *The Wings of the Dove*." In *The Art of Criticism: Henry James on the Theory and Practice of Fiction*, edited by William Veeder and Susan M. Griffin (Chicago: The University of Chicago Press, 1986), 355.

James, William. *The Principles of Psychology*, vol. 1 (Cambridge: Harvard University Press, 1981), 233.

Joyce, James. *A Portrait of the Artist as a Young Man* (New York: Signet, 1991), 28-29, 217.

_____. *Ulysses* (New York: Vintage, 1990), 59, 68, 738.

Rosenthal, Chuck. E-mail to the author, April 22, 2002.

Rushdie, Salman. *Midnight's Children* (New York: Avon Books, 1982), 31.

Sartre, Jean-Paul. "Intimacy," cited in Dorrit Cohn, *Transparent Minds: Narrative Modes for Presenting Consciousness in Fiction* (Princeton: Princeton University Press, 1978), 64.

Schwartz, Delmore. "In Dreams Begin Responsibilities." In *In Dreams Begin Responsibilities and Other Stories* (New York: New Directions, 1978), 3.

Tolstoy, Leo. *War and Peace*, translated by Anthony Briggs (London: Penguin, 2005), 487.

Vargas Llosa, Mario. *Letters to a Young Novelist*, translated by Natasha Wimmer (New York: Farrar, Straus and Giroux, 1997), 8.

_____. *The Perpetual Orgy: Flaubert and Madame Bovary*, translated by Helen Lane (New York: Farrar, Straus and Giroux, 1986), 186-187, 192, 194, 200.

WHAT WE TALK ABOUT WHEN WE TALK ABOUT FLOW

Barthelme, Donald. "Not-Knowing." In *The Pushcart Prize XI: Best of the Small Presses*, edited by Bill Henderson (Wainscott, NY: Pushcart Press, 1986), 28.

Benedict, Helen. "Tone Deaf: Learning to Listen to the Music in Prose," *Poets & Writers* 29, no. 6 (November/December 2001): 14-15.

Biggar, Lisa. Letter to the author, November 17, 2002.

Bly, Robert. Comment during panel on prose poetry at the Associated Writers and Writing Programs conference, Washington, DC, April 1996.

Bosselaar, Laure-Anne. "The Interrogation of Stephen Dobyns," *The Writer's Chronicle* 34, no. 1 (September 2001): 46.

Brown, E.K. *Rhythm in the Novel* (Lincoln: University of Nebraska Press, 1978).

Capote, Truman, cited in *Writers on Writing*, 3rd ed., edited by Jon Winokur (Philadelphia: Running Press, 1990), 294.

Carver, Raymond. "Menudo." In *Where I'm Calling From: New & Selected Stories* (New York: Atlantic Monthly Press, 1988), 338.

Dybek, Stuart. "Magic in Craft." In *Novel Voices*, edited by Jennifer Levasseur and Kevin Rabalais (Cincinnati: Writer's Digest Books, 2003), 64.

Faulkner, William. *Light in August* (New York: Random House, 1959), 121.

Flaubert, Gustave. *The Selected Letters of Gustave Flaubert*, translated and edited by Francis Steegmuller (New York: Vintage, 1953), 174.

Fodor, Jerry A. *The Language of Thought* (Cambridge: Harvard University Press, 1980), 56, 61, 67.

Ford, Ford Madox. *Portraits From Life* (Boston: Houghton Mifflin, 1937), 70-71, 74.

Forster, E.M. *Aspects of the Novel* (New York: Harcourt, 1927), 213, 235, 240-241.

Harding, D.W. *Words Into Rhythm: English Speech Rhythm in Verse and Prose* (New York: Cambridge University Press, 1976), 140-141.

Harrell, Tom, cited in Whitney Balliett, "Tom and Jeru," *The New Yorker* (April 15, 1996): 94.

Hass, Robert. *Twentieth Century Pleasures: Prose on Poetry* (New York: Ecco Press, 1984), 108, 113.

Hemingway, Ernest. "A Clean, Well-Lighted Place." In *The Short Stories of Ernest Hemingway* (New York: Scribner, 1966), 379.

Hempel, Amy. "A Conversation With Amy Hempel." In *Story Matters*, edited by Margaret-Love Denman and Barbara Shoup (Boston: Houghton Mifflin, 2006), 223.

Hopkins, Gerard Manley. 1878 letter to Richard Watson Dixon, cited in Tillie Olsen, *Silences* (New York: Delacorte Press, 1978), 126.

Kundera, Milan. *The Art of the Novel* (New York: HarperCollins, 1993), 75-77, 88-89.

Lacan, Jacques. *Speech and Language in Psychoanalysis*, translated by Anthony Wilden (Baltimore: The Johns Hopkins University Press, 1981), 262.

Lawrence, D.H. "Odour of Chrysanthemums." In *The Complete Short Stories of D H. Lawrence*, vol. 2 (New York: Viking, 1961), 283.

Macauley, Robie and George Lanning. *Technique in Fiction*, 2nd ed. (New York: St. Martin's Press, 1987), 73.

Malouf, David. Interview with Kevin Rabalais, *Writers Ask* 33 (2006): 13.

Maritain, Jacques. *Creative Intuition in Art and Poetry* (Cleveland: World Publishing Group, 1954), 67, 202-203, 205.

Mattison, Alice. Interview with Barbara Brooks, *Writers Ask* 31 (2006): 6.

Max, D.T. "The Carver Chronicles," *The New York Times Magazine* (August 9, 1998): 34-56.

Morris, Wright. *About Fiction* (New York: Harper & Row, 1975), 67, 69-70, 73.

Nabokov, Vladimir. "On a Book Entitled *Lolita*." In *Lolita* (New York: Putnam, 1955), 317.

Pascal, Blaise. *Pascal's Pensées* (New York: Dutton, 1956), 7.

Pound, Ezra. "Vorticism," *Fortnightly Review* 96 (1914): 463.

Queneau, Raymond. *Exercises in Style*, translated by Barbara Wright (New York: New Directions, 1981).

Rich, Adrienne, cited in "A Conversation With Carolyn Ferrell." In *Story Matters*, edited by Margaret-Love Denman and Barbara Shoup (Boston: Houghton Mifflin, 2006), 211.

Rilke, Rainer Maria. December 29, 1908, letter to Auguste Rodin. In *Letters of Rainer Maria Rilke, 1892-1910*, translated by Jane Bannard Greene and M.D. Herter Norton (New York: Norton, 1945), 342.

Russell, Bertrand. *An Inquiry Into Meaning and Truth* (London: George Allen and Unwin, 1940), 347.

Tufte, Virginia. *Grammar as Style* (New York: Holt, Rinehart & Winston, 1971), 8-9, 11, 29.

Wolff, Tobias. "The Chain." In *The Night in Question* (New York: Knopf, 1996), 131-132.

Woolf, Virginia. Letter to Vita Sackville-West, cited in Douglas Bauer, "The Pack Mule of Prose: Thoughts on the Sentence," *The Writer's Chronicle* (September 2003): 40.

Yeats, William Butler. "An Introduction to My Plays." In *Essays and Introductions* (New York: Macmillan, 1961), 530.

REMEMBRANCE OF THINGS PRESENT:
PRESENT TENSE IN CONTEMPORARY FICTION

Baxter, Charles. *The Feast of Love* (New York: Pantheon, 2000), 3, 25, 91, 248.

_____. "On Defamiliarization." In *Burning Down the House: Essays on Fiction* (Saint Paul, MN: Graywolf Press, 1997), 40.

_____. "Saul and Patsy Are Pregnant." In *A Relative Stranger* (New York: Penguin, 1990).

Beattie, Ann. "Secrets and Surprises" and "Waiting." In *Park City: New and Selected Stories* (New York: Knopf, 1998), 185-190, 310.

Beckett, Samuel. *Molloy, Malone Dies, The Unnamable* (New York: Knopf, 1997), 25, 37.

Benson, L.D. "Chaucer's Historical Present, Its Meaning and Uses," *English Studies* XLII (1961): 67.

Bergson, Henri. *Time and Free Will: An Essay on the Immediate Data of Consciousness*, translated by F.L. Pogson (New York: Harper & Brothers, 1960), 99.

Burroway, Janet. *Writing Fiction: A Guide to Narrative Craft*, 4th ed. (New York: HarperCollins, 1996), 240.

Camus, Albert. "Absurd Freedom." In *A Casebook on Existentialism*, edited by William V. Spanos (New York: Thomas Y. Crowell Co., 1966), 298.

Carver, Raymond. "Fat." In *Where I'm Calling From: New & Selected Stories* (New York: Atlantic Monthly Press, 1988).

Cary, Joyce, preface to *Mister Johnson* (London: Michael Joseph, 1967), 9-10.

Casparis, Christian Paul. *Tense Without Time: The Present Tense in Narration* (Bern: A. Francke, 1975), 10, 31-32, 67.

Chute, Carolyn. Interview with Barbara Stevens, *Writers Ask* 10 (2000): 10.

Dodd, Susan. "Potions." In *Old Wives' Tales* (Iowa City: University of Iowa Press, 1984).

Dujardin, Édouard. *We'll to the Woods No More*, translated by Stuart Gilbert (New York: New Directions, 1938).

Földes, Jolán. *The Street of the Fishing Cat*, translated by Elizabeth Jacobi (New York: Farrar & Rinehart, 1937).

García Márquez, Gabriel. "Someone Has Been Disarranging These Roses." In *Collected Stories* (New York: Harper & Row, 1978).

Gass, William H. "A Failing Grade for the Present Tense." In *Finding a Form* (New York: Knopf, 1996), 17, 21, 24, 26, 29.

Genette, Gérard. "Time and Narrative in *A la recherché du temps perdu*." In *Essentials of the Theory of Fiction*, edited by Michael J. Hoffman and Patrick D. Murphy (Durham: Duke University Press, 1988), 284.

Haas, Robert Bartlett. *A Primer for the Gradual Understanding of Gertrude Stein* (Los Angeles: Black Sparrow Press, 1973), 49.

Hempel, Amy. "Church Cancels Cow." In *Tumble Home* (New York: Simon & Schuster, 1997), 22.

Houston, Pam. "Sometimes You Talk About Idaho." In *Cowboys Are My Weakness* (New York: Pocket Books, 1992), 145.

Joyce, James. *Ulysses* (New York: Vintage, 1961), 34.

Lee, Vernon (Violet Paget). "Carlyle and the Present Tense." In *The Handling of Words and Other Studies in Literary Psychology* (Lincoln: University of Nebraska Press, 1968), 176.

Le Guin, Ursula K. "Some Thoughts on Narrative." In *Crafting Fiction: In Theory, In Practice*, edited by Marvin Diogenes and Clyde Moneyhun (Mountain View, CA: Mayfield Publishing Co., 2001), 60-61.

Lewis, Wyndham. *Time and Western Man* (Boston: Beacon Press, 1957), 89.

Macauley, Robie and George Lanning. *Technique in Fiction*, 2nd ed. (New York: St. Martin's Press, 1987), 180, 195, 197-198.

Mailer, Norman. *The Naked and the Dead* (New York: Rinehart, 1948).

Mann, Thomas, cited in A.A. Mendilow, *Time and the Novel* (London: Peter Nevill, 1952), 89-90.

_____. *Doctor Faustus* (New York: Vintage, 1992), 286.

Mansfield, Katherine. "Spring Pictures" and "The Wind Blows." In *The Stories of Katherine Mansfield* (New York: Knopf, 1970).

McCorkle, Kate. "The Last Parakeet." In *Flash Fiction: Very Short Stories*, edited by James Thomas, Denise Thomas, and Tom Hazuka (New York: Norton, 1992).

Mendilow, A.A. *Time and the Novel* (London: Peter Nevill, 1952), 48, 91, 96, 99, 107.

Minot, Susan. "Île Sèche" and "The Man Who Would Not Go Away." In *Lust and Other Stories* (New York: Washington Square Press, 1989), 133, 145.

Moore, Lorrie. "How to Be an Other Woman." In *Self-Help* (New York: Warner Books, 1985).

_____. "People Like That Are the Only People Here: Canonical Babbling in Peed Onk." In *Birds of America* (New York: Knopf, 1998), 212, 219, 222-223, 234, 250.

Munro, Alice. "Labor Day Dinner." In *Selected Stories* (New York: Vintage, 1997).

Noon, William T. "Modern Literature and the Sense of Time." In *The Theory of the Novel*, edited by Philip Stevick (New York: The Free Press, 1967), 296.

Oates, Joyce Carol. "August Evening." In *The Assignation* (New York: Ecco Press, 1988).

_____. "You." In *The Wheel of Love and Other Stories* (Greenwich, CT: Fawcett, 1972), 334.

Porter, Katherine Anne. "Flowering Judas." In *Flowering Judas and Other Stories* (New York: Harcourt Brace, 1958).

Proulx, Annie. "The Wer-Trout." In *Heart Songs and Other Stories* (New York: Simon & Schuster, 1995), 137.

Robison, Mary. "The Nature of Almost Everything." In *An Amateur's Guide to the Night* (New York: Knopf, 1983).

Rueckert, William. "Boxed in the Void: An Essay on the Late Sixties in America," *The Iowa Review* 9, No. 1 (Winter 1978): 62-63, 66-68.

Sartre, Jean-Paul. *Being and Nothingness*, translated by Hazel E. Barnes (New York: Gramercy Books, 1956), 479.

_____. *"What Is Literature?" and Other Essays* (Cambridge: Harvard University Press, 1988), 346.

Schneider, Linda. "Saul and Patsy Teach a Lesson: Charles Baxter's Interpretation and Practice of Defamiliarization," M.F.A. Critical Thesis, Vermont College (Spring 2001), 17.

Schwartz, Delmore. "In Dreams Begin Responsibilities." In *In Dreams Begin Responsibilities and Other Stories* (New York: Norton, 1978).

Shklovsky, Viktor. "Art as Technique." In *Russian Formalist Criticism: Four Essays*, translated and edited by Lee T. Lemon and Marion J. Reis (Lincoln: University of Nebraska Press, 1965).

Spender, Stephen, cited in A.A. Mendilow, *Time and the Novel* (London: Peter Nevill, 1952), 14.

Stein, Gertrude. *A Long Gay Book*. In *GMP* (Barton, VT: Something Else Press, 1972).

_____. "As Fine as Melanctha." In *As Fine as Melanctha* (Freeport, NY: Books for Libraries Press, 1969), 255.

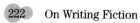

_____. "A Transatlantic Interview." In *A Primer for the Gradual Understanding of Gertrude Stein*, edited by Robert Bartlett Haas (Los Angeles: Black Sparrow Press, 1973), 20.

_____. *Tender Buttons*. In *Writings 1903-1932* (New York: Library of America, 1998).

Tanner, Ron. "The Rain of Nowness: Present-Tense Fiction in America," *Chelsea* 54 (1993): 70, 73, 75.

Thomas, Abigail. "Sisters." In *Getting Over Tom* (New York: Scribner, 1994), 7, 9-11.

Thomas, James, Denise Thomas and Tom Hazuka. *Flash Fiction: Very Short Stories* (New York: Norton, 1992).

Updike, John. Interview with Charles Thomas Samuels. In *Writers at Work: The Paris Review Interviews*, 4th series, edited by George Plimpton (New York: Viking, 1976), 447-448.

_____. "Lifeguard." In *Pigeon Feathers and Other Stories* (New York: Fawcett Crest, 1980), 149.

Warnock, Mary. *Imagination and Time* (Cambridge: Blackwell, 1994), 175.

Welty, Eudora. "Powerhouse." In *Thirteen Stories* (New York: Harcourt Brace Jovanovich, 1977).

Williams, Diane. "Here's Another Ending." In *This Is About the Body, the Mind, the Soul, the World, Time and Fate* (New York: Grove Press, 1989).

Wolff, Tobias. "A Conversation With Tobias Wolff." In *Story Matters*, edited by Margaret-Love Denman and Barbara Shoup (Boston: Houghton Mifflin, 2006), 478.

_____. "The Other Miller." In *The Night in Question* (New York: Knopf, 1996), 99.

Wood, Monica. Interview excerpt, *Writers Ask* 10 (2000): 11.

Woolf, Virginia. "The Evening Party" and "The String Quartet." In *The Complete Shorter Fiction of Virginia Woolf,* edited by Susan Dick (New York: Harcourt Brace, 1982).

SOME EPIPHANIES ABOUT EPIPHANIES

Baxter, Charles. "Against Epiphanies." In *Burning Down the House: Essays on Fiction* (Saint Paul, MN: Graywolf Press, 1997), 53-54, 56-58, 60, 62-63, 65-66.

_____. "Prowlers" and "Saul and Patsy Are Pregnant." In *A Relative Stranger* (New York: Penguin, 1990), 50, 58, 219, 223.

Carver, Raymond. "Fat" and "Cathedral." In *Where I'm Calling From: New & Selected Stories* (New York: Atlantic Monthly Press, 1988), 51-52, 279.

Chekhov, Anton. "A Gentleman Friend" and "The Kiss." In *A Doctor's Visit: Short Stories by Anton Chekhov,* edited by Tobias Wolff (New York: Bantam, 1988), 46, 48, 143.

Chopin, Kate. "The Story of an Hour." In *The Awakening and Selected Stories* (New York: Modern Library, 1981).

Conrad, Joseph. *Heart of Darkness,* edited by Robert Kimbrough (New York: Norton, 1971), 71.

Curtis, C. Michael. *American Stories: Fiction From The Atlantic Monthly* (San Francisco: Chronicle Books, 1990), xii.

Fitzgerald, F. Scott. *The Great Gatsby* (New York: Collier Books, 1986), 111-112.

Hills, Rust. *Writing in General and the Short Story in Particular* (Boston: Houghton Mifflin, 1987), 19.

Joyce, James. "Araby" and "The Dead." In *Dubliners* (London: Jonathan Cape, 1967), 29-32, 36, 249, 255-256.

_____. *Stephen Hero*, edited by Theodore Spencer (New York: New Directions, 1963), 211.

Munro, Alice. "Miles City, Montana." In *Selected Stories* (New York: Vintage, 1997), 376, 392-393.

O'Connor, Flannery. "A Good Man Is Hard to Find." In *The Complete Stories* (New York: Farrar, Straus and Giroux, 1981), 131-133.

_____. "On Her Own Work." In *Mystery and Manners*, edited by Sally and Robert Fitzgerald (New York: Farrar, Straus and Giroux, 1981), 111-113.

Olsen, William. "The Reading Life." Lecture at Vermont College, July 2000.

Prose, Francine. "What Makes a Short Story?" In *On Writing Short Stories*, edited by Tom Bailey (New York: Oxford University Press, 2000), 10.

Schwartz, Sheila M. "Afterbirth" and "Contributor's Note." In *Prize Stories 1999: The O. Henry Awards*, edited by Larry Dark (New York: Anchor Books, 1999), 257, 261-262, 407.

Updike, John. "Pigeon Feathers." In *Pigeon Feathers and Other Stories* (Greenwich, CT: Fawcett Crest, 1962), 85, 88, 105.

Ventrella, Lisa. "Got Epiphany?" Lecture at Vermont College of Fine Arts, January 2008.

STACKING STONES: BUILDING A UNIFIED SHORT STORY COLLECTION

Barrett, Andrea. "The Secret Sharers," *The New York Times Book Review* (April 13, 2003): 20.

Barth, John. *Lost in the Funhouse* (New York: Anchor Books, 1988), vii.

Becker, Leslee. *The Sincere Cafe* (Minneapolis: Mid-List Press, 1997), 26, 27, 34, 38, 76, 130, 146, 151, 154.

Bissell, Tom. "History Is a Nightmare" (review of David Mitchell's *Cloud Atlas*), *The New York Times Book Review* 109, No. 35 (August 29, 2004): 7.

Brown, Rosellen. *Street Games* (Garden City, NY: Doubleday, 1974).

Busch, Frederick. *Domestic Particulars: A Family Chronicle* (New York: New Directions, 1976).

Calisher, Hortense. *The Collected Stories of Hortense Calisher* (New York: Arbor House, 1975), ix.

Chaon, Dan. *Among the Missing* (New York: Ballantine, 2001), 60.

Cisneros, Sandra. *Woman Hollering Creek and Other Stories* (New York: Random House, 1991).

Davis, Lydia. *Almost No Memory* (New York: Farrar, Straus and Giroux, 1997).

Dybek, Stuart. "A Conversation With Stuart Dybek." In *Story Matters*, edited by Margaret-Love Denman and Barbara Shoup (Boston: Houghton Mifflin, 2006), 165.

————. "An Interview With Stuart Dybek," conducted by Jeanie Chung, *The Writer's Chronicle* (October/November 2005): 43.

Erdrich, Louise. *Love Medicine*, new and expanded ed. (New York: Harper Perennial, 1993).

Eugenides, Jeffrey. Jacket blurb, Lydia Davis, *Almost No Memory* (New York: Farrar, Straus and Giroux, 1997).

Flaubert, Gustave, cited in *The Story and Its Writer*, 6th ed., edited by Ann Charters (New York: Bedford/St. Martin's, 2003), 521.

Forster, E.M. *Aspects of the Novel* (New York: Harvest Books, 1956).

Frost, Robert, cited by James Wright in Peter Stitt, *The World's Hieroglyphic Beauty: Five American Poets* (Athens: University of Georgia Press, 1985), 205.

Galvin, James. *Elements* (Port Townsend, WA: Copper Canyon Press, 1988), 18.

Gass, William H. "A Revised & Expanded Preface." In *In the Heart of the Heart of the Country and Other Stories* (Boston: Godine, 1981).

Houston, Pam. *Waltzing the Cat* (New York: Virago Press, 2000).

Jauss, David. *Black Maps* (Amherst: University of Massachusetts Press, 1996).

Jones, Edward P. *All Aunt Hagar's Children* (New York: Amistad/Harper-Collins, 2006).

_____. *Lost in the City* (New York: Amistad/HarperCollins, 2003).

Kaplan, David Michael. *Skating in the Dark* (New York: Pantheon, 1991).

Kundera, Milan. *The Book of Laughter and Forgetting*, translated by Michael Henry Heim (New York: Penguin, 1981), 206-207.

Larkin, Philip, cited in Stephen Metcalf, "An Old-Type Fouled-Up Guy," *The New York Times Book Review* (May 30, 2004): 9.

Lefer, Diane. "Breaking the 'Rules' of Story Structure." In *The Best Writing on Writing*, edited by Jack Heffron (Cincinnati: Story Press, 1994), 11, 13-15.

Longstreet, K.A. *Night-Blooming Cereus* (Columbia: University of Missouri Press, 2002), 30, 34, 38, 69, 72, 116, 125, 158.

Luscher, Robert M. "The Short Story Sequence: An Open Book." In *Short Story Theory at a Crossroads*, edited by Susan Lohafer and Jo Ellyn Clarey (Baton Rouge: Louisiana State University Press, 1989), 149, 157-158.

Mason, Wyatt. "Ballad for Americans: The Stories of Edward P. Jones," *Harper's Magazine* (September 2006): 91.

Mattison, Alice. "A Note to the Reader." In *In Case We're Separated: Connected Stories* (New York: William Morrow/HarperCollins, 2005), 227.

Merrill, James. "Tomorrows." In *Collected Poems,* edited by J.D. McClatchy and Stephen Yenser (New York: Knopf, 2001), 759-760.

Miller, Laura. "And the Winner Is . . .", *The New York Times Book Review* (November 14, 2004): 63.

Mitchell, David. *Cloud Atlas* (New York: Random House, 2004).

_____, cited in Jessica Murphy, "Expect the Unexpected," *Poets & Writers* (May/June 2006), 48.

Murch, Walter, cited in Michael Ondaatje, *The Conversations: Walter Murch and the Art of Editing Film* (New York: Knopf, 2002), 81, 270.

Naylor, Gloria. *The Women of Brewster Place* (New York: Penguin, 1983).

Neville, Susan. "A Conversation With Susan Neville." In *Story Matters,* edited by Margaret-Love Denman and Barbara Shoup (Boston: Houghton Mifflin, 2006), 357.

O'Brien, Tim. *The Things They Carried* (New York: Penguin, 1983), 40, 270.

Olsen, Tillie. *Tell Me a Riddle* (New York: Delta, 1961).

Oness, Elizabeth. *Articles of Faith* (Iowa City: University of Iowa Press, 2000), 89, 106.

Pancake, Ann. *Given Ground* (Hanover, NH: Middlebury College Press, 2001), 52-53.

Pascal, Blaise. *Pascal's Pensées* (New York: Dutton, 1956), 7.

Quammen, David. *Blood Line: Stories of Fathers and Sons* (Saint Paul, MN: Graywolf Press, 1988).

Rawlins, Paul. *No Lie Like Love* (Athens: University of Georgia Press, 1996).

Rose, Mark. *Shakespearean Design* (Cambridge: Harvard University Press, 1972), 14, 65, 69, 72, 76-77.

Shields, David. "There's Only One Rule: Never Be Boring." In *Rules of Thumb: 73 Authors Reveal Their Fiction Writing Fixations*, edited by Michael Martone and Susan Neville (Cincinnati: Writer's Digest Books, 2006), 181.

Shomer, Enid. *Imaginary Men* (Iowa City: University of Iowa Press, 1993), 99, 101, 152.

Silber, Joan. *Ideas of Heaven: A Ring of Stories* (New York: Norton, 2004), 145, 220.

Vannatta, Dennis. *Lives of the Artists* (Livingston, AL: Livingston Press, 2002).

LEVER OF TRANSCENDENCE: CONTRADICTION AND THE PHYSICS OF CREATIVITY

Adams, Henry. *The Education of Henry Adams* (New York: Modern Library, 1931), 406, 451, 497-498.

Aristotle. *Aristotle's Poetics*, translated by S.H. Butcher, edited by Francis Fergusson (New York: Hill and Wang, 1961), 61, 104.

Bachelard, Gaston. *The Poetics of Space*, translated by Maria Jolas (Boston: Beacon Press, 1994), xxxii.

Barthelme, Donald. "Not-Knowing." In *The Pushcart Prize XI: Best of the Small Presses*, edited by Bill Henderson (Wainscott, NY: Pushcart Press, 1986), 24.

Baudelaire, Charles. "Correspondences," translated by Richard Wilbur. In *The Flowers of Evil*, edited by Marthiel and Jackson Mathews, revised ed. (New York: New Directions, 1963), 12.

Beardsley, Monroe C. *Aesthetics: Problems in the Philosophy of Criticism* (New York: Harcourt, Brace, 1958), 138, 141.

Beckett, Samuel. *More Pricks Than Kicks* (New York: Grove Press, 1970), 38.

Bernstein, Leonard. *The Infinite Variety of Music* (New York: Simon & Schuster, 1966), 141.

Bishop, Elizabeth. "Roosters" and "One Art." In *The Complete Poems 1927-1979* (New York: Farrar Straus and Giroux, 1995), 35-39, 178.

Blake, William. "The Marriage of Heaven and Hell." In *The Complete Poetry and Prose of William Blake*, edited by David V. Erdman (New York: Doubleday, 1988), 34.

Bogen, Joseph E. and Glenda M. Bogen. "Creativity and the Bisected Brain." In *The Creativity Question*, edited by Albert Rothenberg and Carl R. Hausman (Durham: Duke University Press, 1976), 257-258.

Bohr, Niels, cited in Bill Becker, "Pioneers of the Atom," *The New York Times Magazine* (October 20, 1957): 52.

Breton, André. "Second Manifesto of Surrealism." In *Manifestoes of Surrealism*, translated by Richard Seaver and Helen R. Lane (Ann Arbor: University of Michigan Press, 1972), 123.

Brooks, Cleanth. *The Well Wrought Urn: Studies in the Structure of Poetry* (New York: Harcourt, Brace, 1956), 3, 7, 18, 81.

Byatt, A.S. *Still Life* (New York: Collier Books, 1985), 85.

Cocteau, Jean. *Cocteau on the Film: Conversations with Jean Cocteau Recorded by André Fraigneau* (New York: Dover, 1972), 63.

Coleridge, Samuel Taylor. *Biographia Literaria*, edited by George Watson (London: J.M. Dent & Sons, 1971), 85.

Conrad, Joseph. *Lord Jim*, edited by Thomas C. Moser (New York: Norton, 1968), 196.

Cox, Mark. "After Rain." In *Natural Causes* (Pittsburgh: University of Pittsburgh Press, 2004), 69.

Crane, Hart. "Voyages." In *The Complete Poems and Selected Letters and Prose of Hart Crane*, edited by Brom Weber (Garden City, NY: Doubleday, 1966), 41.

Dickinson, Emily. Poems 465, 501, and 657. In *The Complete Poems of Emily Dickinson*, edited by Thomas H. Johnson (Boston: Little, Brown, 1961), 223, 243, 327.

Donne, John. "The Flea," "Song," and "Holy Sonnet 14." In *John Donne: The Major Works*, edited by John Carey (Cambridge: Oxford University Press, 2000), 89, 98, 178.

Dostoevsky, Fyodor. Letters to N.A. Lyubimov, May 10, 1879, and June 11, 1879. In *Selected Letters of Fyodor Dostoevsky*, translated by Andrew R. Mac-Andrew, edited by Joseph Frank and David I. Goldstein (New Brunswick, NJ: Rutgers University Press, 1987), 464-465, 470.

_____, cited in Philip Rahv, *The Myth and the Powerhouse* (New York: Noonday Press, 1966), 149.

Dunn, Stephen. "Interview with Stephen Dunn," conducted by Philip Dacey, *The Cortland Review* (www.cortlandreview.com/features/00/03/index.html), March 2000, 6.

_____. "The Past." In *The Insistence of Beauty* (New York: Norton, 2004), 39.

_____. "The Soul's Agents." In *Everything Else in the World* (New York: Norton, 2006), 36.

Ehrenzweig, Anton. *The Hidden Order of Art: A Study in the Psychology of Artistic Imagination* (Berkeley: University of California Press, 1967), 32.

Emerson, Ralph Waldo. "Brahma." In *Collected Poems and Translations*, edited by Harold Bloom and Paul Kane (New York: Library of America, 1994), 159.

Faulkner, William. *Absalom, Absalom!* (New York: Modern Library, 1951), 76.

Fitzgerald, F. Scott. *The Great Gatsby* (New York: Collier Books, 1980), 40.

Freud, Sigmund. "The Antithetical Sense of Primal Words." In *On Creativity and the Unconscious: Papers on the Psychology of Art, Literature, Love, Religion* (New York: Harper & Row, 1958), 54-55.

García Lorca, Federico. "The Irresistible Beauty of All Things," *Harper's Magazine*, 309, No. 1852 (September 2004): 28.

_____. "Somnambule Ballad." In *The Selected Poems of Federico García Lorca*, edited by Franciso García Lorca and Donald M. Allen (New York: New Directions, 1955), 65.

Gass, William H. "The Pedersen Kid." In *In the Heart of the Heart of the Country and Other Stories* (Boston: Godine, 1981), 75.

Graves, Robert, cited in Amy Lowell, "The Process of Making Poetry." In *The Creative Process: A Symposium*, edited by Brewster Ghiselin (New York: New American Library, 1952), 109.

Harries, Karsten. "Metaphor and Transcendence." In *On Metaphor*, edited by Sheldon Sacks (Chicago: The University of Chicago Press, 1979), 71.

Hass, Robert, citing an unnamed source in an interview with Bill Moyers on *The Language of Life*, PBS, July 7, 1995.

Hayles, N. Katherine. *Chaos Bound: Orderly Disorder in Contemporary Literature and Science* (Ithaca: Cornell University Press, 1988), 184.

Hegel, G.W.F. *Hegel's Logic: Being Part One of the Encyclopedia of the Philosophical Sciences*, translated by William Wallace (Oxford: Oxford University Press, 1975), 305.

Hemingway, Ernest. *A Farewell to Arms* (New York: Scribner, 1995), 126.

Hempel, Amy. "A Conversation With Amy Hempel." In *Story Matters*, edited by Margaret-Love Denman and Barbara Shoup (Boston: Houghton Mifflin, 2006), 223.

Herrick, Robert. "Delight in Disorder." In *The Complete Poetry of Robert Herrick*, edited by Douglas Brooks-Davies (New York: Everyman's Library, 1997), 15.

Hirshfield, Jane. "Poetry and Uncertainty," *The American Poetry Review* 34/6 (November/December 2005): 65.

Holton, Gerald. *Thematic Origins of Scientific Thought: Kepler to Einstein* (Cambridge: Harvard University Press, 1973), 121, 148, 150.

Jamison, Kay Redfield. *Touched With Fire: Manic-Depressive Illness and the Artistic Temperament* (New York: Free Press, 1993), 112, 127.

Joyce, James. *Ulysses* (New York: Vintage, 1961), 154, 167, 414, 488.

Keats, John. Letter to George and Tom Keats, December 21 (27?), 1817. In *The Letters of John Keats, 1814-1821*, vol. 1, edited by Edward D. McDonald (New York: Viking, 1936), 193.

Lawrence, D.H. "Preface to *The Grand Inquisitor*." In *Phoenix: The Posthumous Papers of D.H. Lawrence*, edited by Edward D. McDonald (New York: Viking, 1936), 283.

Lee, Li-Young. "An Interview With Li-Young Lee Conducted by Carolyn Alterio," *Poetry Miscellany* 30 (2004): 3.

Marks, Lawrence E., Robin J. Hammeal and Marc H. Bornstein. *Perceiving Similarity and Comprehending Metaphor*, Monographs of the Society for Research in Child Development, Serial No. 215, vol. 52, no. 1 (Chicago: The University of Chicago Press, 1987), 73-74.

Melville, Herman. "Hawthorne and His Mosses." In *Shorter Works of Hawthorne and Melville*, edited by Hershel Parker (Columbus: Merrill, 1972), 225-226.

_____. *Moby-Dick, or The Whale*, edited by Charles Feidelson, Jr. (New York: Bobbs-Merrill Co., 1969), 724.

Merleau-Ponty, Maurice. *Phenomenology of Perception*, 2nd ed., translated by Colin Smith (London: Routledge, 2002), 266.

Merwin, W.S. "The Annunciation." In *The First Four Books of Poems* (New York: Atheneum, 1977), 147.

Milton, John. "Samson Agonistes." In *The Poems of John Milton* (New York: Thomas Nelson and Sons, 1937), 530.

Moore, Marianne. "What Are Years?" In *The Complete Poems of Marianne Moore* (New York: Penguin, 1982), 95.

Nabokov, Vladimir. "The Potato Elf." In *A Russian Beauty and Other Stories* (New York: McGraw-Hill, 1974), 223, 232, 237, 240, 245.

_____. *Speak, Memory* (New York: Putnam, 1966), 34-36.

O'Connor, William Van. "Irony." In *The Princeton Encyclopedia of Poetry and Poetics*, edited by Alex Preminger (Princeton: Princeton University Press, 1974), 407.

Oppenheimer, J. Robert, from a September 1955 talk on BBC radio, quoted as an epigraph in James Schevill, *The Arena of Ants* (Providence: Copper Beech Press, 1977).

Pessoa, Fernando, cited in Richard Zenith, "Introduction: The Drama and Dream of Fernando Pessoa." In *Fernando Pessoa and Co.: Selected Poems*, translated and edited by Richard Zenith (New York: Grove Press, 1998), 11-12.

Plath, Sylvia. "Medusa." In *The Collected Poems*, edited by Ted Hughes (New York: HarperPerennial, 1992), 224-226.

Poe, Edgar Allan. "Al Aaraaf." In *Poe: Poetry, Tales, and Selected Essays* (New York: Library of America, 1996), 45.

Priest, Graham. "What Is So Bad About Contradictions?" In *The Law of Non-Contradiction: New Philosophical Essays*, edited by Graham Priest, J.C. Beall, and Bradley Armour-Garb (Oxford: Clarendon Press, 2004), 23.

Raban, Jonathan, cited in Ian Hamilton, *Robert Lowell: A Biography* (New York: Vintage, 1983), 431.

Rich, Adrienne. "When We Dead Awaken: Writing as Re-Vision." In *On Lies, Secrets, and Silence: Selected Prose 1966-1978* (New York: Norton, 1979), 43.

Rothenberg, Albert. "The Process of Janusian Thinking in Creativity." In *The Creativity Question*, edited by Albert Rothenberg and Carl R. Hausman (Durham, NC: Duke University Press, 1976), 313-316, 322, 325.

Russell, Bertrand. *The History of Philosophy* (New York: Simon & Schuster, 1945), xiv.

Shakespeare, William. *Romeo and Juliet*, Act I, scene i.

Sorensen, Roy. *A Brief History of the Paradox: Philosophy and the Labyrinths of the Mind* (New York: Oxford University Press, 2005), 304.

Stevens, Wallace. "Connoisseur of Chaos." In *Poems by Wallace Stevens*, edited by Samuel French Morse (New York: Vintage, 1959), 97.

Thomas, Dylan. "Vision and Prayer." In *The Collected Poems of Dylan Thomas, 1934-1952* (New York: New Directions, 1957), 165.

Underwood, Anne. "Real Rhapsody in Blue," *Newsweek* (December 1, 2003): 67.

Venturi, Robert. *Complexity and Contradiction in Architecture*, 2nd ed. (New York: The Museum of Modern Art, 1977), 16, 42.

Ward, Brian. "The Literary Appropriation of Chaos Theory," Ph.D. diss., University of Australia, 1998.

Warnke, Frank J. and Alex Preminger. "Oxymoron." In *The Princeton Encyclopedia of Poetry and Poetics*, edited by Alex Preminger (Princeton: Princeton University Press, 1974), 596.

Wasiolek, Edward. *Dostoevsky: The Major Fiction* (Cambridge: MIT Press, 1964), 168.

Weil, Simone. *First and Last Notebooks*, translated by Richard Rees (London: Oxford University Press, 1970), 86, 134, 216.

_____. *Gravity and Grace*, translated by Arthur Wills (New York: Putnam, 1952), 151, 156.

_____. *The Simone Weil Reader*, edited by George A. Panichas (New York: David McKay, 1977), 379.

Whitman, Walt. "Song of Myself." In *Leaves of Grass*, edited by Sculley Bradley and Harold W. Blodgett (New York: Norton, 1973), 88.

Wilde, Oscar. "The Truth of Masks." In *The Prose of Oscar Wilde* (New York: Cosmopolitan Book Corp., 1916), 240.

Wright, Franz. "Untitled." In *Walking to Martha's Vineyard* (New York: Knopf, 2003), 34.

Wright, James. "Lying in a Hammock at William Duffy's Farm in Pine Island, Minnesota." In *Above the River: The Complete Poems* (New York: Farrar, Straus and Giroux and University Press of New England, 1990), 122.

Yeats, William Butler. *A Vision* (New York: Collier Books, 1966), 25.

Zenith, Richard. "Introduction: The Drama and Dream of Fernando Pessoa." In *Fernando Pessoa and Co.: Selected Poems*, translated and edited by Richard Zenith (New York: Grove Press, 1998), 5-7, 16, 28, 31.

INDEX

Index   241

WRITER'S DIGEST

WRITER'S DIGEST
ONLINEworkshops
WritersDigestUniversity.*com*

Our workshops combine the best of world-class writing instruction with the convenience and immediacy of the web to create a state-of-the-art learning environment. You get all of the benefits of a traditional workshop setting—peer review, instructor feedback, a community of writers, and productive writing practice—without any of the hassle.

Save with Writer's Digest Shop!

WritersDigestShop.*com*

Your one-stop shop for great writing instruction at incredible discounts! You'll find books, magazines, downloads and much more!

SUBSCRIBE TO OUR FREE ONLINE NEWSLETTER
for a daily dose of writing advice and special deals and you'll receive a free digital download of **"The 101 Best Websites for Writers."**

SIGN UP TODAY AT WritersDigest.*com/enews*